THE MISEDUCATION OF THE HEBREW AND THE GENTILE

A NATION IN CAPTIVITY, A PEOPLE IN DENIAL

ASAPH MACCABEE

ABOUT THE COVER

The image on the cover of this book is more than a visual—it is a parable.

I don't think much needs to be explained about the man on the left side of the image. The world is very familiar with that visual.

The man on the left represents the Hebrew: a Black man in America, scarred by the brutality of slavery. His wounds are both **literal and symbolic**—they speak to the **physical chains of the past** and the **spiritual, emotional, mental, and generational trauma** still inflicted today on the children of Israel scattered across the earth.

The man on the right represents the Gentile: a white American, bearing **no visible chains or scars**, yet scarred by false history and deception. His lashes are **symbolic**—representing the **mental and spiritual bondage** inflicted upon a people lied to about history, God and God's chosen people. His lashes represent the abuses of his governments, religious institutions, and of his financial systems. They represent his enslavement to a system that he no longer controls. His wounds reveal a truth rarely acknowledged: that **he, too, is just a modern day "slave" to the real elites, a cog in the machine in his**

own country — completely lost about God, history, identity, and power.

These scars, though different, trace back to the same oppressor, which has ruled through lies, manipulation, and spiritual confusion. One was enslaved by force. The other by fraud.

But there is hope for both.

For the Hebrew, this book is a call to remember who you are.

For the Gentile, this book is an invitation to discover who you are not.

Truth has the power to heal all scars.

RUACH PRESS

May the breath of the Ruach Ha'Qodesh be upon these words
HalleluYah

THE MISEDUCATION OF THE HEBREW AND THE GENTILE
A NATION IN CAPTIVITY, A PEOPLE IN DENIAL

A prophetic unveiling for the descendants of Judah in captivity
By Asaph Maccabee

Published by:

Ruach Press LLC

300 Peachtree St. NE Ste CS2 #1025

Atlanta, Ga 30308

(404) 726-8101

Contact@ruachpress.com

https://TheVoiceOfZion.com

ISBN (Hardcover):

979-8-9938544-0-3

ISBN (Paperback):

979-8-9938544-1-0

ISBN (eBook): 979-8-9938544-2-7

ISBN (Audiobook): 979-8-9938544-3-4

First Edition: 2025

Cover Design: Ruach Press LLC

Interior Layout: Vellum

Scripture quotations are used under Fair Use for commentary, study, and education.

Printed in the United States of America.

✻ Formatted with Vellum

FOREWORD

"He that answereth a matter before he heareth it, it is folly and shame unto him."

— Proverbs 18:13

Before you turn another page, let this serve as a warning — not against this book, but against yourself.

If you begin this journey with conclusions already made...

If you clutch your traditions more tightly than the truth...

If you are quick to judge and slow to listen...

Then the Bible — not this author — calls you a fool.

This book is not written for fools.

It is written for seekers of truth, defenders of righteousness, and for the scattered children of Jacob who are finally ready to remember who they are.

Let us reason together.

What you will find in these pages is not hate — it is clarity.

Not anger — but accountability.

Not bitterness — but biblical restoration.

You will not find a single call to violence, vengeance, or division.

But you will find an unapologetic call to truth, repentance, holiness, and justice — not by man's standards, but by YAHUAH's.

We live in a world where uncomfortable truths are often dismissed as hate speech, and where silence about injustice is labeled peace. But truth — by its very nature — will offend those who benefit from lies.

This book is an alarm clock.

It will disturb those who are still asleep.

It will challenge the deceived, agitate the complacent, and awaken the chosen.

To the Hebrew: you will see yourself.

To the Gentile: you will see your choices.

To all: you will see the hand of the Most High, still extended.

This work does not demand blind agreement — it demands honest reflection. If at any point you are tempted to react in emotion, return to this foreword and ask yourself: "Have I truly heard the matter?"

Read every word.

Consider every claim.

Measure it all against Scripture, history, and logic. Pray to the Most High.

Then decide if the world you were taught... is the world that is true.

We are not here to argue.

We are here to testify.

Let the record speak.

Let the blind see.

Let the sleeping rise.

And may YAHUAH receive all the glory.

Generations in Decline

Let's trace the systematic weakening of Hebrew men by generation:

1. Slave Generation –Stripped of Freedom, humanity, liberty, language, land, family, masculinity, and God.
2. First Free – Freed by law, but still enslaved by oppression, poverty, and terror.
3. Migration North – Moved for opportunity, found discrimination in suits instead of whips.
4. Pre-Integration – Built strong, independent communities and businesses.
5. Post-Integration – Lost our schools, our institutions, and our self-determination.
6. Civil Rights & Jim Crow – Demanded justice, received tokenism. Leaders were murdered, co-opted, or exiled.
7. Hip-Hop, Crack, AIDS – Culture shifted from family to fame. From fatherhood to fornication. The street replaced the church.
8. Gen Z & Alpha – Under educated and under developed, over-sexualized, emotionally unstable, mentally weak, screen-raised, biblically illiterate and gender confused. The children of the hip-hop generation, raised by tablets.

Carter G. Woodson, The Miseducation of the Negro:

"If you can control a man's thinking you do not have to worry about his action."

You only have I known of all the families of the earth: therefore I will punish you for all your iniquities."

— Amos 3:2

"In the place where it was said unto them, Ye are not my people, there shall they be called the children of the living God."

— Romans 9:26

Dr. Amos Wilson:

"The greatest threat to a people is when they lose their sense of manhood and womanhood."

"They that hate you shall rule over you." – Leviticus 26:17

"And they will forget all My commandments, even all that I command them, and they will walk after the Gentiles and after their uncleanness and after their shame, and will serve their gods…" – Jubilees 1:8

"Come out of her, My people, so that you will not share in her sins." – Revelation 18:4

Without her alignment (Hebrew Woman), the nation cannot rise. Without her virtue, our future collapses.

We were never meant to be victims. We are the priests, the builders, the protectors, the image of divine masculinity. But until we repent— "If my people, which are called by my name, shall humble them- selves…" (2 Chronicles 7:14)—we will remain in captivity, even if we think we are free.

INTRODUCTION

"The Miseducation of the Hebrew and the Gentile: A Nation in Captivity, a People in Denial"

A prophetic unveiling for the descendants of Judah in captivity

"My people are destroyed for lack of knowledge: because thou hast rejected knowledge, I will also reject thee…"

— Hosea 4:6

"And ye shall know the truth, and the truth shall make you free."

— John 8:32

We begin this book not with comfort, but with conviction.

To the descendants of the tribe of Judah, the so-called Black American descendants of slaves — you are the Hebrews, the chosen seed, the royal priesthood who fell from glory not because you were hated, but because you were disobedient to the Most High.

And to the Gentiles, especially the European-American Gentile: you are not the villain of this book, but you are no longer excused by ignorance either. You have been used as a tool — sometimes willingly, sometimes blindly — in a system older than your nation and darker than your history books dare to tell.

This book is not for cowards.

This book is not for comfort-seekers.

This book is not for the emotionally fragile, or for those who will forsake the fountain of living waters, and hew themselves out cisterns, broken cisterns, that can hold no water.

—Paraphrasing Jeremiah 2:13

WHY THIS BOOK?

Because truth has been buried.
Because culture has been corrupted.
Because a divine people have been reduced to stereotypes, slaves, inmates, entertainers, and consumers.

Because our women are being masculinized, our men are being feminized, our children are being indoctrinated, our families are being erased, and our God has been forgotten.

Because the Most High still speaks — and He is calling His people to repent, return, and rebuild.

WHO ARE THE HEBREWS?

We are the seed of Jacob, descendants of Judah, strangers in a strange land — scattered to the four corners of the earth, but especially to one nation: America.

We are not Africans.

We are not simply "Black."

We are Hebrews — as prophesied in Deuteronomy 28 and across the Scriptures.

"And the LORD shall scatter thee among all people, from the one end of the earth even unto the other…"

— Deuteronomy 28:64

We arrived in ships.

We were sold.

We were branded, broken, and renamed.

We were miseducated by a system that does not want us to know who we are, because to know who we are would be to know that this system is not only fragile — it is condemned.

In every generation, the Most High preserves a remnant.

Not all Hebrews will awaken. Some will cling to Egypt until the bitter end. Some will worship the gods of their oppressors and mock their own prophets. But Yah has always preserved a remnant—those who refuse to bow to Baal, those whose hearts remain tender toward truth, those who hear the call and return.

This remnant carries the burden of awakening the rest. Their job is not popularity—it is prophecy. Their words will not always be welcomed in synagogues or pulpits. Their voices will not be amplified by social media algorithms or mainstream media. They will be misunderstood, misquoted, and mocked. But they are the salt of the earth, the torchbearers of a sleeping nation.

Isaiah prophesied about this remnant long ago:

"And it shall come to pass in that day, that the remnant of Israel… shall stay upon the Lord, the Holy One of Israel, in truth. The remnant shall return, even the remnant of Jacob, unto the mighty God."

—Isaiah 10:20–21

Identity is not just a cultural issue—it is a spiritual weapon. Knowing who you are in the Most High aligns your soul with divine purpose. It restores dignity. It heals generational trauma. It breaks the psychological chains of inferiority, bitterness, and confusion.

This is why the world fears a spiritually conscious Hebrew man. Not a bitter man. Not a carnal man. But a repentant, disciplined, set-apart man of Yah. He is the most dangerous thing in Babylon.

Once the remnant rises, systems will shake. The remnant will raise families rooted in Torah. They will reject the false images of success and manhood and crafted by Babylon. They will stand as righteous husbands, fathers, community builders, and spiritual warriors—not pawns, not thugs, not clowns, not slaves. They will teach their children that their lineage is royal and their future is prophetic.

Healing does not begin in legislation or policy—it begins in identity. When the Hebrew remembers who he is, healing begins. And when healing begins, repentance follows. And when repentance comes, restoration is not far behind.

The plantation never closed—it evolved.

The trauma of slavery did not end with the Emancipation Proclamation. It mutated. It passed down through generations like a virus, embedded in our behaviors, relationships, fears, hopes, and expectations. It shaped our theology. It twisted our view of God, of ourselves, of each other.

Consider the Willie Lynch letter—whether fully authentic or not, the psychological principles within it ring true. The intentional division of Black people by age, color, gender, and status was not an accident—it was policy. The slave master knew that to destroy a people long-term, you must turn them against themselves.

A Hebrew woman taught to mistrust her man. A Hebrew man taught to fear his strength. Children raised to idolize the oppressor and mock their ancestors. This is the legacy of the plantation, still alive today in music videos, school systems, and government programs that reward dysfunction and penalize righteous order.

The trauma is so deep, we often don't even recognize it. We mistake our dysfunction for freedom. We call rebellion "independence." We mistake promiscuity for empowerment. We think we're rising, but we're only sinking into deeper levels of captivity—captivity of the soul.

But Yah is not done with us.

The remnant is rising with eyes wide open. We are confronting the pain head-on. We are naming the generational curses. We are choosing healing over hype. We are choosing truth over trauma. And that truth is setting us free—not because we learned it in a classroom, but because it was always in our blood.

There is a reason Satan has worked so hard to distort our reflection.

If the Hebrew man looks in the mirror and sees only a thug, a criminal, a deadbeat, or a sexual object, then he will behave like one. If the Hebrew woman sees herself only as a loud, angry, overly independent, disposable object of desire, she will act accordingly. If we believe we are cursed, we will live cursed.

This is why the culture is saturated with images of us as broken, violent, reckless, hyper-sexualized caricatures.

Hollywood. The music industry. Fashion. Social media algorithms. These industries are not run by Hebrews. They are run by those who profit from dysfunction. These gatekeepers understand something that many in our communities don't: image shapes behavior. Repetition becomes identity. If you control what a people see, you control what they believe. And if you control what they believe, you can keep them enslaved without ever touching them.

But it's time to break the mirror.

It's time to look deeper—to see past the distortion and into the truth: that you are not the names they gave you. You are not the labels they imposed on you. You are a chosen vessel, a royal priesthood, a peculiar nation (1 Peter 2:9). And once you see yourself as Yah sees you, the chains fall.

This is not just about trauma—it is about transformation.

The war within is the final frontier. Babylon knows this. The enemy understands this. That's why so much money, media, and manpower has been spent on keeping the Hebrew soul in bondage. But the Most High has declared war on the darkness, and He is awakening His people.

This is the call:

Hebrew man, arise.

Hebrew woman, return.

Gentile believer, repent of your complicity and embrace the truth.

We are not victims—we are the remnant. And the war within ends when we remember who we are and return to the covenant of our ancestors. The covenant sealed by blood. The covenant rekindled through repentance. The covenant fulfilled in Yahusha HaMashiach.

This is how we win. Not by weapons of this world, but by the renewal of the mind, the healing of the soul, and the restoration of our true identity.

The war within is real. But the victory is already written.

THE TRAP: MISEDUCATION AND DESTRUCTION

You've been told that success is money, that family is optional, that gender is fluid, that truth is offensive, and that God is whatever you feel like today.

You've been told that we are inferior, lazy, violent, emotional, hypersexual, and godless — and then every image we see reinforces those lies.

Meanwhile, we literally built this country. We bled for it. We died for it. We served in every war, farmed every acre, built prominent parts of infrastructure, invented countless tools, paved the streets, styled the culture and provided the soundtrack. We led the marches and forced moral consciousness on a nation, and yet… we remain hated, feared, and forgotten.

Why?

Because a righteous, awakened, and organized Hebrew people would destroy this entire system — *not with violence*, but with truth, with order, with repentance, and with divine power.

This is why they flooded our communities with drugs, poverty, and propaganda.

This is why they used integration not to lift us up, but to dismantle our independence — because we were thriving. We had our own Banks, hospitals, businesses, schools, cab companies, lawyers, seamstresses, pilots, and power.

"Woe to them that call evil good, and good evil…"

— Isaiah 5:20

Every time we rose, they burned it down — from Tulsa to Rosewood, from Wilmington to Detroit. These were not accidents. These were not riots. These were strategic acts of terrorism against the Hebrews in America.

The War Within – The Psychological Chains of the Hebrew Soul

Captivity Beyond Chains

While the physical yoke of slavery may have been broken by legislation and revolution, a more insidious form of captivity remains —one that binds not the body, but the soul and the mind. This is the psychological war against the Hebrew man and woman, waged through deception, distortion, and spiritual confusion. The oppressor understood long ago that brute force alone could not hold an entire people in subjugation forever. So, they shifted strategies: from shackles to symbols, from whips to whispers, from plantations to programming.

The war we now face is internal—a struggle for memory, identity, and spiritual reconciliation. It is not enough to be physically free while mentally and spiritually imprisoned. As Scripture declares:

"As a man thinketh in his heart, so is he." – Proverbs 23:7

What, then, does a Hebrew man become when he thinks he is a Gentile? Or worse—when he believes he is nothing at all?

WHO REALLY RUNS THIS?

Let us be clear: European-American Gentiles were used, but they are not the masterminds.

They were sold the lie that Black people were their enemy — while the real architects of this system sat in banking halls, media empires, and political offices, untouched.

Let us name names.

Let us speak the truth, even if it costs us everything.

"I know the blasphemy of them which say they are Jews, and are not, but are the synagogue of Satan."
— Revelation 2:9

From Judah P. Benjamin, the "brains of the Confederacy," to the hidden financiers of the Atlantic slave trade, and those who now control the entertainment industry, the record labels, the algorithms, and the educational curriculums — the true puppeteers have remained in the shadows.

But their time is up.

OUR RESPONSE: REPENTANCE AND RECLAMATION

This book is not just a lamentation — it is a battle cry.

We will examine the sickness of our culture, not to shame, but to expose.

We will call out the emasculation of our men, the hypersexualization of our women, and the demonic confusion being forced upon our children.

We will name the propaganda.

We will shatter the false doctrines of "universe spirituality" and New Age deception.

We will speak directly to the LGBTQ+ agenda, with sobriety, truth, and statistics.

We will restore marriage, fatherhood, identity, and scriptural obedience to their rightful place at the center of Hebrew life.

Because we are not victims — we are the remnant, and the Most High is calling us back.

"If my people, which are called by my name, shall humble themselves, and pray, and seek my face, and turn from their wicked ways; then will I hear from heaven, and will forgive their sin, and will heal their land."

— 2 Chronicles 7:14

A FINAL WORD TO THE AMERICAN GENTILE:

We do not hate you. We do not seek revenge. We are not now, nor have we ever been your enemy.

The retribution you should be worried about is from The Most High, not from us .

We carry the oracles of God in our blood. We carry forgiveness even after centuries of torment. But do not mistake our peace for ignorance. The truth is coming, and no one will be able to run from it.

The Hebrews are waking up.

This book is one of many trumpets sounding.

Not to start a race war, but to end a spiritual one.

If you fear this book, ask yourself what you're afraid of: the words, or the truth behind them?

Let the scroll be opened. Let the lies be exposed. Let the truth be heard.

This is The Miseducation of the Hebrew and the Gentile.

And it begins now.

CONTENTS

PART I
THE FOUNDATIONS
OF DECEPTION AND
IDENTITY THEFT

Chapters 1-8

The State of the Hebrew Man

THE GREAT AMNESIA — IDENTITY STOLEN, TRUTH BURIED

"*I* will bless those who bless you, and whoever curses you I will curse."

— Genesis 12:3

THIS BOOK IS about stolen identity — not just of a people, but of the entire biblical narrative.

The world knows Israel, or so it thinks. It celebrates a European Jesus, paints apostles with pale skin and blue eyes, and sings hymns in cathedrals built by slave owners. Meanwhile, the true children of Israel live under curses exactly as the Torah foretold — scattered, oppressed, forgotten even by themselves.

THE HEBREW IN AMERICA, the descendants of slaves ripped from the coasts of West Africa, are not just another African diaspora story. They are the living testimony of Deuteronomy 28. They are Judah, carried on ships to a new Egypt. They are the ones whose identity was so threatening to the world order that it had to be crushed, rewritten, and replaced.

AND THE SECOND GREAT TRAGEDY: the Gentile nations have been equally misled.

They have been taught to bless impostors and curse the true people of YAH, believing lies that will bring judgment on their own heads and nations. Thus both Hebrew and Gentile have been miseducated — one through stolen history, the other through cunning falsehoods and erased and rewritten history.

THIS CHAPTER LAYS bare the foundational theft that shapes every other chapter: the loss of identity, the erasure of history, and the spiritual amnesia that keeps an entire nation — both Israel and those who live among them — blind to the truth.

A STOLEN LEGACY

*O*ur story did not begin on plantations. It began in Jerusalem, in the land of Canaan, under the covenant of Abraham, Isaac, and Jacob. It moved through kings — David and Solomon — and prophets, through captivities under Babylon, Egypt, Persia, and Assyria. It moved through fleeting returns, and occupation by the Seleucid empire. And ultimately ended occupied and destroyed by Rome.

WHEN YAHUSHA WARNED, "There shall not be left here one stone upon another that shall not be thrown down," He was speaking of the destruction that came in 70 A.D. under Vespasian and Titus. Jerusalem fell. The Temple burned. Hebrews fled.

HISTORY RECORDS WHERE THEY WENT:

•First down through Egypt, then deeper into North Africa.

•Avoiding old enemies, they continued into the heart of West Africa, settling around the Niger Valley (modern day Ghana, Benin,Nigeria).

•Some carried on to Spain and Portugal, where the bloodline of King David continued among Iberian Hebrews until the Inquisition drove them out or enslaved them. The Inquisition was 1478-1834. The transatlantic slave trade was 1619-1865.

•Maps from the 1700s and earlier show "Negroland," with the "Kingdom of Judah" (often spelled Wahida) plainly marked on the Slave Coast.

-IN 1492 COLUMBUS sailed the ocean blue …..but also in 1492 Spain expelled the Jew and Mali did too.-

REMEMBER The Spanish and Portuguese were the first European empires to institutionalize the transatlantic slave trade, systematically capturing and exporting Hebrew Israelites from the Iberian Peninsula and West Africa. The first Hebrews enslaved and brought to The Americas we were brought directly from Spain and Portugal while there children were abducted and sent to the African island of São Tomé. And then they started hunting Hebrews in Western Africa.

The Portuguese and Spanish did not hunt generic "Africans."

They hunted Hebrews, descendants of those who fled Rome and related to those they sold into slavery from Spain and Portugal.

That is why the Spanish word for black — "Negro" — became attached to us uniquely. The world knew who we were. Only we forgot.

CLARIFYING THE MYTH — AFRICANS DID NOT SELL AFRICANS

One of the greatest lies ever sold is that Africans simply sold their own into slavery.

The reality is more nuanced and far more sinister.

THE DAHOMEY TRIBE, descendants of Ham (among others) captured people distinct from themselves. These were Hebrews (descendants of Shem)— physically, culturally, and spiritually distinct. So to say that the Dahomey sold Hebrews would be like saying the French sold English. Two distinct groups of people whom share a common skin tone but are completely different. Another way to put It is a portion of the descendent of Ham sold the descendants of Shem.

••EUROPEANS are seen as Germans, Irish, Poles, Italians, etc... each with pride in their national identities. Yet the world compresses all dark-skinned people into one indistinct "African." The fact is there is more diversity in the blood of the two closest tribes in any part of the African continent then there is in the blood of any European across Europe. So while German, Irish, Polish, Italians ,French, Swedish,

Russian, English, ect.. are all considered very different and diverse people. Genetically they actually are not. (At least nowhere near as diverse as the melanin people of the Earth). And while globally all melanin people, meaning the descendants of Ham and the descendants of Shem are considered all the same we actually are very different and very diverse. Please understand this is not said out of hate, and also understand this is not something I am speaking out of opinion. This was the result of research from a National Geographic study titled : Africa's genetic diversity revealed by full genomes of a Bushman and a Tutu published by National Geographic in 2010.

THE BIBLE PROPHESIED these divisions long before colonial borders. The Hebrews were a set-apart people, known by their covenant, by circumcision, by Torah practices. That distinction made them targets. Just as Jacob's sons were targeted by Edom and Ishmael in ancient times, the descendants of Judah were targeted in West Africa.

THE MYTH OF "AFRICANS SELLING AFRICANS" absolves the world of recognizing a strategic hunt for Hebrews.

It also erases the clear prophetic fulfillment:

"YOU SHALL BE SOLD unto your enemies for bondmen and bondwomen, and no man shall buy you (redeem you)."

— Deuteronomy 28:68

WHY ERASE OUR HISTORY?

*T*his is the question at the heart of the conspiracy — and it is not merely political or economic. It is spiritual.

IF THE HEBREW man forgets who he is, he forgets who his God is.

If he forgets YAHUAH, he will not repent.

If he does not repent, the covenant remains broken.

And if the covenant remains broken, the curses continue.

IN THE BIBLE, the entire story of the Hebrew people is disobey the Most high fall into judgment, repentance, RESTORATION, repeat.... Because they knew who they were, when they fell into judgment, they knew what they had to do. The only way to keep the Hebrew cursed is to keep him from repentance. The only way to keep him from repentance is to make him forget who he is, recreate his identity.

THAT IS why Psalm 83 says:

.   .   .

"THEY HAVE SAID, Come, and let us cut them off from being a nation; that the name of Israel may be no more in remembrance."

THIS HAS ALWAYS BEEN the strategy of Satan: sever the Hebrews from their heritage, keep them in perpetual sin, so that judgment continues and restoration is delayed.

BUT YAH PROMISED,

"IF MY PEOPLE, which are called by my name, shall humble themselves, and pray, and seek my face, and turn from their wicked ways; then will I hear from heaven, and will forgive their sin, and will heal their land."

— 2 Chronicles 7:14

THIS IS why national repentance matters. This is why knowing who we are matters. It is the path to forgiveness, to restoration, to the breaking of generational curses, and to the return of blessings long withheld.

THE STRATEGIC ERASURE of Memory

WHY WAS it so important for the powers of this world to erase the identity of the true Hebrews?

BECAUSE IDENTITY IS the gateway to repentance. And repentance is the gateway to restoration.

. . .

THE ADVERSARY UNDERSTANDS SCRIPTURE. Satan does not fear Blackness—he fears repentant Hebrews. He fears a people who awaken, remember who they are, and cry out to their Elohim in truth. That is why identity theft is not just historical—it is spiritual warfare.

"IF MY PEOPLE, who are called by My Name, shall humble themselves and pray, and seek My face and turn from their wicked ways, then will I hear from heaven and forgive their sin, and will heal their land."
– 2 Chronicles 7:14

EVERY SYSTEM OF OPPRESSION—WHETHER religious, educational, or governmental—has worked overtime to keep the Hebrew people from reaching this verse. If you don't know you're the "people called by His Name," how will you ever know to repent as a nation? The crime wasn't just slavery—it was spiritual sabotage.

ACCORDING to the Book of Jubilees:

"AND THEY WILL FORGET ALL My commandments, even all that I command them, and they will walk after the Gentiles and after their uncleanness and after their shame, and will serve their gods..." –
Jubilees 1:8

THE STRIPPING of memory was not accidental—it was prophetic.

SPIRITUAL &
PSYCHOLOGICAL WARFARE

*C*aptivity is more than chains. It is mind control.

•The trauma of being stolen from our land, renamed, and forced to worship a god who looked like our oppressors has not left our DNA.

•The policies of breaking families on plantations, separating children from parents, teaching only enough to obey but never to question, left scars deeper than skin.

•The "white-washed" Hebrew who denies his people, scorns his own skin, and strives to prove to Gentiles that he is "not like us" is the greatest trophy of psychological warfare.

•Likewise the Hebrew woman who sees her men as beneath her or just a vehicle for monetary or physical gain, aligning herself with the very systems that crushed her fathers, is a product of the same sinister engineering.

This is about rejecting your own people to embrace a culture that despises your God and your heritage.

That is the ultimate victory of the enemy: when the children of Zion despise Zion, worship Egypt, and curse their own reflection in the mirror.

From Negro to Nigger – The Evolution of a Weaponized Word

I. Introduction: The Power of a Word

There are few words in the English language more volatile, more emotionally charged, and more historically bloody than the word "nigger." It is a word soaked in humiliation, baptized in blood, and sharpened like a sword to cut into the psyche of a people. But before it became a dagger, it was a chain. Before it was a chain, it was a label. And before it was a label, it was a word—Negro—born not out of hate, but out of the tongue of the Spaniard. That tongue, however, would become the linguistic whip that lashed the backs of the Hebrews scattered to the coasts of Africa and across the Atlantic.

How did we go from being Hebrews—the chosen people of the Most High—to Negroes, and from Negroes to niggers? This chapter will trace the devolution of identity through the evolution of language. Words are spiritual. Words carry power. And in this case, words have become weapons.

II. The Spanish and Portuguese Origin of "Negro"

The term Negro originates from the Spanish and Portuguese word for "black." In a purely linguistic sense, the word simply denotes color. But history doesn't exist in a vacuum, and neither does language. The Spanish and Portuguese were not just explorers or traders—they were among the earliest and most aggressive slavers in the transatlantic trade. And who were they targeting?

The Hebrew people who had migrated over centuries into Western Africa—many of whom had originally fled from the destruction of Jerusalem in 70 A.D., carrying with them the sacred traditions, oral history, and remnants of a shattered kingdom.

Spain and Portugal were not strangers to the Hebrews. The lineage of David had even found its way into Iberia and history is rich with facts about the Moors and Jews of Spain. In fact, in Portugal it became considered such an insult to call someone the word "Jew" that the government enacted a law forbidding the term altogether. They instead started calling them the black Portuguese or Negro Portuguese and eventually just Negro. But as Catholic monarchies rose to power and Inquisitions began to purge the land of all non-conforming faiths, the Hebrew presence in Spain and Portugal became a target. Many were exiled, enslaved, or murdered. From there, the hunt expanded to the African continent—specifically to the coasts they labeled Negroland and the Slave Coast, territories rich with Hebrew refugees who had long since fled Roman persecution.

Thus, the word Negro was applied not just to anyone with dark skin, but specifically to those Hebrews who were now being sold en masse from Spain and Portugal and there relatives in Western Africa (Negroland). The world began to call the scattered children of Jacob by the name Negro, because that was how the Spanish and Portuguese had labeled them.

III. From Identity to Insult: The Birth of "Nigger"

As the slave trade evolved and spread into the British colonies of the Americas, the word Negro crossed the Atlantic and underwent a sinister metamorphosis. In the mouths of Anglo-Saxon slaveholders, the word began to change—phonetically corrupted, twisted by accents, and poisoned by prejudice.

Negro became nigger.

This was not a neutral linguistic shift. This was a spiritual assassination. The word was intentionally malformed to become a slur—short, sharp, and brutal. Where "Negro" could once be spoken in a bureaucratic or even clinical tone, nigger was always spit like venom.

It became the label of subhuman status, the justification for murder, rape, chains, whips, dogs, alligators, hangings, beatings, and psychological annihilation. It was the word screamed as the noose was tied, as Gentile families cheered with their children at what they called "picnics". The word hissed through clenched teeth by plantation overseers. The word that reminded every stolen Hebrew that they were no longer people—they were property.

IV. The Word as a Curse and a Spell

In biblical culture, names matter. Words have weight. The Most High gave names with meaning. He changed names when destinies shifted: Abram became Abraham. Jacob became Israel. Words could bless—or curse.

To call someone nigger is not just to insult them. It is to curse them. It is to cast a demonic spell over their identity. It is to erase their royal lineage and inscribe instead the lie of inferiority, criminality, and godlessness.

The term nigger is not just offensive—it is occultic. It replaces "Hebrew" with "beast," "chosen" with "chattel," "image of God" with "animal."

The enemy understood this well. By cursing us with a name, they severed us from our own. And many of us believed the lie. We wore the curse like a name tag. Some of us still do.

V. Reclaiming or Reinforcing? The Modern Confusion

In the 20th and 21st centuries, the word nigger (or its variant nigga) has been reappropriated by many in the Hebrew community as a form of endearment, kinship, or solidarity. In rap music, in movies, on the streets—it became a badge of resilience for some, a middle finger to oppression.

But can poison ever nourish?

Can a curse become a crown?

This is where the spiritual discernment of a reawakened Hebrew must rise. *Just because we can flip the word doesn't mean we've broken the spell.* Just because we say it with love doesn't mean it's lost its power to harm.

When we continue to refer to ourselves by a name the oppressor gave us, we tether ourselves to the trauma. We keep singing the songs of Babylon with Babylon's tongue. And we wonder why our communities remain spiritually disoriented.

VI. The Scriptural Demand for Renaming

Isaiah 65:15 (KJV) declares:

"And ye shall leave your name for a curse unto my chosen: for the Lord God shall slay thee, and call his servants by another name."

The time has come to cast off the names given in slavery. The time has come to renounce the curses. We are not niggers. We are not Negroes. We are Hebrews—descendants of Abraham, Isaac, and Jacob. A royal priesthood. A holy nation. A people of covenant.

Revelation 2:17 speaks of a new name given to the faithful:

"…To him that overcometh will I give… a white stone, and in the stone a new name written, which no man knoweth saving he that receiveth it."

The true restoration of our people begins when we reject the name the slave master gave and embrace the name the Father ordained.

VII. Conclusion: Break the Spell, Speak the Truth

LET US BE CLEAR: the word nigger is not just profanity—it is prophecy fulfilled (Jeremiah 24:9) and identity defiled. It is a reminder of captivity, but also a wake-up call to reject it. The Hebrew man must rise and remember. The Hebrew woman must teach her children to speak truth and not repeat the incantations of oppression.

This is not just about a word. It's about warfare—spiritual, cultural, and generational.

The spell must be broken. Our true name must be reclaimed. The truth must be restored.

We are not Niggers.

We are not Negroes.

We are not African-Americans

We are Hebrews. We are Judah.

Post-Traumatic Slave Syndrome: The Unhealed Wound

Dr. Joy DeGruy coined the term Post-Traumatic Slave Syndrome (PTSS) to describe the multigenerational trauma passed down from slavery that remains unhealed. Symptoms include:

• Self-hatred and internalized racism

• Disconnection from spiritual identity

• Hypermasculinity in men, hypersexualization in women

• Violence toward one another

• Distrust of each other and of authority

• Emotional numbness, hopelessness, and generational despair

This syndrome was not accidental—it was cultivated. Just as the trauma was intentional, so too was the denial of healing. Even when freedom was declared, therapy was not provided. Compensation was not granted. Land was not given. Reconciliation was not pursued. Instead, the Hebrew man was left to drown in memories too painful to recall and too scarred to forget.

The Enemy's Strategy: Miseducate, Entertain, Destroy

Let us be clear: a people who know who they are cannot be controlled. So the Hebrew had to be miseducated. The truth had to be hidden beneath centuries of lies, and replaced with entertainment, shame, and confusion.

•The school system told us we were "from Africa," nothing more.

•The media showed us as criminals, buffoons, or slaves.

•The church erased our names from the Book of Life and handed it to Europe.

•The music taught our sons to kill each other and our daughters to twerk for approval.

We were not just colonized—we were reprogrammed. Our spiritual operating system was overwritten with European theologies, Greco-Roman philosophies, and capitalist obsessions.

From Proverbs to Profanity: The Shift in Language and Vision

In the Scriptures, the Hebrew man was known for wisdom, strength, and divine favor. He was called:

•A priest

•A king

•A prophet

•A warrior

•A servant of the Most High

Today, he is called:

•A "hood nigga"

•A "thug"

•A "baby daddy"

•A "yn"

•A "inmate"

This is no coincidence. Language is a tool of dominion. By changing what we're called, they changed what we become.

"Death and life are in the power of the tongue." — Proverbs 18:21

When we stopped calling ourselves kings and started calling ourselves killers, the spirit of the Most High was grieved. The lies of the enemy were no longer outside us—they had taken root inside us.

The Only Cure: Remembering and Repenting

If forgetting is what keeps us cursed, remembering is what will heal us. And not just remembering the pain—but the promise.

We are not defined by our captivity. We are defined by our covenant. The Most High made a covenant with Abraham, Isaac, and Jacob— and He is not a man that He should lie.

"If my people, which are called by my name, shall humble themselves, and pray, and seek my face, and turn from their wicked ways; then will I hear from heaven, and will forgive their sin, and will heal their land." — 2 Chronicles 7:14

The enemy's greatest fear is not our protest, but our repentance.

If the Hebrew man returns to the Most High…

If the Hebrew woman rejects the lies of Babylon…

If the Hebrew family rebuilds its altar of prayer and truth…

Then the curses will break. The heavens will open. And the dry bones will rise.

Conclusion: Victory Begins in the Mind

We must not underestimate the war we're in. This is not just physical, financial, or political. It is mental. It is spiritual. It is generational.

The good news is: this war has already been won—but only for those who return. Only for those who remember and repent.

THE RISE OF THE CRIMINAL
IMAGE & THE CULTURAL HIJACK

*L*ong before there was a Hebrew gangster, America made criminals its heroes. Let's not forget that America's first blockbuster movie, A Birth Of A Nation (1915) was about abolitionist and the birth of the KKK.

From Jesse James to Al Capone. From Irish mobs to Italian mafias. All the way to national, and indeed global crime syndicates controlled by Meyer Lansky and Lucky Luciano, organized crime was romanticized. Hollywood minted legends from thieves and murderers. Newspapers wrote them into folklore. America spread the culture of Bonnie and Clyde, Babyface Nelson, and public enemy number one John Dillinger to the whole world. The original Scarface movie was made in 1932. America has always idolized its criminals and gangsters.

Hebrews arrived in this land under chains, subjected to laws meant to criminalize them for simply existing. Vagrancy laws, pig laws, and Black codes turned survival into crime. As time passed and systems evolved, the power that ruled the plantations shifted to rule the airwaves.

. . .

RECORD EXECUTIVES AND MEDIA CONGLOMERATES, largely tied to the same elite families who once owned slave ships and plantations, now owned record and movie studios. They choose who would be made famous, what songs would be played, and what movies would be produced.

SO THE IMAGE of the Hebrew man transformed from slave to sharecropper to shuffling servant to violent gangster.It was not organic. It was designed.

MEANWHILE, Hebrews imitated what Babylon rewarded. Italian mafia films were box office gold; soon Hebrews imitated their swagger, names, codes, and even their criminal enterprises. The gangster mentality is not a Hebrew invention — it is an American export. It's the American dream.

THE TRAGEDY IS that we embraced this lie, internalized it, and built our own destruction around it, never realizing who profited from the spectacle.

BABYLON'S PUPPET STRINGS — The Entertainment Industry and the Crafting of the Black Psyche

"THE KINGS of the earth set themselves, and the rulers take counsel together, against YHWH, and against His anointed, saying, 'Let us break their bands asunder, and cast away their cords from us.'"
— Psalm 2:2–3

"And no marvel; for Satan himself is transformed into an angel of light."
— 2 Corinthians 11:14

. . .

I. THE REAL CONTROLLERS: Behind the Curtain

MOST BELIEVE the entertainment industry is driven by talent, creativity, and public demand. But in truth, it is a meticulously engineered machine, governed by the elite power structures—what Scripture calls the synagogue of Satan.

THIS MACHINE IS NOT DESIGNED to entertain—it is designed to:

•Program/degrade/profane/

desensitize / and sexualize the mind

•Condition behavior,

•Shape the values,

•And destroy the Hebrew and Gentile soul.

Who owns the labels? Who finances the films?
Who approves the scripts?
Who signs the artists?
Who censors the truth?

It is not Judah. It is not Zion.
It's Babylon—and Babylon knows exactly what it's doing.

II. Hip-Hop: The Weaponized Soundtrack of a Lost Generation

ONCE A FORM of resistance and storytelling, hip-hop was born in the Bronx, NY—infused with rhythm, pain, hope, and truth.

Early rappers spoke of partying and fun but also social issues such as:

•Police brutality,

•Poverty,

•Community unity,

•Black empowerment.

BUT BY THE late 1980s and early 90s, there was a sinister pivot.

Behind closed doors, a memo was sent. A meeting was held.

THE PRIVATE PRISON AGENDA & The Industry Takeover

The entertainment industry colluded with private prison investors to promote music that would:

•Glorify gang violence,
•Promote drug use,
•Normalize criminal behavior,
•Sexualize youth,
•And ultimately fill prison beds.

Once conscious rap was buried, the new era of:
•Gangsta rap,
•Trap music,
• Drill rap,
took the stage—mass distributed, corporately funded, and globally exported.

It was no longer "music by us, for us."

It became "music by them, against us."

III. From Lyrics to Lifestyle: Programming the Hebrew Mind

HEBREW BOYS GROW UP BELIEVING:

•Manhood equals sexual conquest.

•Success equals drug dealing or rapping or being a professional athlete.

•Conflict must be resolved with violence.

•Womanhood equals twerking, thirst traps, and submission to men with money. We are taught to objectify our woman, that they are things for us to use, conquer, and disregard. Not love, cherish, and protect.

THIS IS NOT ACCIDENTAL.

EVERY TIME A RAPPER MENTIONS:

•Killing another Black man,

•being a "crash out"

•Materialism

•Murdering someone over colors a hood or a block,

he is rewarded with:

•Grammy nominations,

•BET Awards,

•Streaming deals,

•Corporate sponsorship.

BUT THE MOMENT A RAPPER:

•Quotes Scripture,

•Speaks against homosexuality,

•Critiques systemic racism,

•Calls for repentance or responsibility,

HE IS DEPLATFORMED, shadowbanned, or blacklisted.

BABYLON PAYS for your destruction but censors your deliverance.

IV. The Jezebel Agenda: The Assault on Hebrew Women

IT'S NOT JUST the men. The system has launched an all-out psychological war on Hebrew women.

ENTER THE NEW ARCHETYPES:

•The City Girl,

•The Baddie,

•The OnlyFans Queen,

•The Independent Woman Who Needs No Man.

. . .

THIS IS NOT EMPOWERMENT. This is enslavement disguised as freedom.

THE HEBREW WOMAN, once a Proverbs 31 queen, is now fed lies:

•That she is a god unto herself,

•That submission to a man is weakness,

•That motherhood is a burden,

•That modesty is oppression,

•That marriage is a trap. That men are the enemy and that men should submit to them.

MUSIC VIDEOS, social media influencers, and scripted reality shows have become the new Torah for our daughters.

THEY'VE REPLACED SARAH, Rebecca, and Deborah with Nicki, Cardi, and Meg.

And what does Babylon call it?

Freedom. Expression.
Representation.

BUT IT IS REALLY REGRESSION—A return to spiritual prostitution and emotional bondage.

V. Rituals in Plain Sight: Occult Symbolism in Media

. . .

IF YOU HAVE eyes to see, you'll notice the rituals:

•Pyramids, one-eye symbolism, and checkerboard floors in music videos.

•Artists being "reborn" through fire, water, or blood.

•Red carpets symbolizing sacrifice.

•Performances full of sexual perversion, mock crucifixions, or Baphomet imagery.

THIS IS NOT ART. This is witchcraft in plain sight.

"THOU SHALT NOT SUFFER a witch to live."

— Exodus 22:18

WE ARE NOT WITNESSING ENTERTAINMENT—WE are witnessing public indoctrination.

Demons with choreographers and makeup artists.

AND THE HEBREW MASSES?

They clap. They sing along. They imitate.

Just as Pharaoh intended.

VI. The Solution: Starve the Machine

WHAT HAPPENS WHEN WE:

•Stop streaming the filth?

•Stop funding the madness?

•Stop dancing to our own destruction?

WE BREAK THE MACHINE.

WE MUST:

•Raise up righteous artists.

•Teach our children to critically analyze lyrics.

•Reclaim our gifts and platforms for the glory of Yah.

•Support content that heals instead of harms.

We don't need more idols.
We need more prophets.

Let us remember:
The Levites sang. David wrote psalms. Miriam danced.
Worship has always been part of Hebrew culture.

But now our music must be warfare.
Our art must be prophecy.
Our platforms must be pulpits.

SUMMARY:

THE ENTERTAINMENT INDUSTRY has become the modern-day plantation—rich white owners, exploited (hand picked) Black performers, and a system designed to destroy the minds and spirits of the Hebrew people. From rap to reality TV, the media has been used to normalize dysfunction and disguise it as culture. But we are not powerless. We can and must unplug from the matrix, expose the deception, and rebuild a righteous media culture that glorifies YAH and uplifts Zion.

GOVERNMENT-
SPONSORED DESTRUCTION

*I*f you think the rise of drugs in Hebrew neighborhoods was coincidental, think again.

IN THE 1980s, crack cocaine flooded Los Angeles' Black communities. This was not simply the work of greedy cartels and ambitious drug dealers. CIA operatives, tied to the Iran-Contra affair, funneled cocaine profits to fund illegal wars in Central America.

This is not conspiracy — Lieutenant Colonel Oliver North testified to it!

OLIVER NORTH TESTIFIED for the Iran-Contra affair in Washington, D.C. in July 1987. His week-long testimony was delivered before a joint congressional committee convened to investigate the scandal and was broadcast live on network television.

KEY REVELATIONS from the Iran contra affair

•Secret arms sales to Iran: The Reagan administration, in contradiction to its publicly stated policy of not negotiating with terrorists and adhering to an arms embargo against Iran, facilitated the sale of arms to Iran. The goal was to secure the release of American hostages held in Lebanon by Hezbollah, an organization linked to Iran.

•Diversion of funds to the Contras: Profits from these illegal arms sales were then secretly diverted and channeled to the Contra rebels in Nicaragua. This directly violated the Boland Amendment, a congressional ban on U.S. military aid to the Contras, who were fighting against the Marxist Sandinista government.

•Covert operations and lack of oversight: These actions were orchestrated by members of the National Security Council (NSC), including Lieutenant Colonel Oliver North, without the knowledge or approval of Congress. The NSC's involvement in these operational activities, rather than its traditional advisory role, raised serious questions about executive overreach and accountability.

•Misleading and lying to Congress:Several senior administration officials, including then-National Security Advisor Robert McFarlane and his successor John Poindexter, initially lied to Congress during investigations into the affair.

•Obstruction of justice: Evidence was deliberately destroyed and altered by individuals involved in the affair, including Oliver North and his secretary, Fawn Hall. This attempt to impede investigations further compounded the scandal and indicated a cover-up.

•Use of private networks and foreign entities: To circumvent congressional restrictions, a network known as "the Enterprise," headed by retired Air Force Major General Richard Secord, was established to carry out the operations and channel funds to the Contras. Funds were also solicited from third-party countries, further complicating the oversight process.

•Contra involvement in drug trafficking: A 1998 report by the CIA inspector general confirmed that the Contras were involved in drug trafficking and that the US government transported those drugs back to the United States to be sold to Americans to continue funding the war. And that the Reagan administration had shielded their activities from law enforcement.

INVESTIGATIONS REVEALED *government awareness and complicity. This means the American government started the crack epidemic in the streets of Los Angeles and later across the nation.*

HEBREW COMMUNITIES WERE the chosen testing ground.

Crack was cheaper, more addictive, and far more destructive than powdered cocaine. Laws were written to ensure Hebrew men received longer prison sentences for smaller quantities. Families shattered, children grew up fatherless, and a new wave of trauma began.

THE SAME HANDS that once held whips now controlled legislation, policing, and economic policies to ensure Hebrews remained a captive people — this time behind bars and inside projects, rather than on plantations.

THE PROPHETIC CLOCK — 400 YEARS AND THE SHIFT OF POWER

*W*hen YAH spoke to Abraham, He gave a chilling prophecy:

"KNOW of a surety that thy seed shall be a stranger in a land that is not theirs, and shall serve them; and they shall afflict them four hundred years."

— Genesis 15:13

THE TRANSATLANTIC SLAVE trade is generally marked from 1619, when the first ship arrived in Virginia. For four centuries, Hebrews in America endured slavery, Jim Crow, lynchings, redlining, police brutality, business, economic, and educational racism, mass incarceration, cultural and spiritual warfare.

As THE PROPHETIC clock approached its fulfillment, we began to see shifts:

•European Gentile churches fell into apostasy — embracing homo-sexuality, prosperity scams, and outright rejection of biblical truth.

•Meanwhile, the true Hebrews began to awaken, rediscovering their identity, Torah, and the name of their King: Yahusha

This is the shift of dispensations.
The age of Gentile dominance is closing.
The time of Jacob's trouble transitions into Jacob's triumph.

"For Esau is the end of the world, and Jacob is the beginning of it that followeth"
2 Esdras

Knowing who Israel is matters. It is not just historical curiosity; it is an eschatological necessity.
Blessing or cursing the true Israel is how nations secure blessing or invite wrath.

The Awakening of Judah — From Dry Bones to a Mighty Army

"Then He said to me, 'Prophesy to these bones and say to them, O dry bones, hear the word of the Lord!'"
— Ezekiel 37:4

"AND WHEN I BEHELD, lo, the sinews and the flesh came upon them... but there was no breath in them."

— Ezekiel 37:8

"THEN HE SAID UNTO ME, Son of man, these bones are the whole house of Israel..."

— Ezekiel 37:11

. . .

I. FROM DEATH TO AWAKENING: The Prophetic Fulfillment

THE PROPHET EZEKIEL stood in a valley full of dry bones.
Scattered. Lifeless. Forgotten.

AND THE MOST High asked him, "Can these bones live?"

THAT VALLEY WASN'T JUST metaphorical. It was prophetic.
It represented the house of Israel, and more specifically, the tribe of
Judah—cut off from its heritage, severed from its land, and spiritually
asleep in the lands of captivity.

THE BLACK MAN and woman in America are those dry bones:
•Stripped of language.
•Erased of lineage.
•Shamed into forgetting who they are.
•Forced to believe they're African, cursed, thugs, or just "Black."

BUT NOW—SOMETHING is happening.

II. The Rattling Begins: The Identity Crisis is Breaking

FOR CENTURIES, Judah has walked in a fog of confusion:
•They sang in the church but didn't know their name.

•They shouted "HalleluYah " but didn't know the Hebrew behind it.

•They prayed to Jesus (Yahusha) but didn't know they were His blood.

AND NOW THE fog is lifting.

THE BONES ARE RATTLING.

ALL OVER THE WORLD, a once-slumbering people are waking up and asking questions that shake kingdoms:

•Why do Deuteronomy 28 curses match our history perfectly?

•Why were we enslaved for 400 years like Genesis 15:13 foretold?

•Why do the people in Israel not match the descriptions in the Bible?

•Why is our history only told starting at slavery—and never before it?

THE ANSWERS ARE POURING in like rain, and the breath is beginning to return.

III. Breath of Life: The Spirit is Reviving the Remnant

EZEKIEL SAW the bones come together.

He saw flesh return.

He saw structure without life.

BUT IT WASN'T until the breath entered them that the army stood.

· · ·

TODAY, that breath is the Ruach Ha'Qodesh—the Holy Spirit of the Most High—blowing across a people long forgotten.

•Torah and The Gospel is being studied.

•Hebrew is being spoken again.

•Feasts are being kept.

•Identity is being restored.

AND MOST IMPORTANTLY: Repentance is breaking out.

"IN THE LAND of their captivity, they shall remember themselves."
— Baruch 2:30 (Apocrypha)

THIS IS NOT A MOVEMENT.

This is not a trend.

This is prophecy unfolding.

IV. Repentance, Not Revenge: Judah's True Rise

THE WORLD FEARS A RISING Black nation.

They imagine vengeance, riots, and racial war.

BUT THE TRUE rise of Judah is not revenge against the nations—it is reunion with their Elohim.

. . .

"IF MY PEOPLE, who are called by My name, shall humble themselves and pray..."

— 2 Chronicles 7:14

THE MOST HIGH is calling His people not to march in anger—but to bow in repentance.

THE CURSES ARE BREAKING because the people are returning.

THIS IS SPIRITUAL WARFARE.

Not a revolution with guns—but a resurrection of truth.

V. The Role of the Gentiles in the Awakening

AS JUDAH RISES, the Gentiles face a choice:

•Mock or support.

•Dismiss or investigate.

•Persecute or bless.

"THE GENTILES SHALL COME to thy light, and kings to the brightness of thy rising."

— Isaiah 60:3

THE AWAKENING of Judah is not the rejection of Gentiles.

It is their invitation to truth—to stand with the people of YAH and walk in His covenant.

. . .

THERE ARE Gentiles who will join the remnant.

There are Gentiles who will defend the truth.

And there are Gentiles who will fall for rejecting it.

"I WILL BLESS those who bless thee, and curse those who curse thee."

— Genesis 12:3

VI. From Slave to Soldier: Judah as a Holy Army

Let it be known:

The Black man in America is not a thug.
He is not a criminal by default.
He is not a failed African experiment.

He is Judah—the kingly tribe.

His DNA is divine.
His blood is covenantal.
His awakening is inevitable.

The same Judah who was shackled in chains will one day:
•Judge the nations (Psalm 149:6–9)
•Rule with righteousness (Isaiah 11)
•Be regathered from every nation (Isaiah 11:11–12, Jeremiah 23:8)
•Sing a new song in Zion (Revelation 14)

HE IS NOT RISING ALONE.

. . .

JUDAH IS BECOMING AN ARMY.

VII. This Is That Prophecy — The Time Is Now

MAKE NO MISTAKE: this is that valley.

THE PRISON YARDS, ghettos, hoods, barrios, favelas, and slums—they are the modern valley of dry bones.

But the Word has gone forth.
And now the bones are shaking.
The flesh is returning.
And the breath of YAH is blowing.

WHAT YOU ARE SEEING IS NOT a trend.

IT IS THE FULFILLMENT OF:

•Ezekiel 37

•Deuteronomy 30

•Baruch 2

•Isaiah 11

•Revelation 7

•Joel 3

•Zechariah 12

. . .

JUDAH IS AWAKENING.

And once he stands—nothing can stop the Most High's plan.

SUMMARY:

JUDAH, long forgotten and spiritually dead, is now rising. The awakening of the so-called African American, the scattered Hebrew Israelites, is not a passing trend —it is the fulfillment of prophecy. A remnant is returning to their Elohim. Repentance is replacing rage. Identity is replacing confusion. And the breath of YAH is reviving a holy army that will stand in the last days—not to rule through violence, but through righteousness and truth.

PART II
THE SYSTEM THAT KEEPS US CAPTIVE : FROM CHAINS TO CONFUSION THE CONTINUATION OF CAPTIVITY

Chapters 9-16

When the physical shackles were removed, mental ones were forged in their place. It was no longer necessary to beat a Hebrew body when you could bind a Hebrew mind. The slave masters knew this well. As the plantation transformed into the prison, and the whip into the schoolbook, the enemy changed his form—but never his goal.

To this day, the world does not really fear a violent Hebrew—it fears an awakened one. Not the one who marches, but the one who remembers. Because if he remembers, he repents. And if he repents, he is restored.

"The fear of the LORD is the beginning of wisdom." — Psalm 111:10

. . .

The system wasn't afraid of us because we were strong. It was afraid because we are chosen. So the agenda became to distract, distort, and dilute.

CHURCH CHURCH CHURCH

I. The Gospel of White Supremacy – Christianity's Complicity in the Cover-Up

II. The Catholic Church — A Counterfeit Authority

III. The Black church — False Prophets and Fallen Pulpits – The Spiritual Betrayal of the Hebrew Church

—

I THE GOSPEL of White Supremacy – Christianity's Complicity in the Cover-Up

"WOE unto them that call evil good, and good evil; that put darkness for light, and light for darkness..." – Isaiah 5:20

. . .

I. The Hijacking of the Gospel

What began as a movement of oppressed Hebrews under Roman occupation—the good news of the Kingdom preached by a brown-skinned Messiah named Yahusha—was transformed into a tool of conquest, colonization, and control.

The early followers of Christ were Hebrews, not Europeans. The apostles spoke Hebrew and Aramaic, not Latin. They worshipped in synagogues, not cathedrals. They celebrated Passover, not Easter. They followed Torah, not tradition. But as time passed and the faith spread into Gentile lands, something dark began to unfold: the gospel was hijacked.

When Rome adopted Christianity under Emperor Constantine in the 4th century, the gospel stopped being a message of deliverance and became a weapon of domination. *The oppressors now claimed to serve the same Messiah who came to set captives free.*

What followed wasn't revival—it was revision.

II. From Yeshua to White Jesus: The Great Image Swap

Perhaps no deception has done more damage to the identity of the Hebrews than the image of the white Jesus.

"Whose image is this?" – Matthew 22:20

. . .

THAT QUESTION WAS ORIGINALLY about Caesar's coin. But it now echoes through centuries of spiritual confusion.

THE BIBLICAL MESSIAH is described in Revelation 1:14-15:

"HIS HEAD and his hairs were white like wool... and his feet like unto fine brass, as if they burned in a furnace."

WOOLLY HAIR. Burnished bronze skin. The Son of Man looked like His people. Yet centuries later, we were handed images of a soft-skinned, blue-eyed, European "Savior" named Jesus—modeled after Cesare Borgia, the morally corrupt son of Pope Alexander VI.

THIS WASN'T JUST artistic interpretation. It was calculated erasure.

BECAUSE IF YOU change the image of God, you change the image of those made in His likeness.

III. The Catholic Church: Architect of Apostasy

THE ROMAN CATHOLIC CHURCH didn't just spread Christianity—it rebranded it.

•Idolatry was introduced: statues, rosaries, relics.

•Paganism was baptized: Christmas (Saturnalia), Easter (Ishtar), saints replacing ancestral reverence.

•Papal supremacy replaced Scripture.

•Confession to priests replaced direct prayer.

•Mary was elevated almost to goddess status, while the true identity of Mary—a young Hebrew woman—was buried.

ALL WHILE CONTINUING to persecute the very people the Messiah came from.

THE SAME INSTITUTION that claims the authority of Peter once funded slave ships, blessed crusaders, tortured heretics, and silenced dissent.

AND WHAT OF their legacy today? Billions follow a faith system built not on truth, but paganism and tradition. Meanwhile, the descendants of the apostles are still in captivity—taught to view themselves as cursed, criminal, or cursed-by-Ham (we do not descend from Ham we descend from Shem) footnotes in their own spiritual story.

THIS ISN'T CHRISTIANITY. This is counterfeit.

IV. Slave Bible and the Preacher on the Plantation

LET US GO DEEPER.

DURING SLAVERY, many plantation owners gave their enslaved Hebrews a special Bible—called the Slave Bible—which had over 90% of the Old Testament and 50% of the New Testament removed. Verses about freedom, justice, and deliverance were cut out. What remained? Passages about obedience, submission, and servants obeying their masters.

. . .

"IT WAS NEVER ABOUT SALVATION. It was about subjugation."

THEY ERASED Exodus but kept Ephesians 6:5:

"SERVANTS, obey your earthly masters with fear and trembling..."

THIS WAS psychological warfare dressed in holy robes. The slave master was painted as Moses. The Hebrew became Pharaoh's brick-maker. The preacher on the plantation was often handpicked— (just like our modern day entertainers) trained not to stir the spirit, but to pacify the pain.

AND THIS IS WHY, to this day, many Hebrew men and women sit in church buildings under systems that continue to erase their identity— systems that preach Jesus but hide Yahusha, that promise heaven but offer chains.

V. Modern-Day Miseducation: Pulpits Without Prophets

THE DECEPTION DIDN'T END in the 1800s. Today, many predominantly Black churches are still following Eurocentric theology and denomi-national doctrine rather than truth.

THEY PREACH PROSPERITY, but not prophecy.

They talk about tithes, but not about repentance.

They praise Caesar's government, but never expose its wickedness.

They teach forgiveness, but never call for justice.

. . .

THEY CELEBRATE MLK but forget Moses.

AND PERHAPS MOST TRAGICALLY, they don't teach salvation or repentance— They preach prosperity and manifestation and a Jesus that loves everyone no matter what. Telling Hebrews to love Jesus, but never revealing who they are in His bloodline. As a result, many Hebrew believers remain spiritually awakened, but historically amnesiac.

VI. The True Church vs. The Institutional Church

THERE IS A REMNANT RISING—A generation of Hebrews awakening to the truth. They are not content with emotional services and shallow sermons. They want meat, not milk. They want Scripture, not superstition. They want Yah, not tradition.

THESE ARE the voices crying out in the wilderness:

"COME OUT OF HER, MY PEOPLE." – Revelation 18:4

THE TRUE CHURCH is not a denomination. It's not a building. It's not 501(c)(3). It's a body of believers who walk in truth, keep the commandments, and follow the Messiah in spirit and in truth.

THE INSTITUTIONAL CHURCH, however, is often entangled in political loyalty, cultural compromise, and theological colonization.

ONE CHURCH UPLIFTS ZION. The other defends Babylon.

. . .

VII. A Call to the Hebrew Believer: Come Out of Her

To every Hebrew brother and sister still in churches that suppress their identity—this is your wake-up call.

You are not cursed—you are chosen.
You are not an afterthought—you are the apple of His eye.
You are not just "Black Christians"—you are Hebrew believers rediscovering your covenant.

It's time to come out of Babylon.
Out of confusion.
Out of spiritual Stockholm Syndrome.
Out of the plantation gospel.

Return to your roots. Reclaim your name. Walk in covenant. Teach your children. Expose the lies.

The Messiah is not returning for a confused bride—He's returning for a restored nation. A people who know who they are. A people who have come out of deception and into divine truth.

II The Catholic Church — A Counterfeit Authority

It is impossible to discuss spiritual deception without further confronting the Roman Catholic Church.

•The Catholic institution is built on a lie — that Peter was its first pope, that the pope is infallible, that tradition overrides Scripture.

•Its halls are filled with statues, sunbursts, and pagan imagery borrowed from Babylon and Rome.

•Its record is stained with homosexual pedophilia scandals that have ruined countless lives.

CONTRAST this with the early Hebrew church.

The first followers of Yahusha were Torah-keeping Hebrews who worshiped in synagogues, kept feast days, and rejected idolatry.

It was only after Roman emperors hijacked the faith that images of a white Jesus, graven statues, and Sunday worship replaced the lunar Sabbath.

THE CATHOLIC CHURCH became a global empire, baptizing slavery, colonization, and genocide in the name of Christ.

To this day, it stands as a counterfeit — a spiritual Babylon clothed in purple and scarlet, drunk on the blood of the saints.

III THE BLACK Church

False Prophets and Fallen Pulpits – The Spiritual Betrayal of the Hebrew Church

"Her priests have violated my law, and have profaned mine holy things: they have put no difference between the holy and profane... and I am profaned among them."
— Ezekiel 22:26

The betrayal did not begin in the streets. It began in the sanctuary. While the Hebrew man was being lynched in the fields, poisoned in

the ghettos, imprisoned in the courts, and emasculated by the media—
where were the shepherds?

The Black church, once the heartbeat of resistance and the echo of
prophetic fire, has in many cases become a stage for performers, a
platform for cowards, and a safehouse for traitors.

**THE BETRAYAL of the Hebrew people has not only come from
without—it has erupted from within.**

I. THE MODERN Plantation Church

WHAT WE NOW CALL THE "Black church" was born under the
surveillance of slaveholders. Enslaved Hebrews were allowed to
worship only when it reinforced obedience to their earthly masters.
Any mention of freedom, justice, or prophetic truth was violently
suppressed.

BUT THE TRAGEDY IS THIS: long after physical chains were broken,
mental chains remained—and many pulpits were passed down not as
altars of truth, but as tools of pacification.

•Prosperity Gospel replaced prophetic truth.
Instead of warning of judgment or calling for repentance, pastors
began preaching comfort: "sow a seed," "claim your blessing," "name it
and claim it"—while ignoring injustice, sin, and identity.
•501(c)(3) status silenced righteous boldness.
Many churches traded truth for tax exemption. Once registered under
government authority, the pulpit was neutered. Pastors would speak
about heaven but not about real-life hells on Earth: racism, injustice,
or national repentance.
•Preachers became celebrities, not servants.

Designer suits, luxury cars, mega buildings(not that there is inherently anything wrong with these things. In fact, we are called to be blessed) — but little spiritual substance. Preaching became entertainment. Worship became a concert. The altar became a runway. And the sheep? Scattered, starving, and sedated.

II. From Moses to Pharaoh: Pastors Who Became Gatekeepers

EVERY GENERATION HAS ITS MOSES—BUT it also has its Pharaohs wearing shepherd's robes.

These are not just false prophets who fail to lead—they are gate-keepers of the Babylonian system, keeping the Hebrew people asleep. They are like the false priests in Jeremiah's day who cried "peace, peace" when there was no peace (Jeremiah 6:14).
•They reject truth-tellers:
Any prophet who speaks on Hebrew identity, repentance, or judgment is branded "divisive" or "a conspiracy theorist."
•They endorse wickedness:
Some pulpits now openly affirm sin—from homosexuality to gender confusion—claiming "love" while ignoring the Most High's commandments.
•They protect whitewashed doctrine:
They refuse to question Roman Catholic influence, the image of white Jesus, or the historical lies that erased the true Hebrews from Scripture.

THESE MEN ARE NOT SHEPHERDS—THEY are hirelings. And when the wolf comes, they flee—or worse, they aid him.

. . .

THE JEZEBEL SPIRIT in the Church

IT IS NOT ONLY the men who have compromised. Many pulpits are now ruled by the spirit of Jezebel—a spirit of disorder, rebellion, and self-worship.

JEZEBEL IS NOT JUST A WOMAN—IT is a system. It speaks through male and female alike. It elevates emotion over truth, feelings over Scripture, power over purity.

Under Jezebel's influence:
•The church becomes sensual, not sacred.
Worship becomes erotic. Lyrics become romanticized pleas not to Christ, but to a "lover." Sanctuaries look like nightclubs. Holiness is mocked as "old-fashioned."
•Women rule over men spiritually.
Just as in Isaiah 3:12, women are exalted while men are diminished. The order of YAH is reversed—and chaos always follows.
•Correction is outlawed.
Anyone who speaks of sin, repentance, or gender order is labeled "judgmental." The modern church has become allergic to truth.

SELLING Out to the Synagogue of Satan

Some of the most prominent Black pastors and bishops are now tools of elite manipulation, controlled by political funding, media ties, and corporate sponsorships. They are elevated not for their righteousness, but for their compliance.
•They host politicians who support abortion, LGBTQ+ agendas, and Zionist lies.

•They attend ecumenical gatherings with Catholic bishops and global elites.
•They endorse "interfaith unity" while denying the exclusivity of YAH and the true Gospel.

THIS IS the spiritual whoredom described in Revelation. These are churches who have become "harlots," drinking from Babylon's cup.

AND YES, many of these so-called leaders know exactly what they are doing. This is not ignorance—it is idolatry.

A CALL BACK to the Ancient Path

BUT NOT ALL IS LOST. The Most High always preserves a remnant— faithful men and women who will not bow to Baal, who will not sell their voice for silver.

The call is simple but costly:
•Repent.
False prophets must either humble themselves or be removed. Judgment begins in the house of YAH (1 Peter 4:17).
•Restore righteousness.
We must return to the commandments, the true Gospel of the Kingdom, and the identity of the true people of Israel.
•Reclaim the pulpit.
The pulpit is not for politicians, celebrities, or cowards—it is for the watchmen, the prophets, the Levites who cry aloud and spare not.
•Rebuild the people.
The purpose of the church is not to pacify but to prepare. Prepare the Hebrew man to be a priest again. Prepare the Hebrew woman

to be a holy vessel again. Prepare the children to walk in covenant.

THIS GENERATION IS CRYING OUT NOT for another motivational speech —but for a word from YAH.

THE HEBREW CHURCH has been infiltrated, compromised, and in many cases, completely hijacked. False prophets have traded truth for popularity, purity for profit, and identity for influence. But the Most High is raising up a remnant of leaders who will return to the ancient path —unapologetically Hebrew, unshaken in truth, and anointed to tear down altars built in Babylon's name.

FROM THE PLANTATION to the Pulpit — The Black Church's Role in Perpetuating the Lie

"HAVING A FORM OF GODLINESS, but denying the power thereof: from such turn away."
— 2 Timothy 3:5

"MY PEOPLE ARE DESTROYED for lack of knowledge: because thou hast rejected knowledge, I will also reject thee..."
— Hosea 4:6

I. PREACHERS IN CHAINS: Religion Born in Captivity

THE BLACK CHURCH was born in the belly of the beast.

. . .

Stripped of names, languages, and culture, the enslaved Hebrew was given Christianity not through the voice of the prophets, but through the whip of the plantation master. Early Black preachers were:
•Selected by slave owners,
•Forced to recite pacifying scriptures,
•Prohibited from knowing the entire Bible,
•And often illiterate—trained to repeat, not to understand.

WHAT EMERGED WAS a systemic religious structure, not rooted in liberation, but in submission.

THE ENEMY KNEW:

IF WE CAN'T KILL their spirit, we'll control it.

II. The Slave Bible: A Gospel Without Exodus

SLAVEHOLDERS EDITED the Word of God.

Known as the Slave Bible, this wickedly abridged version:
•Removed the Book of Exodus—no story of Moses, no deliverance from Egypt,
•Deleted most of the prophets,
•Omitted scriptures about freedom, justice, and Hebrew identity,
•Highlighted only obedience, humility, and eternal reward.

THE MESSAGE WAS SIMPLE:

STAY IN YOUR PLACE. God wants it this way. Heaven will reward your suffering.

THIS WAS NOT the gospel of the Kingdom.

This was the gospel of Rome, tailored to keep Hebrews in mental, spiritual, and generational bondage.

III. The Evolution of the Pulpit: From Shackles to Suits

AFTER EMANCIPATION, the Black church became a vital center of community, education, and resistance.

It was in the Black church that:
•Schools were founded,
•Civil rights movements were launched,
•Voices like Martin Luther King Jr., Medgar Evers, Marcus Garvey, and others echoed.

But over time, something shifted.

As influence grew, so did compromise:
•Prosperity replaced prophecy,
•Emotionalism replaced revelation,
•Tradition replaced truth.

Pastors began to mimic the same systems that once oppressed them:
•Building major congregations, while neglecting the community,

•Preaching prosperity, while ignoring justice,
•Preaching the word of God out of context to further personal agendas,
•Singing praises to a whitewashed Christ while denying their Hebrew Messiah.

IV. Sunday Service and Spiritual Sleepwalking

Let us not be deceived—much of modern church culture is nothing more than spiritual entertainment.
•The choir sings.
•The preacher shouts.
•The people dance.
•But repentance is absent.
•Identity is concealed.
•And truth is avoided.

Many pastors today:
•Know the truth about the Hebrews,
•Know that the real Israelites are the descendants of the transatlantic slave trade,
•Know the lies embedded in seminary doctrines...

...BUT REMAIN SILENT TO PRESERVE:

•Position,

•Paychecks,

•Popularity.

THEY FEAR man more than they fear YHWH.

. . .

"FOR THEY LOVED the praise of men more than the praise of God." —
John 12:43

V. The Pimping of the Gospel

WE MUST SAY IT PLAINLY: some preachers have become pimps of the
pulpit.

They:
•Sell hope while ignoring repentance,
•Manipulate emotion to secure offerings,
•Preach miracles but never teach identity,
•Exploit poverty while living in luxury,
•Speak of heaven while forsaking justice on earth.

This is not the church of Acts.
This is not the ministry of Yahusha.
This is not truth. It is Babylon dressed in clergy robes.

VI. What Must Change: A Call to the Watchmen

We are living in a prophetic hour. And judgment begins in the house
of God.

Pastors, prophets, bishops, and ministers—return to your post as
watchmen on the wall.
Preach repentance.
Proclaim identity.
Cast down the whitewashed lies and lift up the true Hebrew Messiah.

It is time for:
•The Black Church to become the **Hebrew Assembly**,
•The pulpit to return to truth,
•And for the people to walk in the fullness of the Covenant.

"Cry aloud, spare not, lift up thy voice like a trumpet, and show my people their transgression..." — Isaiah 58:1

SUMMARY:

THE BLACK CHURCH, though birthed in pain and hope, was manipulated to become a tool of suppression. Today, it faces a divine ultimatum—continue preaching lies for comfort, or awaken the people with the truth of their identity, calling, and covenant. The pulpit must return to the prophets. The church must become a holy remnant. And the pastors must once again become shepherds of the Most High—not performers for Pharaoh.

S.O.S

*L*et us now pull the veil back on one of the darkest, most controversial, and deliberately hidden truths of our time—a truth that Yahusha Himself warned us about. This is not conspiracy. This is Scripture. This is history. This is war.

WHO ARE THE REAL JEWS? Exposing the Synagogue of Satan

"I KNOW THY WORKS, and tribulation, and poverty, (but thou art rich) and I know the blasphemy of them which say they are Jews, and are not, but are the synagogue of Satan."

— Revelation 2:9

"THE WORLD HAS BEEN DECEIVED, not by accident, but by design. And the truth, once buried, is rising like a lion awakened from sleep."

I. A BOLD DECLARATION: Not All Who Say They Are Jews… Are

. . .

FOR CENTURIES, the world has been led to believe that the people occupying the land of Israel today, and those who dominate Jewish religious, financial, and political institutions globally, are the biblical Jews.

But Scripture,(specifically, Jesus Yahusha) cuts through this confusion with surgical precision:
There are those who say they are Jews, but are not—and are instead the synagogue of Satan.

This is not antisemitism.
This is anti-deception.

We do not hate the "Jewish" people—most of whom are themselves deceived.
But we must reclaim the truth: The true descendants of Judah, the tribe from which the term "Jew" derives, are the very people the world has mocked, enslaved, and dismissed—the so-called "Negroes" of America and the Western world.

II. Scripture Confirms It: Judah in Captivity, Not in Power

"AND HE SHALL SCATTER thee among all people, from the one end of the earth even unto the other... and among these nations shalt thou find no ease..."

— Deuteronomy 28:64–65

Ask yourself:
•Are the modern "Jews" scattered and oppressed—or wealthy and powerful?
•Do they suffer poverty and systemic racism—or control major banking systems and media empires?
•Are they forgotten, erased, and mocked—or promoted, protected, and revered?

THE TRUE HEBREWS are in captivity just like the Bible says they would be, not in control.

THE TRUE JEWS are poor in the world's eyes, not sitting on thrones of global influence.

III. Ashkenazi, Sephardi, and the Khazarian Question

Let's look at the historical record—not just Scripture:
•Ashkenazi Jews trace their lineage to Eastern Europe, especially Germany and Poland—not ancient Israel.
•Sephardic Jews have roots in Spain and North Africa—but were often converts or intermarried with Iberian royalty.
•The Khazars were a Turkic people who converted to Judaism en masse in the 8th century A.D.—not descendants of Abraham, Isaac, and Jacob.

THE 13TH-CENTURY Jewish historian Yehuda Halevi and the famed convert king Bulan of Khazaria openly confirmed this mass conversion.

. . .

AND TODAY, the majority of those who identify as "Jews" trace their lineage not to Abraham—but to these converted Gentile groups.

<u>Ashkenazi name origin</u>
<u>Biblical Background: The Sons of Noah</u>

NOAH WAS NOT the only person to survive the flood. Noah had three sons: Japheth, Shem, and Ham

FROM ZONDERVAN BIBLE DICTIONARY:

SHEM— (shĕm, name, fame), second son of Noah, and progenitor of the Semitic race, was born 98 years before the Flood (Gen. 11:10)

HAM— (hăm, perhaps hot). 1. The youngest son of Noah, born probably about 96 years before the Flood; and one of eight persons to live through the Flood. He became the progenitor of the dark races; not the Negroes, but the Egyptians, Ethiopians, Libyans and Canaan-ites (Gen. 10:6-20).

JAPHETH— (ja'feth, God will enlarge), son of Noah (Gen. 5:32; 6:10; 7:13; 10:21); had seven sons (Gen. 10:2); descendants occupied "isles of Gentiles" (Gen. 10:5);

SO...

•Shem – the ancestor of Semitic peoples including the (Hebrews).
•Ham – the ancestor of African and some Middle Eastern peoples.
•Japheth – the ancestor of Indo-European peoples (Greeks, Medes, Scythians, Europeans).

WHO WAS ASHKENAZ?

ASHKENAZ IS EXPLICITLY MENTIONED in Genesis 10:3 as a descendant of Japheth:

"AND THE SONS OF GOMER; Ashkenaz, and Riphath, and Togarmah."

(Genesis 10:3, KJV)

•Gomer was Japheth's son.
•Ashkenaz was Gomer's son — making Ashkenaz a grandson of Japheth, not Shem.

ASHKENAZ IS HISTORICALLY ASSOCIATED with peoples from regions around the Black Sea, particularly Scythians, and later with Germanic and Slavic regions. In medieval Jewish literature, "Ashkenaz" became associated with Germany and Northern Europe.

WHY A DESCENDANT of Shem Would Not Be Called Ashkenazi

THE HEBREWS DESCEND FROM SHEM, not Japheth.

•Abraham is a descendant of Shem → Arphaxad → Eber → Peleg → Abraham (Genesis 11).

•Thus, Israelites are Shemites (Semitic), not Japhethites.

SO BY BIBLICAL LOGIC:

A SHEMITE (SEMITIC PERSON) — such as a Hebrew — would not be named after a Japhethite (like Ashkenaz), just as a Chinese person wouldn't be called a Germanic surname in their original culture.

SO AGAIN, who are the real Jews?

IV. Historical Witnesses Agree

Even beyond Scripture and genetics, history testifies:
•Arthur Koestler, an Ashkenazi Jew, wrote the book **The Thirteenth Tribe** to expose that modern Jews are Khazarian converts.
•Herodotus, Josephus, and early Arab and African historians recorded the presence of black Hebrew tribes in Africa—long before the transatlantic slave trade.
•Slave ship records, old maps, and colonial documents identified the Slave Coast as "The Kingdom of Judah."

"THEY WEREN'T JUST SELLING Africans. They were selling Hebrews. That's why the ships docked near a region called 'Wahida'—Judah."

— Historical map archives, 17th century.

· · ·

V. The Theft of Identity and the Inversion of Truth

Here lies the most diabolical crime in human history:
The identity of the chosen people was stolen, and their place was given to others—so the world would never know who Israel truly is.

If Satan can confuse the world about who the true Jews are,
then he can divert the blessings, redirect prophecy, and hinder repentance.

Thus:
•The fake Jews receive blind support from the church and the government.
•The true Hebrews are mocked, marginalized, and mass incarcerated.
•The world blesses the wrong people, and curses the right ones.

"Woe unto them that call evil good, and good evil..." — Isaiah 5:20

VI. Modern Power, Ancient Prophecy

Who controls:
•The international banking institutions?
•Hollywood?
•Major sports and media corporations?
•Pharmaceutical industries?
•Political lobbies like AIPAC?

These are not poor, oppressed people.
They are powerful, wealthy, and shielded by governments.

Meanwhile, the Black man in America—the real Judahite—is:
•Gunned down in the streets.
•Mocked in entertainment.
•Locked in prisons.
•Systematically erased from his past and barred from his future.

THIS IS NOT COINCIDENCE. This is fulfillment of prophecy.

VII. The Synagogue of Satan: Not All Jews—But a Specific Elite

We must make this clear: Not every Jewish person is part of the synagogue of Satan.
Most are sincere. Most are deceived. Most are victims of generational lies.

But there is a ruling elite—a group deeply embedded in the financial, religious, and media empires of the world—who are:
•Occultic behind closed doors.
•Loyal to globalism, not God.
•Enemies of the true Messiah (Yahusha), and enemies of His true people.

THIS GROUP WEARS the cloak of religion—but serves Lucifer.

THAT IS the Synagogue of Satan.

AND REVELATION CALLS THEM OUT.

· · ·

VIII. Why This Deception Matters

IF YOU DON'T KNOW who Israel is, you cannot:

•Understand prophecy,

•Interpret Scripture properly,

•Bless who YAH has called you to bless.

CHURCHES SUPPORT MODERN ISRAEL BLINDLY—SENDING money, prayers, and political allegiance—while ignoring the cries of the Black American community.

But YAH never forgets His people.
The time is coming when the world will know—and many will mourn that they backed the wrong side.

"THE FIRST SHALL BE LAST, and the last shall be first..." — Matthew 20:16

SUMMARY:

THE GREATEST IDENTITY theft in human history has blinded the world. Those who claim to be the Jews today are converts, not covenant people. The true children of Judah have been hidden in plain sight—marginalized, oppressed, and erased. But the Most High is not mocked. He is uncovering the truth, exposing the counterfeit synagogue, and reawakening His true people. Judah will rise—not to dominate, but to worship, repent, and reign in righteousness.

. . .

71

<u>THE SYNAGOGUE OF SATAN</u> – Exposing the Global Imposters and
Their Agenda

"I KNOW the blasphemy of them which say they are Jews, and are not,
but are the synagogue of Satan."

— Revelation 2:9

"THE EARTH IS GIVEN into the hand of the wicked: he covereth the
faces of the judges thereof."

— Job 9:24

I. THE BLASPHEMY That Shakes the Nations

WHEN YAHUSHA UTTERED the words "synagogue of Satan," He wasn't
speaking in riddles.

HE WAS MAKING A DIRECT ACCUSATION—AGAINST a group of imposters
who had infiltrated His people, claimed their identity, and twisted the
covenant of Yah into a system of global control.

These are not just fake Jews.
These are the architects of deception.
They wear the mask of God's people, but serve the prince of this
world.

And yet, nearly every pulpit avoids this topic. Why?

Because the synagogue of Satan owns the systems that punish those
who speak truth:

•They own the banks.
•They own the media.
•They control Hollywood.
•They fund the wars.
•They influence governments.
•They finance religious institutions.

To expose them is to declare war on the world's power structure.
But the remnant must not be silent.

II. Who Are the Imposters? Tracing the Ashkenazi and Khazar
Connection

Today, when the world says "Jew," it points to:
•European-looking men in black hats and fake curls.
•Families who fled the Holocaust.
•Citizens of the modern state of Israel.

But history, genetics, and Scripture all tell a different story.

The Ashkenazi Jews:
•The term Ashkenaz appears in Genesis 10:3 as a descendant of
Japheth—not Shem.
•Therefore, Ashkenazi Jews are Japhethic Gentiles, not Semitic
Hebrews.
•Most modern Jews trace their lineage through the maternal line,
often of European descent.

The Khazar Empire:
•In the 8th century, a Turkic people called the Khazars in what is now modern day Ukraine, converted to Judaism.
•This was a political conversion, not a spiritual inheritance.
•The Khazars adopted the customs and texts of the Hebrews—but not the bloodline.
•After their empire collapsed, they migrated into Eastern Europe and became the core of modern-day "Jewry."

THIS MEANS that the majority of so-called Jews today are converts, not descendants of Abraham, Isaac, and Jacob.

"AND IF YE be Christ's, then are ye Abraham's seed..." (Galatians 3:29)

IDENTITY CANNOT BE CLAIMED by land or language—but by covenant and blood.

III. The Cover-Up: Why the Impostor Agenda Matters

SO WHY HAS the world been programmed to believe a lie?

Because if the world blesses the wrong people, it will be cursed.
Because if the true Hebrews never know who they are, they will never repent.
Because if Satan can masquerade as an angel of light, so can his children.

Tactics of the Synagogue of Satan:

•Whitewashing of Scripture: turning Moses, David, Mary, and Christ into Europeans.
•Perverting the Gospel: replacing the covenant with Christ with man-made traditions (Talmud, Kabbalah).
•Creating Counterfeit Israel: establishing the state of Israel in 1948 through war and bloodshed—not prophecy.
•Controlling the narrative: using film, news, and academia to redefine history.

They hid the true Hebrews (Black descendants of slaves)
And exalted a counterfeit image—
To rob the world of prophetic clarity.

IV. Zionism: Politics Masquerading as Prophecy

THE MODERN STATE of Israel is not the fulfillment of biblical prophecy.

It was:
•Engineered through the Balfour Declaration (1917),
•Funded by Rothschild banking empires,
•And legitimized through United Nations decree, not divine regathering.

Biblically, Israel is to be:
•Gathered by Yah Himself (Isaiah 11:11–12),
•In repentance and obedience (Deuteronomy 30:1–3),
•And live in peace and righteousness, not war and secularism.

Today's Israel:
•Denies Christ,
•Embraces LGBTQ+ parades in Jerusalem,
•And weaponizes its identity for political domination.

This is not Zion.
This is Babylon in Hebrew costume.

V. The Real Antisemitism: Against the Real Semites

When awakened Hebrews speak truth, they are labeled:
•Antisemitic,
•Dangerous,
•Extremist.

But how can the real Semites be antisemitic?

This manipulation is designed to:
•Silence the awakening of Judah.
•Shield imposters from scrutiny.
•Maintain global power without question.

The term "antisemitism" is weaponized to protect the synagogue of Satan, not the covenant
people of Yah.

VI. Scriptural Clues to the Deception

"You are of your father the devil... he is a liar and the father of it."
(John 8:44)

Yahusha wasn't speaking to Romans.
He was speaking to religious leaders (Pharisees and Sadducees,
different from the Essenes whom were born Hebrew. That is why
they say they are "Abraham's seed and were never in bondage" even
though the Hebrews who were born Hebrews came from a bloodline
that had been in bondage. These are Edomites, descendants of
Abraham and Issac but not Jacob.) who had perverted the Law, killed
the prophets, and were plotting His crucifixion.

These were not the sons of Abraham in spirit, even if they rightly
claimed the bloodline.
And today, the same spirit of deception continues through:
•The Talmud, which calls Christ a sorcerer and Mary a prostitute.
•Kabbalah, which introduces mysticism, numerology, and gnosticism
into faith.
•The banking system, (Usury) ruled by elite bloodlines posing as Yah's
people.

VII. Why This Truth Must Be Told

This chapter is not about hate.
It's about truth and identity.

The Synagogue of Satan does not refer to all or even most of the
people identifying as Jews around the world.
It refers to a small specific elite class of imposters who:
•Claim to be Yah's chosen,
•Twist His Word for profit,

•And wage war against the true saints and indeed against the whole world.

"THE DRAGON WAS wroth with the woman, and went to make war with the remnant of her seed..." (Revelation 12:17)

We are not calling for hate or violence in any way, shape, form, or fashion —we are calling for discernment.
Let the reader examine the facts, pray, and seek the Spirit of Truth.

SUMMARY:

THE TRUE IDENTITY of the Hebrews has been suppressed. In their place, Satan has elevated a counterfeit—a synagogue that wears the name of Yah's people but serves the agenda of global deception. The remnant must wake up, not with hatred, but with holy clarity. Because only when the imposters are unmasked, can the world begin to see who Israel really is—and who Yah truly reigns through.

THE SYNAGOGUE OF SATAN — Global Elites, Deception, and the War Against the True Israel

"I KNOW the blasphemy of them which say they are Jews, and are not, but are the synagogue of Satan."

— Revelation 2:9

. . .

"FOR WE WRESTLE NOT against flesh and blood, but against principalities, against powers, against the rulers of the darkness of this world, against spiritual wickedness in high places."

— Ephesians 6:12

I. WHO IS the Synagogue of Satan?

THE TERM IS NOT symbolic or abstract. It refers to a real, organized, elite class of individuals—many masquerading as Jews—who control institutions, manipulate nations, and wage war against the true seed of Abraham, Isaac, and Jacob.

•These are not everyday European Jews who attend synagogue on Saturday.
•These are Kabbalistic, occultic, Luciferian elites, who know they are not the biblical Hebrews.
•Their power is not rooted in Torah—but in Babylon, Talmud, Freemasonry, Zionist politics, and banking empires.

This elite cabal is behind:
•The theft of Hebrew identity
•The whitewashing of the Bible
•The enslavement of Judah
•The confusion of the Gentile church
•The manipulation of governments and media

"YE ARE of your father the devil, and the lusts of your father ye will do... he is a liar, and the father of it."

— John 8:44

.   .   .

79

II. The False Claim to Israel

1. Khazaria and the Conversion to Judaism (8th Century A.D.)
•The Khazar Empire was a Turkic nation in Central Asia.
•In the 700s A.D., its ruling class converted to Judaism—not by faith, but by politics.
•Historian Arthur Koestler (himself Jewish) documents this in The Thirteenth Tribe, stating:
"The mainstream of modern Jewry did not originate in Judea but in the Caucasus…"

THIS EMPIRE, after its fall, scattered into Eastern Europe—primarily Poland, Russia, and Germany.

THE RESULT: a large population of Ashkenazi Jews who had no ancestral connection to Abraham, Isaac, or Jacob.

2. The Rise of Political Zionism
•In the 19th century, leaders like Theodor Herzl promoted a movement to establish a Jewish homeland.
•Zionism, however, was not spiritual—it was secular and nationalistic, aiming to place European Jews in Palestine under British and later U.S. protection.

This movement:
•Took land from Palestinians,
•Rebranded European converts as "God's chosen,"
•And used the Bible as a political tool to manipulate Gentile Christians into blind allegiance.

. . .

TODAY, many Christians support the state of Israel under the belief that doing so fulfills Bible prophecy. But ask yourself this:

"HOW CAN the people who own Hollywood, the pornography industry, Wall Street, the media, and global finance also be the oppressed 'chosen people'?"

HOW CAN anyone believe that the imposters are the true people of YAH when they've turned the Promised Land into a war zone? Gaza lies in ruins, its children buried beneath rubble — and yet the world is told to believe these are the Most High's anointed people. Would the true people of the Most High rule with hate, terror, and maliciousness? No. The fruit exposes the root. And this tree is rotten.

III. The Identity Theft of the True Israel

The greatest heist in history was not just of land or money, but of identity.
•Biblical Hebrews were people of melanin, not Europeans.
•They fled Roman persecution into Africa, not into Europe.
•They were captured, sold, and enslaved—not exalted into power.

YET SOMEHOW, the world believes the opposite when the Bible is very clear.

This is the deception of the synagogue of Satan:
•They have taken the name of Israel without the blood.

81

•They have rewritten the history of Zion. (Literally rewritten history because they own the publishing houses that publish the text books for the schools of America).

•They have blinded the Gentile church and kept the true Hebrews asleep.

"TRULY IN VAIN is salvation hoped for from the hills, and from the multitude of mountains: truly in YHWH our Elohim is the salvation of Israel."

— Jeremiah 3:23

IV. Their Control of Systems

LET'S BE SPECIFIC. The Synagogue of Satan operates by controlling systems, not just ideas. These include:

1. Media and Entertainment

•90% of American media is controlled by six conglomerates, many of which are led by Zionist executives.

•These industries promote:

•Sexual perversion,

•Violence,

•Anti-Hebrew masculinity,

•Feminism divorced from Torah,

•Anti-Christ ideology wrapped in "freedom."

2. Finance and Banking

•The Federal Reserve, the World Bank, and the IMF are deeply rooted in families like the Rothschilds, who funded both sides of world wars and established centralized banking systems.

•The dollar is debt-based and controlled by unelected oligarchs—most of whom claim "Jewish" identity.

3. Politics and Foreign Policy

•The U.S. Congress regularly sends billions in aid to the State of Israel.

• AIPAC manipulates U.S. politics to secure unwavering support for Israel through money, lobbying, and influence amongst other methods.

•Meanwhile, Black American descendants of slaves—true Hebrews—are given crumbs, trauma, and blame.

4. Education and History

•School systems glorify European history while minimizing and in most cases, eliminating Hebrew societal contributions and scriptural roots.

•The role of Black Hebrews in shaping global civilizations is erased or suppressed.

V. The War on True Israel

THIS ISN'T JUST POLITICAL—IT'S spiritual.

THE SYNAGOGUE of Satan does not merely deny the true Hebrews—they despise them. Why?

. . .

BECAUSE THE AWAKENING of Judah signals the end of their reign.

"AND WHEN THESE things begin to come to pass... lift up your heads; for your redemption draweth nigh."

— Luke 21:28

They fear:
•The restoration of Torah obedience,
•The rise of true prophets and watchmen,
•The return of Hebrew men as leaders and priests,
•The revival of a set-apart nation, no longer ruled by wicked systems.

VI. Exposing Without Hating

LET IT BE CLEAR: this is not a message of hatred. The true Hebrews are not calling for vengeance, but truth and repentance.

We do not hate Gentiles.
We do not hate European Jews (who are also Gentiles).
We hate deception.

YAHUSHA REBUKED THE RELIGIOUS ELITE—NOT because they were Jews —but because they had become tools of the enemy.

LIKEWISE, this book speaks out against systems, not souls.

. . .

"FOR WE WRESTLE NOT against flesh and blood, but against principalities, against powers, against the rulers of the darkness of this world, against spiritual wickedness in high places."

Ephesians 6:12

BUT MAKE NO MISTAKE: the truth must be declared.

VII. The Call to the Nations

To the Gentile Christian:
•Wake up. You've been taught to bless modern Israel without knowing who true Israel is.
•Study the Scriptures and ask the Father to open your eyes.
•Bless the true people, not just the political state.

To the Hebrew:
•Come out of her, My people. Leave Babylon.
•Know who you are.
•Return to your covenant.

Summary:

The synagogue of Satan is not an ancient mystery—it is a modern empire of deception. Through lies, theft, and sorcery, they have rebranded themselves as God's people while imprisoning the real children of Zion. The Most High is calling for exposure, not excuses. *The war is not against skin but against systems*—and it is already starting to be won by the power of truth.

THE MISEDUCATION OF THE HEBREW WOMAN – BEAUTY, BETRAYAL, AND BABYLON'S LIES

"*S*he openeth her mouth with wisdom; and in her tongue is the law of kindness." – Proverbs 31:26

I. DAUGHTER OF ZION: Royal Bloodline and Spiritual Power

Before Babylon whispered its lies, before Hollywood distorted her beauty, before the curriculum rewrote her history—she was royal. The Hebrew woman was not a side character in the divine narrative; she was a central pillar of the nation. She was Sarah, who birthed a nation in old age. She was Miriam, who danced in victory. She was Deborah, who judged Israel under the palm tree. She was Ruth, whose loyalty preserved a bloodline. And she was Mary, chosen to birth the Messiah.

The Hebrew woman walked with dignity, wisdom, and spiritual power. Her womb bore kings and prophets. Her voice echoed with counsel and comfort. She was eshet chayil—a woman of valor—not because Babylon said so, but because the Most High ordained her so.

But in a world governed by confusion (Babel), her identity had to be targeted. Because to wound a nation, you must first deceive its women.

II. Weaponizing Her Womb: From Birthgiver to Battleground

The Most High designed the Hebrew woman's womb to give birth to a holy nation. But Babylon turned it into a war zone.

The transatlantic slave trade didn't just shackle bodies—it aimed to corrupt the generational seed. Hebrew women were raped to breed slaves. Children were torn from their arms and sold. The enemy understood spiritual laws: destroy the family, sever the inheritance.

Later, under the guise of "freedom," eugenics policies arose. In the early 20th century, thousands of Black women were forcibly sterilized in the United States. In North Carolina alone, over 7,600 steriliza-tions occurred—many of them Hebrew women targeted by a system convinced they were "unfit to reproduce."

Even today, Planned Parenthood clinics are disproportionately located in Black neighborhoods. While abortion is a deeply sensitive and personal topic, we must tell the truth: over **20 million** Black babies have been aborted since Roe v. Wade. Babylon disguised geno-cide as choice. The seed of Jacob was declared "optional."

But what did the Most High say?

"Before I formed thee in the belly I knew thee." – Jeremiah 1:5

Her womb is not a convenience—it is a consecrated vessel. But Babylon has tried to convince her otherwise.

III. Beauty as a Curse: The Manufactured Image of the Hebrew Woman

Hollywood, music videos, and magazine covers have long conspired to recast the Hebrew woman—not as a Proverbs 31 queen, but as a

hypersexual, angry and aggressive, loud caricature independent from
need of the Hebrew man

In the days of slavery, her beauty was either mocked or exploited. The
story of Sarah Baartman, paraded around Europe in the 1800s as a
freak because of her body, is a tragic reminder of how the world has
both desired and degraded the Hebrew woman.

Today, the same spirit lives on—in lyrics, images, and influencers. The
Hebrew woman is told she is only valuable if she is desired, not
honored. She is taught to weaponize her body, not protect her soul.
Modesty is mocked as oppressive. Righteousness is "boring." Virginity
is outdated, oppressive, and not even a consideration. Jezebel is the
blueprint, not Esther.

And while the world applauds her sexual freedom, it remains silent about
her emotional brokenness, mental confusion and spiritual enslavement.

"As for my people, children are their oppressors, and women rule over
them. O my people, they which lead thee cause thee to err, and
destroy the way of thy paths." – Isaiah 3:12

IV. The Babylonian Brainwash: Feminism and the Lie of
Independence

In the 1960s and 70s, the Hebrew woman was strategically targeted
by white feminist ideology. While her Gentile counterparts sought
liberation from oppressive husbands in suburban homes, the Hebrew
woman had a different struggle—she had been raising children alone
due to mass incarceration and government-imposed fatherlessness.

Yet the feminist movement told her, "You don't need a man." And she
believed it.

But what really happened?

Government programs offered welfare—but only if the man was
absent. So the state became the provider, and the man was removed.

At the same time, music and media began promoting a new archetype: the independent woman who "don't need nobody." Especially not a man. It sounded empowering, but it was a trap.

The strength of the Hebrew woman is undeniable. But strength without order becomes rebellion. And rebellion is what Babylon wanted.

The Most High never called her to carry the nation alone. He called her to walk beside a righteous Hebrew man under His covenant. The enemy's goal wasn't just to make her "strong" it was to make her believe that Hebrew man were weak—it was to make her estranged from her covering.

"Every wise woman buildeth her house: but the foolish plucketh it down with her hands." – Proverbs 14:1

V. Betrayal and the Division from the Hebrew Man

The strongest weapon Babylon forged was division. It sowed seeds of mistrust between the Hebrew man and woman. Through historical trauma, economic stress, and media programming, it turned partners into enemies.

Movies portray the Hebrew man as absent, abusive, or unworthy. Talk shows ridicule him. Music degrades him (and Hebrew artist reinforce this by degrading themselves). Social media mocks him. And the Hebrew woman, hurt and hardened, often absorbs those lies-mixed with real life experiences dealing with lost and broken Hebrew men- and turns them inward.

Some Babylon has seduced into laying with another woman as if she were a man

Some are seduced by the idea that love outside their nation offers "stability" or "status."

This is a pattern of disconnection—This is us forgetting the purpose of our pairing.

When the Hebrew woman no longer loves, trusts, honors or respects the Hebrew man, the nation cannot stand.

But here's the deeper betrayal: Babylon knows the Hebrew woman is the cultural transmitter. If she teaches her children to hate their fathers, the next generation is already lost.

What do your children hear you say about their father?

What did you hear your mother say about your father that shaped your view on not only your father but Hebrew men in general?

VI. Healing the Daughter of Zion: A Call to Return

The Most High is not done with the Hebrew woman. No matter how many lies Babylon told, her identity remains untouched beneath the ashes.

"Shake thyself from the dust; arise, and sit down, O Jerusalem: loose thyself from the bands of thy neck, O captive daughter of Zion." – Isaiah 52:2

She is still chosen. Still set apart. Still beautiful—not because of curves, lips, or hair—but because the Most High adorned her in right-eousness. She was never meant to twerk for Babylon. She was meant to dance in His courts in praise of the Most High.

To the Hebrew woman reading this: you are not what culture says you are. You are not what trauma made you. You are not broken beyond repair.

Return. Repent. Be healed.

The Most High is not just calling back the Hebrew man. He's calling you, daughter of Zion. Because when the woman returns to her role, the household begins to rise. And when the household rises, the nation will follow.

Feminism — A Weapon Against the Hebrew Home

Feminism was never designed for the Hebrew woman.

The original suffragettes marched alongside eugenicists who advocated sterilizing "undesirable (melanin) races." Margaret Sanger, champion of birth control, openly targeted "Negro populations" for reduction.

As feminism evolved, it taught women that husbands were oppressors, children were burdens, and that fulfillment could only be found in careers outside the home. It taught that life was only fulfilled by living a life that was free and independent of a man and that only when you achieve the status symbols of Babylon, should a husband and family even be considered. What resulted was instead of women getting married and having families women were chasing careers but still getting pregnant without marriage.

For Hebrews, this was catastrophic. Unlike European women, who still often had family wealth and supportive social structures, Hebrew women were left to navigate motherhood alone — as welfare laws penalized marriage, and the state rewarded single households.

Today, Hebrew women are told they don't need their men. Internet, music, movies, podcast and talk shows all praise hyper-independence. But Scripture says:

"It is not good that the man should be alone."

— Genesis 2:18

Family is the divine order. A strong man, a virtuous woman, children raised in truth — this is how nations are built.

Feminism was a trap to dismantle that. And it worked.

THE JEZEBEL CONSTRUCT – How the Hebrew Woman Was Weaponized

"And I find more bitter than death the woman, whose heart is snares and nets, and her hands as bands: whoso pleaseth God shall escape from her; but the sinner shall be taken by her."

— Ecclesiastes 7:26

I. Introduction: A Queen Turned Against Her Kingdom

There is no threat more potent to the spiritual rise of a nation than the division between its men and women. When a woman turns against the man she was created to love, help and honor, the entire foundation of the household—of the nation—begins to collapse. What we now face is a generation of Hebrew women who, rather than being the nurturers of righteous legacy, have been conditioned and weaponized to destroy their own house. This did not happen by accident. This was a strategy.

From slavery to modern feminism, from welfare dependency to media manipulation, the Hebrew woman has been targeted—first as a victim, then as a tool of division. She has been seduced into a counterfeit power, encouraged to see her man as the enemy, and convinced that submission to God's design is oppression. The spirit behind this transformation is ancient, seductive, and lethal. It is Jezebel—revived, repackaged, and deployed.

II. Jezebel in the Scriptures: A Spirit, Not Just a Woman

The name Jezebel often evokes imagery of sexual immorality, manipulation, and pride. But Jezebel was more than a licentious queen—she was a strategic destroyer of prophetic order and national identity. In 1 Kings 16-21, Jezebel, a Phoenician princess married to Israel's King Ahab, infiltrated the nation of Israel with idolatry, witchcraft, and persecution of the prophets. She replaced the worship of YHWH with Baal, silenced righteous voices, and castrated masculine spiritual authority.

This spirit—marked by rebellion, seduction, control, and deception—did not die with Jezebel. As Revelation 2:20 warns, it was alive and active in the church of Thyatira and remains a spiritual force today. The modern world has simply renamed it: feminism, sexual liberation, independence, boss chick, baddie culture, and "divine feminine energy." But its goal is the same—destroy the prophetic order of YAH by corrupting the woman and silencing the man.

III. The Hebrew Woman: From Royalty to Rebellion

The Hebrew woman was once the epitome of strength, dignity, and grace. Sarah, Ruth, Esther, Deborah, Miriam—these were women of faith, obedience, humility, and discernment. They supported the mission of the Hebrew man and elevated the covenant through their reverence for the Most High. Their beauty was internal and eternal, flowing from a quiet strength and godly fear.

But what was once beautiful has now been made grotesque by a world that hates the Hebrew legacy.

Let us be clear: the weaponization of the Hebrew woman was not an accident—it was an act of war.

•During slavery, she was raped, humiliated, and made to nurture her oppressor's children while her own were sold away. She was stripped of protection and forced to survive without her man.

•During Reconstruction and Jim Crow, she watched as her men were lynched, imprisoned, emasculated, and economically disabled—forcing her to become both mother and father to her children.

•In the 1960s and 70s, she was targeted with welfare systems that removed the man from the home.

•In the 1980s and 90s, she was seduced by feminism and media to see herself as superior to her man.

•In the 2000s and beyond, she was glamorized as a hypersexual icon, praised for her independence, education and degrees but silent on her brokenness and her mental and emotional struggles.

The Hebrew woman became both idol and executioner—placed on a pedestal by the world, while tearing down her own kingdom.

IV. Feminism Was Never for the Hebrew Woman

Feminism was birthed out of white women's frustration with white men—not Hebrew women's oppression under Hebrew men. *Before feminism, the Hebrew man was not her oppressor; the white supremacist system was.* But the lie of feminism seduced her into believing she needed to "liberate" herself from the very man who was trying to rebuild their broken communities.

Feminism told her that children were a burden, submission was slavery, and the man was the enemy. She was told she needed to be a boss, not a helpmeet. She could be lewd and loud, sexually promiscuous, twerk, curse, expose her body, and emasculate men and still be considered "empowered." She became Eve all over again—deceived by the serpent while walking away from divine order.

Let's be crystal clear: feminism was not liberation. It was infiltration.

V. Media and the Modern Jezebel: The Manufacturing of Rebellion

Who profits from the sexualization of the Hebrew woman? Who funds the reality shows, the rap music, the stripper anthems, and the "independent woman" propaganda? Who benefits when the Hebrew woman no longer values marriage, modesty, or motherhood?

These are not Hebrew-owned narratives. These are media empires—often owned and controlled by people outside the covenant—who elevate Jezebel because Jezebel destroys order. Jezebel weakens the Hebrew home. Jezebel silences Elijah. Jezebel turns the nation upside down.

From Sexy Red to Glorilla and Ice Spice , from The Real Housewives to Love & Hip Hop to Baddies, our sisters have been trained to confuse vulgarity with strength, disrespect and having no self respect with confidence, and being a whore with independence. The Hebrew woman has been given a throne—but not to reign in righteousness. It is the throne of the dragon.

VI. The Cost of Rebellion: Broken Homes, Broken Children, Broken Covenant

What has this Jezebel construct produced?

•70% of Hebrew children born into fatherless homes.

•A generation of emotionally unstable, spiritually confused, and sexually exploited daughters. And sons who want to be daughters.

•A widening war between Hebrew men and women—fueled by bitterness, distrust, and pain.

•A rejection of biblical womanhood and manhood in favor of a toxic counterfeit.

The Hebrew family is broken because the divine order has been rejected. Where the woman was called to be a crown to her husband (Proverbs 12:4), she has become a chain around his neck. Where she was created to nurture, she now neglects or even abuses. Where she was designed to build, she has become the voice and vehicle of destruction.

Hebrew woman I love you.

This is not condemnation. This is truth. And truth is the beginning of healing.

<u>The Path to Restoration – The Healing of the Hebrew Woman</u>

"Who can find a virtuous woman? For her price is far above rubies. The heart of her husband doth safely trust in her… Strength and honour are her clothing; and she shall rejoice in time to come."

— Proverbs 31:10–11, 25

The enemy has done his work well. But the Most High has not forgotten the daughters of Zion. Though the Hebrew woman has been deceived, defiled, and weaponized, she has not been destroyed. A remnant remains—righteous daughters who are awakening from the spell of Jezebel and returning to their original glory.

The healing begins with truth. Not surface-level affirmations, but deep spiritual accountability. The Hebrew woman must understand that she has not only been hurt, but in many cases, she has also hurt—herself, her children, and her man. Yet even in her pain, the Most High has not abandoned her.

This generation of Hebrew women must repent, release, and rebuild.

•Repent of embracing the Jezebel spirit—rebellion, pride, sexual immorality, manipulation, and hatred of godly order.

•Release the pain of the past—acknowledge past sins and trauma, yes, but no longer allow it to govern identity or justify destruction.

•Rebuild from the ashes—through humility, submission to YAH, love for the Hebrew man, and the nurturing of righteous children.

Her beauty must become holy again. Not in drag queen make up, wigs, lashes, nails, filters, and twerking, but in wisdom, modesty, discernment, and fear of the Most High. She must recover what the world told her was weakness: softness, quietness, gentleness, and grace. These are not chains—they are crowns.

A healed Hebrew woman is a dangerous threat to the kingdom of darkness. She raises kings and shields prophets. She crushes serpents under her heel. She does not chase clout or attention for validation— she builds legacy. She does not compete with her man—she completes him. She does not seek attention—she walks in authority.

This is not the Jezebel of pop culture. This is Sarah. This is Deborah. This is Hannah. This is Mary. This is the Proverbs 31 woman in Hebrew skin.

VIII. A Message to the Daughters of Zion

To the daughters of Zion—this is your wake-up call. You were never meant to be exploited sex symbols or slaves to materialism and culture. You were never meant to be twerk queens or feminist mascots. You were never meant to destroy your men with your tongue or compete with your sons in masculinity. You were never meant to share soul ties with multiple sexual partners and you were never meant to have children out of wedlock.

You were created to reflect the glory of the Most High. You were designed to be a sanctuary of life, a well of wisdom, and a pillar of strength—not by domination, but by righteousness.

Return to your power—not the counterfeit "divine feminine" and "baddie" culture of TikTok and tarot cards, but the sacred femininity of Scripture. Return to your role—not as a slave, but as a queen and a helpmeet. Return to your destiny—not as an agent of rebellion, but as a daughter of Zion and a mother to a nation.

The kingdom cannot rise without you. But you must decide: Will you remain Jezebel, or will you become Judah's jewel?

SUMMARY:

The weaponization of the Hebrew woman is one of the most devastating strategies the enemy has employed to destroy the Hebrew nation. Through systems of slavery, government policy, feminism, and media seduction, many of our women have been turned against their men and against themselves. This chapter exposes the spirit of Jezebel and its modern disguises, offering a bold but redemptive path back to righteousness, legacy, and spiritual power for the daughters of Zion.

LET us now enter this sacred chamber—where we refocus the lens on the Hebrew woman, her divine role, her strategic targeting by Babylon, and her coming restoration.

The Hebrew Woman – From Target to Treasure

"Every wise woman buildeth her house: but the foolish plucketh it down with her hands."

— Proverbs 14:1

"Give her of the fruit of her hands; and let her own works praise her in the gates."

— Proverbs 31:31

SHE HAS BEEN the cradle of nations, the pillar of strength in the storm, the prayer warrior in the shadows, the mother of the Messiah's bloodline.

She is not just a woman—she is Zion in flesh. And because of who she is, Babylon has unleashed a relentless, generational war against her.

The Hebrew woman has not just been forgotten.

She has been weaponized.

I. THE ORIGINAL Glory of the Hebrew Woman

Before the lies, before the trauma, before the agenda—she was royalty.

Her reflection was not shaped by TV screens or rap lyrics, but by Torah scrolls and temple altars. The daughters of Zion were raised with purpose, clothed in modesty, and honored as the vessels of legacy.

In ancient Israel:

• She was the keeper of the home—but also the keeper of the culture.

• She was both nurturer and warrior—like Deborah, like Miriam, like Esther.

• She carried the covenant in her womb, and wisdom in her mouth.

The Hebrew woman was never a background character in the biblical narrative.

She was a co-laborer in the Kingdom—not masculine, not subservient, but gloriously distinct.

II. The Babylonian Assault on the Hebrew Woman

If you want to destroy a nation, you don't just kill the men—you corrupt the women.

And Babylon knows this all too well.

The strategy has always been clear: if the Hebrew woman can be pulled away from her identity, her values, her divine order—then the whole house falls.

1. The Welfare State and the Removal of the Hebrew Man

In the 1960s and 70s, U.S. social policies incentivized the Hebrew woman to reject the presence of a man in the home:

•Housing and food assistance were contingent on the absence of the father.

•Government became the new provider, replacing the biblical family model.

•Independence was praised—but only as long as it meant isolation from the Hebrew man.

What seemed like help was actually a Trojan horse—the state sowing division between man and woman under the banner of support.

2. Media Manipulation and the Rebranding of Femininity

Hollywood, hip-hop, and television began to redefine what it meant to be a Hebrew woman.

•From "Proverbs 31" to "Hot Girl."

•From prayer cloths to booty shorts.

•From nurturer to narcissist.

The once regal image of the Hebrew woman was replaced with hypersexual caricatures—loud, combative, entitled, and disconnected from spiritual depth.

This was not accidental. It was programming.

Black women were praised for being "strong," but only when that strength meant rejection of divine order and hostility toward the Hebrew man.

. . .

III. Turning the Hebrew Woman Against the Hebrew Man

This is the crown jewel of Babylon's plan: divide and conquer through emotional manipulation.

The world applauds the Hebrew woman—but only when she aligns herself against her own men.

•If she calls out the Hebrew man's flaws, she's "strong."

•If she praises him, submits to him in righteousness, or honors him— she's "pick me."

Mainstream culture exalts the heavily tattooed, masculinized, combative, independent woman—not the feminine, modest, spiritually submitted daughter of Zion.

This isn't empowerment.

It's witchcraft disguised as liberation.

Even within the church, the Jezebel spirit has crept in—teaching women to compete with men rather than walk beside them.

"As for my people, children are their oppressors, and women rule over them..."

— Isaiah 3:12

IV. The Psychological Toll on the Hebrew Woman

Let's be clear: *the Hebrew woman is not the villain—she is the battlefield.*

She has endured:

•Generational trauma from rape, enslavement, and objectification.

•Centuries of being told she was ugly, loud, unworthy, or "too much."

•A modern culture that only validates her when she conforms to Babylon's image (Wigs to mimic European hair, contouring their face to slim their nose and highlight features that make them look more European.)

The pain is real. The scars are deep. And most of her choices—though wrong—come from wounds, not wickedness.

But we must now speak truth in love:

Her healing must include repentance. Her strength must return to the Source.

V. The Return of the Virtuous Daughter

YAH is not finished with the Hebrew woman.

He is calling her out of the system, out of rebellion, out of confusion, out of shame, out of vanity, and back into her royal role.

"Who can find a virtuous woman? For her price is far above rubies."

— Proverbs 31:10

The return begins when the Hebrew woman:

•Rejects Babylon's image of femininity and embraces biblical womanhood.

•Honors the Hebrew man who walks in righteousness—not because he's perfect, but because he's hers.

•Takes back her womb from the world and restores it to covenant.

•Teaches her daughters truth, modesty, and virtue instead of trends.

•Uses her influence to build, not emasculate; to edify, not seduce.

VI. The Power of the Hebrew Woman in the Last Days

Make no mistake: the enemy fears her return.

A righteous Hebrew woman is a weapon:

•She builds up households and generations.

•She gives birth to prophets, warriors, and kings.

•She carries wisdom and discernment that disrupts Babylon's plans.

Her prayers shake nations.

Her submission to YAH restores order.

Her loyalty to her people heals division.

SUMMARY:

The Hebrew woman has been targeted, tempted, and traumatized—but she has not been defeated. Babylon's agenda to corrupt her has worked for a season, but a righteous remnant of women is rising—bold, modest, spiritually awakened, and ready to build the Kingdom alongside the Hebrew man. She is not forgotten. She is not lost. She is royalty in exile, returning to her throne.

The Role of the Woman in the Hebrew Nation — Virtue, Betrayal, and Redemption

"A virtuous woman is a crown to her husband: but she that maketh ashamed is as rottenness in his bones."

— Proverbs 12:4

"Every wise woman buildeth her house: but the foolish plucketh it down with her hands."

— Proverbs 14:1

"Thy daughters shall be nursed at thy side… Then shalt thou see, and flow together, and thine heart shall fear, and be enlarged."

— Isaiah 60:4–5

I. THE HEBREW WOMAN: Her Sacred Role in Nationhood

In the divine blueprint, the woman is not second-class, nor is she independent of the man. She is the life-bearer, the first teacher of the child, and the foundation of the home.

In Hebrew culture:

•A woman's womb births generations.

•Her tongue sets the tone of the household.

•Her virtue stabilizes the tribe.

She is the first battlefield of the enemy—because when the woman is compromised, the entire future is at stake.

That's why Babylon reprograms the Hebrew woman.

If the enemy can turn the heart of the woman, he can disarm the man, divide the home, and derail the nation.

II. Betrayal: How Babylon Turned the Daughters Against Their Brothers

Let's be clear. This betrayal is not about skin color or relationships—it is about identity abandonment.

The system told Hebrew women:

•"You don't need a man."

•"You are the victim, and he is the oppressor."

•"You are strong and independent."

•"Choose education and career over family."

•"Engage in sexual activity with as many people as you want and their race or gender doesn't matter."

But while Black women were encouraged to forsake their own men,

•White and Latino women were told to preserve their lineage.

•Asian and Arab women were told to honor their culture.

•Only Hebrew women were taught to despise their own men.

From government welfare policies that forced the father out of the home,

To TV shows that caricatured the Hebrew man as lazy, violent, or childish,

To music that glorified sex, materialism, and female domination...

Babylon weaponized the womb.

Babylon programmed betrayal.

When the woman trades her crown for control, the house collapses.

III. The White-Washed Woman: A Crown Lost in the Mirror of Babylon

Some Hebrew women, like their brothers, have been white-washed. Not in skin, but in soul.

They speak the tongue of Babylon, dress like Babylon, and mimic the Gentile woman, believing her superior to herself.

"For they shall be ashamed of the oaks which ye have desired, and ye shall be confounded for the gardens that ye have chosen."

— Isaiah 1:29

They believe the lie that being "liberated" means being disconnected from family, from headship, and from righteousness.

They mock their own brothers for:

•Having multiple children (but say nothing when the Gentile does it).

•Wanting a submissive wife (but celebrate it in Asian or Arab homes).

•Being "too Black," "too Hebrew," or "too masculine."

The white-washed Hebrew woman isn't just disobedient—she is used as a tool of sabotage against her own people.

The whitewashed Hebrew women has a certain tolerance for being degraded by their Gentile partners. Whitewash Hebrew women will put up with the most inhumane behavior and treatment, all for the social validation of having their Gentile man.

The white washed Hebrew woman, exactly like the white washed Hebrew man, has a distain for Hebrew men and Hebrew women. They work hard to appear to any available gentile eye, as having no visible cues of what is considered blackness other than their skin. They go out of their way to say the most disrespectful things about their own people in front of Gentiles, hoping for their approval. They make it a point to let it be known that they do not listen to Hebrew music or Hebrew artist or watch Hebrew movies, TV shows, or any content with Hebrew people, only Gentile. They have a fascination with Gentile movie stars and Gentile movies. They have an obsession with the Gentile woman whome they believe is far more superior than themselves or in the case of white washed Hebrew men whose obsession stems from the belief that the Gentile woman is more superior than the Hebrew women.

And I definitely want to clarify that being in an interracial marriage doesn't denote being white washed. I am speaking of the heart of a people not who they physically desire. Marry who you please as long as they are a believer.

IV. The Jezebel Spirit: Feminism's Spiritual Mask

This betrayal is spiritual.

The Jezebel spirit—not just a woman, but a principality—has always sought to:

•Usurp male authority,

•Seduce the righteous,

•Promote idolatry and sexual confusion,

•Dominate through manipulation and control.

Modern feminism is the mask Jezebel wears today.

While the early movements addressed valid issues (like voting or workplace abuse), modern feminism:

•Encourages sexual freedom but not family order.

•Demands equality but rejects accountability.

•Celebrates promiscuity, abortion, rebellion, and same-sex intimacy.

•Preaches that Hebrew men are the enemy, not the ally.

"Notwithstanding I have a few things against thee, because thou sufferest that woman Jezebel... to teach and to seduce my servants..."

— Revelation 2:20

This isn't empowerment. It's enslavement in disguise.

V. Redemption: The Return of the Virtuous Daughter

But here is the power of grace: The Hebrew woman can return.

The Father is not looking for perfection. He is calling for submission and alignment.

The virtuous woman is not silent—she is wise.

She is not oppressed—she is honored, respected, and protected

She is not weak—she is righteous.

She reclaims her role by:

•Dressing with modesty and dignity.

•Rejecting the culture of promiscuity and lust.

•Honoring Hebrew headship (not as oppression, but as divine order).

•Teaching her daughters to walk in virtue, not vanity.

•Covering her household in prayer and obedience.

"She openeth her mouth with wisdom; and in her tongue is the law of kindness... Her children arise up, and call her blessed; her husband also, and he praiseth her."

— Proverbs 31:26, 28

A righteous Hebrew woman doesn't compete with her man—she completes him.

And together, they rebuild the nation.

VI. Modern Examples and Misconceptions

1. The Lie of Swirl Culture:

Hebrew, marrying outside your nation is not inherently wrong as long as the person you are marrying is a believer in the Most High Yahuah and our Messiah, Yahusha.

But what is dangerous is the systematic campaign to steer Hebrew women away from Hebrew men.

•Corporate ads push interracial relationships (specifically Black woman + white man).

•Films rarely portray strong Black love.

•Hebrew men are vilified as "toxic," "broke," or "abusive."

But this is not random—it's strategic warfare.

2. The Trap of the "Boss Chick" "Baddie" Culture:

The glorification of "independent woman" status often translates to spiritual rebellion.

Scripture doesn't condemn ambition or skill—it condemns pride and disorder. The Most High blessed women like Deborah, Abigail, and Esther.

But all walked in humility, not arrogance.

. . .

VII. The Daughters of Zion Will Rise Again

Despite the chaos, many Hebrew women are awakening.

They're putting away the wigs and weaves.

They're leaving the clubs and churches of compromise.

They are deleting social media accounts and deleting apps.

They are turning off the music, podcasts reality TV.

They are choosing not to lay with another man who is not their husband.

They're learning the commandments, the holy days, and the ancient paths.

They're building homes, supporting their men, and raising righteous children.

These women are not loud.

They are not viral.

But they are dangerous to the enemy.

"Give her of the fruit of her hands; and let her own works praise her in the gates."

— Proverbs 31:31

The restoration of Zion is not just about Hebrew men standing up.

It's about Hebrew women standing with them—in purpose, in prayer, and in purity.

SUMMARY:

The Hebrew woman has been betrayed by a system designed to pit her against her own people. But now, in this hour of awakening, the Most High is calling her back to her royal identity. Not as a slave to

Babylon, but as a daughter of Zion. Her return to virtue is not optional—it is essential for the nation to rise.

WAKING THE DAUGHTERS OF ZION — Restoring the Honor, Modesty, and Power of the Hebrew Woman

"Rise up, ye women that are at ease; hear my voice, ye careless daughters; give ear unto my speech. Many days and years shall ye be troubled, ye careless women…"

— Isaiah 32:9–10

I. THE FALL of the Hebrew Woman

In the beginning, Hebrew women were queens, prophetesses, warriors, and matriarchs.

They were the backbone of the nation, the first teachers of children, and the guardians of the covenant.

But today, many have fallen into deep deception.

They are:

•Worshiping self instead of the Most High,

•Trading in modesty for hypersexuality,

•Trading in virtue for vanity,

•Trading in submission to Yah for submission to Babylon.

The system has trained her to:

•Hate the Hebrew man,

•Raise her sons without discipline,

•Sell her beauty and body for profit,

•And call rebellion "independence."

She no longer births prophets—she births prisoners.

She no longer raises queens—she raises "baddies".

She no longer walks with power—she walks with pride.

This is not who she is.

This is who Babylon turned her into.

II. The Targeted Destruction of the Black Woman

The Hebrew woman—especially the Black American descendant of slaves—was intentionally targeted for psychological, cultural, and spiritual destruction.

Planned Parenthood, founded by Margaret Sanger (a known eugenicist), was not created to "liberate" women—it was created to exterminate them.

"We do not want word to go out that we want to exterminate the Negro population."

— Margaret Sanger, 1939 (Letter to Dr. Clarence Gamble)

In the last 50 years, over 20 million Black babies have been aborted in America—more than any genocide in modern history.

The entertainment industry, under the control of Gentile elites, pushed:

•Doja Cat over Deborah,

•Cardi over Hannah,

•Meg over Mary.

Hollywood told her she was a "bad b****"—but never a daughter of Zion.

She was conditioned to:

•Reject natural hair as ugly and "unprofessional,"

•Expose her body for validation,

•Mock submission as weakness,

•Embrace masculine energy as "empowerment."

The Hebrew woman became Babylon's prized weapon—not because of her weakness, but because of her power. They feared her if she ever woke up.

III. The War Between the Hebrew Man and Woman

The system engineered division between the Hebrew man and woman:

•Welfare laws rewarded single motherhood but punished marriage.

•Media promoted tropes: the absent father, the angry Black woman, the strong independent queen who "don't need no man."

•Music glorified "baby mama" culture and promoted Hebrew men as dogs, players, and "ain't s***."

A wedge was driven. Respect turned into resentment. Love turned into lust. Unity turned into competition.

But this war was never ours. It was theirs.

The serpent whispered in Eve's ear in Eden. He's been whispering to her daughters ever since. Not to liberate them—but to weaponize them against their own men and their own nation.

"Every wise woman buildeth her house: but the foolish plucketh it down with her hands."

— Proverbs 14:1

IV. Modesty Is Power, Not Oppression

The world teaches women that modesty is oppression and nakedness is freedom.

But Hebrew women were never called to:

•Chase lust,

•Impress the Gentile gaze,

•Compete with other women for validation.

They were called to:

•Be holy vessels,

•Set apart in appearance,

•Covered in dignity and grace.

Modesty is not weakness—it is royalty. The Queen Mother of a nation doesn't need to twerk on social media. She walks with power because she knows who she is.

The Hebrew woman must reclaim:

•Her crown,

•Her voice,

•Her purpose.

V. The Return of the Daughters of Zion

But the Most High is not finished with the daughters of Zion.

"In that day the Lord will take away the bravery of their tinkling ornaments about their feet..."

— Isaiah 3:16–24

Yah will strip Babylon's glamor from them. The wigs, the BBLs, the fake nails, the designer labels, the artificial confidence—it will all crumble.

But after the pruning, He will restore them.

"Thy people also shall be all righteous: they shall inherit the land for ever..."

— Isaiah 60:21

The Hebrew woman will rise again as:

•Worshipers, not entertainers,

•Teachers of Torah, not TikTok influencers,

•Mothers of nations, not childless career chasers, or absent mothers chasing lust.

•Holy, not Hollywood.

She will become like:

•Sarah, full of faith,

•Deborah, a righteous judge,

•Esther, bold and strategic,

•Mary, humble and chosen,

•Anna, a prophetess waiting for the Redeemer.

VI. The Role of the Hebrew Woman in Restoration

The nation cannot rise without her.

She must:

•Return to modesty and honor,

•Raise her children in righteousness,

•Cover her man in prayer, not curses,

•Teach younger women holiness, not hustling, narcissism and manipulation.

The Hebrew woman is not weak—she is the womb of the nation, the wisdom of the home, and the warrior in the Spirit.

When she walks in righteousness, her entire household is covered. Her sons become kings. Her daughters become queens.

"A gracious woman retaineth honour…"

— Proverbs 11:16

Summary:

The daughters of Zion have been lied to, manipulated, and weaponized—but the Most High is calling them home. Modesty is power. Holiness is beauty. Submission to Yah is liberation. The Hebrew woman is not the bottom—she is the foundation. And when she awakens, the whole nation will rise.

THE FEMINIZATION OF MEN & MASCULINIZATION OF WOMEN

*I*f Satan can't destroy family by attacking the woman, he attacks the man.

From music to movies, from public policy to private indoctrination, Hebrew men are encouraged to be:

•Soft and passive when they should lead.

•Hyper-emotional, governed by feelings over principle.

•Or the opposite extreme — violent, irresponsible, unreliable, abandoning families.

(A combination of the second two are the ones Hebrew women love.)

MEANWHILE, Hebrew women are pushed to be aggressive, competitive, sexually dominant, and spiritually unsubmissive.

The culture is upside down. Men become like women; women become like men.

. . .

YAH NEVER DESIGNED the home to run on reversed roles.

Weak men produce broken communities.

Masculinized women breed broken homes.

Together, they raise confused children who perpetuate the cycle.

ONLY BY RETURNING to YAH's blueprint — humble, strong men leading in love, and wise, gracious women building the home — can the Hebrew nation be healed.

THE EFFEMINIZATION of the Hebrew Man – Castrating Kings in the Land of Captivity

"THEY HAVE TAKEN the young men to grind, and the children fell under the wood. The elders have ceased from the gate, the young men from their music... The crown is fallen from our head: woe unto us, that we have sinned!"

— Lamentations 5:13–16

THE ENEMY'S final blow is not death, but deconstruction. It is not merely to kill the Hebrew man's body—but to erase his identity, silence his voice, distort his nature, and ultimately feminize his spirit. Why? Because a feminized man cannot lead. A feminized man cannot war. A feminized man cannot reflect the glory of YAH as priest, protector, and provider.

IF THE HEBREW woman has been weaponized, then the Hebrew man has been emasculated—slowly, subtly, strategically.

· · ·

I. THE ANCIENT STRATEGY: Castration of Kings

THROUGHOUT ANCIENT HISTORY, conquering nations often castrated the men they enslaved—physically or symbolically. Eunuchs were placed in the courts of kings not as servants, but as neutered watch-dogs—harmless, obedient, and loyal to their masters. This same pattern can be traced from Egypt to Babylon, from Rome to America.

TODAY, physical castration has evolved into psychological and spiritual emasculation. They have not removed our organs—they have removed our honor. They have not stolen our testosterone—they have stolen our identity.

WE WERE BORN FOR DOMINION, but bred into docility. Born to roar like lions, but trained to purr like housecats.

II. Slavery and the Destruction of Masculinity

THE SLAVE SYSTEM was engineered to break the Hebrew man:

•Forced subjugation before wife and children: A man whipped or lynched in front of his family was not just injured—he was dishonored.

•Stripped of fatherhood and headship: Men were often separated from their offspring, leaving generations of children to be raised by mothers alone.

•"Buck Breaking": A horrific yet documented practice where enslaved Hebrew men were publicly raped by slave masters to humiliate and feminize them before others.

. . .

THIS WAS NOT MERELY CRUELTY. It was intentional spiritual warfare.

A MAN CANNOT LEAD his family if he has been taught he is not a man. He cannot protect his people if he fears his oppressor more than he fears YAH. He cannot govern a nation if he is convinced his only worth is in his physical strength or sexual performance.

III. Feminism, Media, and the New Eunuchs

IN THE 20TH and 21st centuries, the war against Hebrew masculinity took a new shape—cloaked in culture and politics.

•Welfare Policy & Government Dependency: Systems were introduced that removed the man from the home. To receive benefits, women were often required to live without a present male partner.

•Feminism (2nd and 3rd Wave): Hebrew women were recruited into feminist ideologies not designed for them. Unlike white feminists, who rebelled against their own powerful husbands, Hebrew women were taught to rebel against their already-oppressed men.

•Hollywood & Hip-Hop: The glorification of hypersexuality, irresponsibility, drug culture, and materialism replaced images of strong, wise Hebrew fathers with clowns, criminals, and cowards.

•The "Strong Black Woman" & the "Weak Black Man" Tropes: TV and film continue to normalize the idea that the Hebrew woman must always lead, fight, and fix, while the Hebrew man stumbles, fails, and follows.

•Effeminate Role Models: From the rise of emasculated male fashion to the celebration of entertainers who blur gender norms, our boys are taught that manhood is either aggression or submission—nothing sacred, nothing balanced.

. . .

WE ARE WITNESSING the rise of a new generation of eunuchs—men who look like lions but roar like lambs.

IV. The Spirit of Jezebel Needs an Ahab

JEZEBEL, the spirit of rebellion and disorder, thrives only when her counterpart—Ahab—abdicates his authority. In Scripture, Ahab was not weak in appearance, but in spiritual conviction. He compromised truth for comfort, peace for passivity. And because he refused to lead, Jezebel ruled.

THE SAME DYNAMIC plagues our communities. The spirit of Jezebel is allowed to reign because too many Hebrew men have become passive, silent, or spiritually dead.

A NATION without strong men is a nation without walls. A home without a priest is a home without protection. A family without a father is a field left to wolves.

V. Restoring the Roar of the Hebrew Man

THE HEALING BEGINS WITH REPENTANCE, identity, and purpose:

•Repentance – The Hebrew man must first return to YAH, confessing not only personal sin but generational compromise. He must reject the lust, laziness, and lies he's been fed.

•Identity – He must reclaim his role: son of the Most High, seed of Abraham, spiritual warrior, protector of his nation.

•Purpose – He must build, lead, teach, correct, and cover. He is not a sidekick to his woman, nor a rival—he is her shield, her covering, her head in righteousness.

THE MOST HIGH is raising up mighty men of valor—men who do not bow to Babylon, who do not lust after Sodom, who do not remain silent while their families are devoured.

WE ARE NOT THUGS.

We are not gangsters.

We are not fakes.

We are kings, priests, and warriors in the army of the Most High.

SUMMARY:

THE SYSTEMATIC EFFEMINIZATION of the Hebrew man—through slavery, psychological warfare, cultural manipulation, and spiritual confusion—has devastated the Hebrew family and nation. This chapter exposes how society has worked to castrate our kings, leaving our people vulnerable. But the Most High is calling His sons back into righteous manhood: bold, holy, protective, and unapologetically masculine.

RECLAIMING THE SEED — Fatherhood, Legacy, and the Rebirth of Hebrew Masculinity

"AS FOR ME, this is My covenant with them," saith YHWH; "My Spirit that is upon thee, and My words which I have put in thy mouth, shall not depart out of thy mouth... nor out of the mouth of thy seed's seed..."

— Isaiah 59:21

"I GO the way of all the earth: be thou strong therefore, and shew thyself a man; and keep the charge of YHWH thy Elohim."

— 1 Kings 2:2–3

I. THE FALL of the Hebrew Father

THE ASSAULT on Hebrew masculinity has been relentless and calculated. From slavery to the present, Babylon has done everything in its power to remove the man from the home, from the heart of his woman, and from the mind of his children.

1. The Plantation Era:

•Hebrew men were publicly humiliated, whipped, and broken.

•Families were intentionally split apart—children sold off, wives raped.

•The enslaved father was seen as powerless and disposable.

2. The Welfare Era:

•By the 1960s, U.S. government policies penalized Hebrew women for having a man in the home.

•Lyndon B. Johnson's "Great Society" programs, including Aid to Families with Dependent Children (AFDC), paid mothers more if they were unmarried and fatherless.

•The result: the emasculation of the Black man and the institutional-ization of fatherlessness.

. . .

3. The Incarceration Era:

•Under Bill Clinton's 1994 Crime Bill, and earlier Reagan-era policies, Hebrew men were locked up in record numbers for non-violent drug offenses.

•Today, 1 in 3 Black men can expect to be incarcerated in his lifetime —compared to 1 in 17 white men.

THIS WAS NOT JUST POLICY. This was prophecy. The curse of Deuteronomy 28 was manifesting:

"THY SONS and thy daughters shall be given unto another people, and thine eyes shall look... but there shall be no might in thine hand." (Deut. 28:32)

II. The Crisis of Seed Without Legacy

BABYLON HAS REDUCED the Hebrew man to a sperm donor instead of a seed-bearer.

•Children are raised without fathers.

•Men boast about "baby mamas" instead of building homes.

•Masculinity is redefined by hyper sexuality or violence.

BUT BIBLICALLY, seed is not about ejaculation—it's about continuity.

"AND I WILL ESTABLISH My covenant between Me and thee and thy seed after thee in their generations..." — Genesis 17:7

. . .

A MAN'S SEED IS:

•Spiritual – a legacy of faith and obedience.

•Cultural – passing down the history, language, and law of the Hebrews.

•Relational – being physically present, emotionally stable, and spiritually anchored.

A HEBREW MAN is not a breeder. He is a builder.

III. The Restoration of the Hebrew Man

THE DRY BONES ARE RATTLING. The men of Judah are waking up.

1. He Returns to the Covenant

THE REBORN HEBREW man is not a thug, a simp, or a savage. He is a priest and protector.

HE LEARNS Torah and The Gospel.

He honors the Sabbath.

He teaches his children.

He leads his wife in righteousness.

He walks like David, speaks like Moses, and serves like Yahusha.

"AND YE SHALL TEACH them [My commandments] to your children, speaking of them... when thou walkest by the way, when thou liest down, and when thou risest up."

— Deut. 11:19

2. He Reclaims His Authority

MASCULINITY IS NOT TOXIC. Sin is.

The reborn man is not domineering—he is righteous in leadership.

THE HEBREW FATHER:

•Sets the spiritual tone in the home.

•Corrects his children with firmness and love.

•Protects his family from deception and danger.

•Walks in humility before YHWH and is honored in the gates.

3. He Rebuilds the Family

A STRONG NATION begins in the house. The man returns home—not just physically, but spiritually.

HE MARRIES HIS WOMAN—NOT just legally, but covenantally.

He raises sons who honor, not imitate Babylon.

He raises daughters who value modesty and purpose.

He stops creating children and starts creating legacy.

. . .

IV. What the Enemy Fears Most

THE IMAGE that terrifies Babylon is not the Hebrew man with chains or sagging pants.

WHAT THEY FEAR MOST IS:

•A Hebrew man praying with his children,

•Teaching Torah and the Gospel at his dinner table,

•Refusing to take the mark of the beast,

•Walking in strength, self-control, and spiritual power.

THIS MAN CANNOT BE BOUGHT with money, sex, drugs, or fame.

This man cannot be controlled with fear or flattery. A man with morels and biblical values. This man answers to YHWH and no one else.

"AND THEY SHALL BE like mighty men... they shall march every one on his ways, and they shall not break their ranks."

— Joel 2:7

V. Repentance and the Call to Legacy

EVERY HEBREW MAN must look in the mirror.

HAVE I left my children fatherless?

Have I forsaken righteousness for pleasure?

Have I abandoned my post as priest of the home?

THERE IS STILL time to return.

THE FATHER IS NOT CALLING for perfection—He is calling for repentance and restoration.

•It's not too late to contact your children .

•It's not too late to marry the mother of your children.

•It's not too late to turn off the music and turn to the Scriptures.

•It's not too late to become the man you were created to be.

Summary:

The fall of the Hebrew father was not just personal—it was prophetic. But the rebirth of the Hebrew man is the key to national resurrection. Fatherhood is not just a social issue—it is a spiritual assignment. The men of Zion must reclaim their authority, their seed, and their destiny. The time for excuses is over. The kingdom needs fathers again.

Hebrew Masculinity — The Rebuilding of the Royal Priesthood

"The glory of young men is their strength: and the beauty of old men is the gray head."
— Proverbs 20:29

"And hath made us kings and priests unto God and his Father; to him be glory and dominion for ever and ever."
— Revelation 1:6

I. The Hebrew Man Has Been Broken

He was once a king.
He was once a priest.
He was once the spiritual covering for his household and a warrior for his nation.

NOW HE IS:

•Fatherless,

•Jobless,

•Faithless,

•Clueless about who he truly is.

He has been reduced to a stereotype:
•The thug,
•The baby daddy,
•The hustler,
•The lost boy seeking validation through money, sex, or violence.

He has been falsely labeled toxic, dangerous, and worthless.
But none of this is who he truly is.

He is Judah—the lion who forgot how to roar.

II. The Psychological Castration of the Hebrew Male

THE ENSLAVEMENT of the Hebrew man wasn't just physical—it was psychological.

THE SLAVE MASTERS broke his body, but more importantly, they broke:

•His mind (stripped of history and self-worth),

•His spirit (removed from his Creator),

•His authority (emasculated in front of his woman and children).

THE WILLIE LYNCH LETTER, revealed a long-term strategy:

"Take the biggest and strongest male, beat him, break him, and let all the others watch."

HE WAS TAUGHT TO:

•Fear authority,

•Submit to the oppressor,

•Distrust his own brother,

•And worst of all—distrust himself.

IN BABYLON, a strong Hebrew man is seen as a threat, not a leader.

III. False Models of Manhood: From Kings to Criminals

BABYLON GAVE him false idols to emulate:

•Scarface instead of Solomon,

•Kodak instead of Paul,

•NBA YoungBoy instead of Nehemiah,

•Ghost and Tommy instead of Joshua and Caleb.

MASCULINITY WAS TWISTED INTO:

•Violence,

•Sexual conquest,

•Emotional repression,

•Materialism.

INSTEAD OF LEARNING how to protect, he learned how to possess.
Instead of being taught to lead, he was taught to dominate.

THE RESULT?
A generation of men who are physically grown—but spiritually infantile.
Strong in body—but weak in character.

Gifted—but directionless.

Free in the flesh—but still chained in the mind.

IV. The Rebirth of the Royal Priesthood

BUT YAH IS CALLING the Hebrew man back to order.

Not just to be a king—but to be a priest.

THIS MEANS:

•Knowing Torah and The Gospel ,

•Living in righteousness,

•Walking in authority,

•Covering his family,

•Fighting in the spirit,

•Building up his community.

"BE WATCHFUL, stand firm in the faith, act like men, be strong."
— 1 Corinthians 16:13 (ESV)

HE MUST BECOME:

•A student of the Scriptures,

•A husband who washes his wife in the Word,

•A father who disciplines in love,

•A leader who serves.

. . .

THIS IS BIBLICAL MASCULINITY—NOT domination, but sanctification.

Not ego, but example.

V. The Restoration of Brotherhood

ONE OF THE deepest wounds among Hebrew men today is the loss of brotherhood.

Jealousy, betrayal, and competition plague our communities.

BUT IN ANCIENT TIMES:

•David had Jonathan.

•Moses had Aaron.

•Yahusha sent the disciples out two by two.

WE WERE NEVER MEANT to walk alone.

TRUE BROTHERHOOD IS:

•Accountability without condemnation,

•Correction without humiliation,

•Encouragement without flattery,

•Prayer and protection in times of weakness.

WE MUST SHATTER the crab-in-a-barrel curse.

If I see my brother fall, I must lift him.

If I see my brother shine, I must support him.

. . .

"BEHOLD, how good and how pleasant it is for brethren to dwell together in unity!"

— Psalm 133:1

VI. Hebrew Masculinity Is Both Lion and Lamb

TOO OFTEN, masculinity is painted as one-dimensional—loud, aggressive, and emotionally unavailable.

BUT YAHUSHA SHOWED us the full spectrum:

•He wept.

•He prayed all night.

•He flipped tables in righteous anger.

•He laid down His life for His bride.

HE WAS MEEK, not weak.

Bold, not boastful.

Gentle, not soft.

Warrior and worshiper.

THE HEBREW MAN is called to reflect that same balance.

HE IS NOT A SAVAGE.

He is a son of the Most High.

. . .

VII. The War for the Seed

SATAN KNOWS if he can destroy the man, he can destroy the nation.

THAT'S WHY THE ENEMY:

•Over-incarcerates us,

•Targets us with abortion and violence,

•Confuses us with gender identity lies,

•Tempts us to abandon our post as protectors.

BUT WE WILL RISE.

THE HEBREW MAN MUST SAY:

"NOT ON MY WATCH. Not my family. Not my seed."

HE WILL RETURN TO:

•Fasting,

•Studying,

•Building,

•Covering,

•Fighting on his knees before he fights with his hands.

. . .

SUMMARY:

THE HEBREW MAN was never meant to be a thug, gang member, or illegal hustler. He is a king, a priest, and a son of the covenant. He has been broken—but now he will be rebuilt. Through studying the Bible, brotherhood, and spiritual discipline, the royal priesthood will rise again, and the lion will remember how to roar.

DESTROYED BLACK CITIES
AND FORCED INTEGRATION

*H*ebrews prospered most when left alone.

After slavery, despite every obstacle, we built our own communities which included:

•Our own schools, churches, hospitals.

•Our own barbers, tailors, restaurants, banks.

•Our own entire thriving cities — Black Wall Street in Tulsa, Rosewood in Florida, thriving districts in Chicago, Durham, and dozens more.

BUT EACH TIME, jealous mobs burned them down. Or highways were carved straight through the business centers. Or rivers were redirected to flood them.

When brute force wasn't enough, the government mandated integration.

Integration was sold as equality. In reality, it was control.
By forcing us into their schools, under their curriculums, under their economic systems, they ensured we would learn to depend on Babylon, not ourselves.

Integration was the death of the self-sustaining Hebrew economy. From that point on, our communities never fully recovered.

Hidden Beneath the Surface – When Cities Vanish, But the Truth Remains

What happens when a thriving Hebrew town is not burned,

BUT BURIED—UNDER water or under the lies of urban progress?

SENECA VILLAGE: The First Black Landowners in New York

BEFORE CENTRAL PARK was ever a concept, there stood Seneca Village, a Black settlement in Manhattan founded in 1825 by freed African-Americans. Families owned land. Children went to school. It was peaceful and self-sustaining. And yet, it was systematically erased from history.

WHEN THE CITY decided to build Central Park, officials used eminent domain to seize over 225 plots of land—many owned by Black residents. The city framed it as "removal of squatters," but these were tax-paying landowners with deeds, churches, and schools. Their generational wealth was stolen. Their memory was paved over by winding paths and green lawns.

IT WASN'T until archaeological excavations in the 1990s that New Yorkers even learned of Seneca Village's existence again.

. . .

THIS WAS NOT A ONE-TIME INJUSTICE. This was a blueprint: destroy, deny, disappear.

BLACK WALL STREET – Tulsa, Oklahoma (1921)

TULSA'S GREENWOOD DISTRICT, nicknamed "Black Wall Street," was one of the most affluent Black communities in the early 20th century. It featured:

•Over 300 Black-owned businesses: banks, hotels, cafes, movie theaters, and more.

•Professionals like doctors, lawyers, and educators—all within a self-sustained community.

•By 1921, over 10,000 residents thrived in Greenwood.

DESTRUCTION:

•On May 31–June 1, 1921, a white mob—fueled by a false accusation of assault against a Black teen—attacked Greenwood.

•Planes dropped firebombs, this isn't the only time in U.S. history where American citizens were bombed by air on U.S. soil.

(We will soon discuss the

Philadelphia MOVE Bombing in 1985)

•Over 1,200 homes and 35 city blocks were destroyed.

•Up to 300 Black people were murdered.

•The community never fully recovered, and insurance companies refused to pay out damages.

. . .

Rosewood, Florida (1923)

Rosewood was a small, Black town in Levy County.

•Residents owned land, homes, schools, churches, and farms.

•It was relatively prosperous and self-reliant.

Destruction:

•In January 1923, after a white woman falsely accused a Black man of assault, mobs from neighboring towns burned the town to the ground.

•Entire families were massacred or driven into hiding in swamps.

•Survivors never returned, and the land was abandoned.

Thriving Districts in Chicago and Durham

Durham, NC – Hayti & Parrish Street ("Black Wall Street of the South"):

•Home to North Carolina Mutual Life Insurance, the nation's largest Black-owned insurance company.

•Mechanics, Farmers, Banks and dozens of businesses thrived in the early 1900s.

•Systematic redlining and highway construction split the community, leading to economic decline.

Chicago – Bronzeville:
•In the early-mid 1900s, Bronzeville was a cultural mecca.
•Hosted businesses, newspapers like the Chicago Defender, and major music venues.
•Over time, disinvestment, racist zoning, and urban renewal dismantled its infrastructure.

Philadelphia MOVE Bombing (1985)

•MOVE was a Black liberation group founded in the 1970s promoting back-to-nature, anti-government views.

•In May 1985, the Philadelphia police dropped a bomb from a helicopter onto the group's rowhouse.

•The resulting fire killed 11 people, including 5 children, and destroyed 61 homes in the neighborhood.

•The city let the fire burn. No one was criminally charged.

•It was a blatant act of state-sponsored terrorism against a Black group.

Bruce's Beach – Manhattan Beach, California

•In 1912, Willa and Charles Bruce, a Black couple, bought beachfront land in Manhattan Beach, CA, to create a seaside resort for Black families—one of the few places they were allowed.

•By the 1920s, white residents and city officials pressured them to sell, eventually seizing the land using eminent domain, falsely claiming it would be a public park.

•The land remained unused for decades.

•In 2022, after decades of activism, LA County returned the land to Bruce descendants, acknowledging the racist land theft.

. . .

ASAPH MACCABEE

Lake Lanier: A Reservoir Built on Ruins

In Georgia, just northeast of Atlanta, Lake Lanier is a popular recreational spot—but beneath the surface lies another erased Black town: Oscarville.

In the early 1900s, Oscarville was a prosperous Black farming community. That all changed in 1912 after a racially motivated lynching followed by the forcible expulsion of over 1,000 Black residents. Homes, churches, and livelihoods were stolen overnight. The land was eventually submerged under Lake Lanier in the 1950s by the U.S. Army Corps of Engineers.

Strangely, Lake Lanier is infamous for its abnormally high death tolls, eerie drownings, and tales of hauntings—almost as if the ground beneath it cries out.

Bombings, Burnings, and Brutality: The War on Hebrew Churches and Communities

We are taught that churches are sanctuaries. For Black Hebrews in America, even that has been violently violated.

•1921 – Tulsa, Oklahoma: During the attack on Black Wall Street, Mount Zion Baptist Church, a massive symbol of spiritual and economic strength, was firebombed by planes—a premeditated act of terror.

•1951 – Florida: Harry T. Moore, a civil rights leader and educator, was murdered alongside his wife when a bomb exploded beneath their home—on Christmas Day—planted by white supremacists.

140

•1963 – Birmingham, Alabama: The 16th Street Baptist Church was bombed by Ku Klux Klan members, killing four little Hebrew girls—Addie Mae Collins, Cynthia Wesley, Carole Robertson, and Denise McNair.

•1995 to 1997: Over 30 Black churches were burned across the South, most of them intentionally set. These were not isolated hate crimes—they were part of a coordinated effort to undermine Hebrew spiritual centers.

•2015 – Charleston, South Carolina: At Mother Emanuel AME Church, a historic Hebrew church dating back to the 1800s, nine believers were gunned down by a white supremacist during Bible study.

EACH OF THESE attacks was not just on buildings, but on hope and expectation—on healing, on community, on spiritual power.

INTEGRATION: A Trojan Horse Wrapped in Promise

INTEGRATION WAS MARKETED AS PROGRESS. But what did we integrate into?

THE SCHOOL SYSTEMS we were forced into stripped away any curriculum that taught our true heritage. The neighborhoods we moved into saw white flight and plummeting investment. The jobs we were allowed to pursue were limited and controlled. We were systematically disarmed of our independence.

MARTIN LUTHER KING JR., long held as the face of integration, came to realize this painful truth before his death. In 1967, he is reported to have said:

. . .

"I FEAR I have integrated my people into a burning house."

WHAT HE SAW WAS that social acceptance came with spiritual compromise, and legal equality came with economic dependency. Integration helped dissolve Black-owned banks, schools, and insurance companies. Black teachers were fired en masse. Black institutions folded. Why? Because Babylon wanted our bodies, not our autonomy.

BEHIND THE CURTAIN: Who Funded the Movement?

THE CIVIL RIGHTS movement had many brave Hebrew leaders—but the machinery behind it was often financed by Jewish donors and organizations with their own agendas.

NOTABLY:

•The American Jewish Congress and the Anti-Defamation League (ADL) offered significant funding and legal support.

•Stanley Levison, a Jewish businessman, was not only a key financial backer of Martin Luther King Jr. but also a speechwriter and strategist.

•The Jewish Labor Committee and National Council of Jewish Women lent institutional power and press coverage.

THOUGH SOME WERE SINCERE, others were not fighting for Hebrew liberation, but for alignment with broader liberal agendas—including later LGBTQ advocacy and secularism, which were at odds with Hebrew biblical values.

. . .

WHILE KING'S heart was pure, the pipeline of money and media surrounding him ensured the movement evolved into something beyond his control—eventually mutating into a beast of integration, assimilation, and spiritual compromise.

CONCLUSION: The Cost of Forced Dependency

FROM SENECA VILLAGE TO OSCARVILLE, from bombed churches to "progressive" integration, one pattern is clear:

WHEN THE HEBREWS THRIVED, Babylon struck.

SOMETIMES WITH TORCHES. Sometimes with policy. Sometimes with propaganda. But the goal remained the same:

DISRUPT THE IMAGE OF SELF-SUFFICIENCY, and replace it with dependency.

THEY FEARED A SELF-SUSTAINING, unified, and spiritually awakened Hebrew nation.

Because a nation that remembers who they are... will remember who their God is.

And when that happens—deliverance is inevitable.

SOCIAL PROGRAMS, WELFARE & HOUSING — MODERN SLAVERY

*S*lavery never ended. It evolved.

THE EMANCIPATION PROCLAMATION was a declaration on paper, not a deliverance in reality. Once the chains were removed from the wrists, they were fastened to the soul by new systems designed to keep the Hebrew man bound and broken.

SHARECROPPING: Slavery by Another Name

AFTER THE CIVIL WAR, freed Hebrews were given no land, no reparations, and no tools to start anew. Instead, they were funneled into sharecropping — a system that allowed them to farm a portion of a white landowner's property in exchange for a share of the harvest.

. . .

BUT HERE'S THE TRUTH:

Sharecropping was slavery in disguise.

THE WHITE LANDOWNERS — often former slaveholders — controlled the seeds, the tools, the land, and the market. The sharecropper did all the labor, but by harvest time, they owed so much in "debts" that they often ended the year poorer than they began.

AND BEHIND MANY of these stores — the general stores where sharecroppers bought supplies on credit — were Jewish merchants, strategically positioned as the financial gatekeepers of the rural South. These merchants charged exorbitant interest rates, often up to 70%, ensuring that sharecroppers never escaped the cycle of debt. The system was rigged so tightly that a man could work dawn to dusk, six days a week, twelve months a year, and still owe more than he earned.

CONVICT LEASING: Legalized Slavery

NEXT CAME CONVICT LEASING. With new Black Codes and vagrancy laws, Hebrew men were arrested for crimes like "loitering" or "not having a job." Once imprisoned, they were leased out to private corporations and state governments for free labor. They were beaten, starved, and worked to death — often in conditions mimicking slavery.

THE 13TH AMENDMENT'S CLAUSE — **"except as a punishment for crime"** — **allowed slavery to continue, hidden in plain sight.**

Redlining and Economic Entrapment

With the rise of urbanization, Hebrews moved into cities — but freedom still eluded them. Redlining policies by the FHA and banks denied mortgages to Black families, forcing them into overcrowded, underfunded ghettos and housing projects. Property values were suppressed. Public schools were neglected. Economic growth was stunted by design.

MEANWHILE, white families were granted loans and benefits to build generational wealth — wealth that Hebrews were systemically denied.

WELFARE: A New Plantation System

BY THE MID-20TH CENTURY, the government had designed a new leash: social programs that seemed like help but functioned as control mechanisms.

WELFARE PROGRAMS LIKE:

•AFDC (Aid to Families with Dependent Children)

•Section 8 housing

•Food stamps

•Medicaid

...ALL CAME WITH A CATCH: the Hebrew father had to leave the home.

. . .

To qualify for benefits, the mother had to declare that no man was present. Welfare officers would even inspect closets and pantries to make sure no adult male was living there.

This created a perverse incentive: destroy the family to feed the children.

Children grew up watching their mothers rely on a government check, not a husband. Marriage rates plummeted. Dependency soared. A culture of survival replaced a culture of vision.

The Hebrew woman began to see the government as the provider, not the Hebrew man. With subsidized rent, free medical care, food assistance, and childcare vouchers, the father became optional. Worse — he became unwelcome.

The Cost of Dependency

But the cost of that "free" help was catastrophic:
•A community without fathers is a community without protection.
•A generation raised without discipline is a generation raised for destruction.
•The loss of self-reliance meant the loss of economic power.

When the Hebrew man is replaced by the state, the state controls the destiny of the family. No longer do we create and support our own. No longer do we depend on one another. No longer are we builders — we become beggars.

But when the government check stops… the father becomes necessary again.

. . .

No more Section 8 means we must own land and homes.

No more food stamps means we must grow, buy, and cook our own.

No more Medicaid means we must pursue education, health, healing, and fitness.

No more dependency means we must return to each other — man, woman, and child — in divine order.

No more government assistant means more Hebrew family and community self-reliance. It means depending on one another again. It means creating our own and supporting our own. It means every man is responsible for who he creates. And he is also responsible for the woman he procreates with.

Conclusion: Return to Responsibility, Reject the Chains

What they gave us was never freedom — it was a leash wrapped in paperwork and handouts. But true liberty is found in covenant, not contracts. In self-determination, not dependency.

The Most High never designed the Hebrew family to rely on Pharaoh for bread. He designed us to walk in unity, with the man as the covering, the woman as the crown, and the children as the heritage of YAH.

The systems of Babylon were never made to bless us — only to manage us.

. . .

IT IS time we tear up their contracts and return to our covenant.

It is time the Hebrew man stands again.

It is time the Hebrew woman sees her value again.

It is time we rebuild, not with bricks of dependence, but with the cornerstone of righteousness.

BECAUSE A NATION that depends on its oppressor will never be free.

But a nation that returns to its God will never be broken again.

STANDARDIZED
EDUCATION & TRADES

*T*he public school system in America was never meant to produce free thinkers.

It was modeled on Prussian systems designed to create obedient workers for factories and soldiers for wars.

HEBREWS INTEGRATED INTO THIS STRUCTURE, hoping for equality.

Instead, we received:

•Inferior schools, underfunded and overcrowded.

•Curriculums that erased our history, celebrated European conquests, and demonized independent thought.

•Guidance counselors who steered us away from trades and ownership into endless cycles of consumerism.

MEANWHILE, we stopped teaching our children skills that sustain families and communities.

We abandoned carpentry, masonry, metal work, tailoring, farming.

We stopped building, so we started begging.

A RETURN TO TEACHING TRADES, entrepreneurship, and above all the Torah of YAH and the Gospel, is not optional.

It is essential for breaking the dependency Babylon created.

SCHOOLS OF SERVITUDE — Rockefeller, Indoctrination & the Death of Skill

"I DON'T WANT a nation of thinkers. I want a nation of workers."

— Attributed to John D. Rockefeller

THAT QUOTE, whether literal or symbolic, reveals the true DNA of the American school system.

JOHN D. ROCKEFELLER, one of the wealthiest men in modern history, was instrumental in shaping American education into what it is today. In 1903, he founded the General Education Board, which laid the foundation for a national curriculum aimed not at enlightenment— but at industrial efficiency.

THE BOARD'S stated mission wasn't to raise philosophers, entrepreneurs, or visionaries. It was to create a compliant, punctual, obedient, and uncritical workforce. A population trained to follow orders, meet quotas, and support the machinery of capitalism without ever questioning the system that consumed their time and their lives.

. . .

FACTORIES FIRST, Freedom Never

BEFORE THE AGE of public schooling, education was largely localized, biblically grounded, and family-led. After Rockefeller's intervention, schools began to resemble factories:

•Rows of students in straight lines.

•Bells that rang like factory shifts.

•Memorization of arbitrary facts, rather than cultivation of critical thought.

•A growing emphasis on obedience, not originality.

THIS SYSTEM WASN'T BROKEN—IT was built that way.

AND IT WORKED. Generations of Americans were trained to be good workers—but not free thinkers. They were taught how to do a job, but never why. They were given information, but not truth.

Integration & the Erasure of Hebrew Excellence

BEFORE INTEGRATION, many Hebrew schools—though underfunded—were led by passionate educators who infused children with cultural pride, discipline, faith, and skill. Trades were taught. Practical knowledge was passed down. Community was central.

BUT AFTER FORCED INTEGRATION:

•Black teachers were fired en masse, replaced with teachers unfamiliar and hostile to Hebrew children.

•Trade programs began to vanish—plumbing, carpentry, welding, electrical work, masonry, tailoring—all disappeared.

•For the Hebrew child higher education was not realistic for most, often with no financial literacy, no backup plan, and no skill-based career path.

•The school-to-prison pipeline became the unspoken

track for too many.

TODAY, we have degrees with debt, but no tools in hand. We have classrooms without truth, campuses without conviction, and diplomas that hold little value in the real world.

WHERE DID THE TRADES GO?

AFTER WORLD WAR II, America boasted thousands of vocational programs in its public schools. These programs created generations of electricians, mechanics, builders, and craftsmen—Black and white.

BUT BEGINNING in the 1970s and accelerating after the 1980s, trade education was stripped from public schools, especially in urban communities. Why?

BECAUSE A SKILLED MAN is a free man.

He doesn't need to beg for a job.

He doesn't need a resume to eat.

He can create, build, provide.

.   .   .

BUT IF YOU remove the trades, then he becomes dependent again—on employers, on politicians, on systems that neither love him nor honor him.

THE REMOVAL of trades was no accident. It was a strategic disarmament—especially of the Hebrew man.

THE PUBLISHERS of Propaganda

MOST AMERICAN TEXTBOOKS are published by a handful of multibillion-dollar corporations, many of them with Jewish owner-ship and editorial leadership. These companies have held near-monopolies over K–12 curriculum for decades:

MAJOR TEXTBOOK PUBLISHERS:

1.Pearson Education (UK/US) – Formerly owned Addison-Wesley, Longman, and Prentice Hall. One of the largest textbook publishers globally.

2.McGraw-Hill Education – Founded by James H. McGraw and John A. Hill. At times connected to Jewish financiers and editorial boards.

3.Houghton Mifflin Harcourt – Acquired Holt, Rinehart and Winston. In the early 2000s, Jewish-owned capital groups held majority shares.

4.Scholastic Corporation – Founded by Maurice R. Robinson, a Jewish businessman. Major supplier of educational materials to U.S. schools.

5.Simon & Schuster Education Division – Originally part of Paramount Global, with longstanding Jewish editorial influence.

6.Jewish Publication Society (JPS) – While not a school publisher, JPS has influenced many biblical and historical texts used in private and religious schools.

These are the companies who thought you everything you (think you) know and have ever learned in life......

These companies:

•Whitewashed slavery, turning it into "indentured servitude" or "migration."

•Erased black inventors, warriors, entrepreneurs, and freedom fighters.

•Taught Hebrews that their story began in chains, not with kings.

•Promoted Eurocentric heroes while vilifying or erasing indigenous, African, and Hebrew leaders.

ENTIRE MAPS of Africa have been redrawn. Slave rebellions have been omitted. Hebrew contributions to society, science, law, medicine, and politics have been minimized or eliminated. The truth was not just neglected—it was buried.

They have completely rewritten history. They have completely omitted there atrocities.

THE CURE: Trade, Truth, and Torah

TO REBUILD, we must retrain:

•Learn the trades. Farming, hunting, welding, carpentry, mechanics, electrical work, digital media, coding, construction, plumbing, HVAC —these are modern weapons.

•Teach the truth—starting in our homes, then in our communities. Let no Hebrew child be taught that their history began with cotton.

•Return to Torah. The Scriptures command us to teach our children diligently, not to outsource their minds to Babylon.

"AND YE SHALL KNOW the truth, and the truth shall make you free."
— John 8:32

IT IS time to tear down the mental shackles forged by Rockefeller's model and rebuild schools that don't just graduate workers—but raise up kings, priests, builders, thinkers, and leaders.

CONCLUSION: From Indoctrination to Liberation

THE MODERN SCHOOL system was never designed to elevate the Hebrew or Gentile mind—it was designed to contain it.

BY STRIPPING AWAY OUR HISTORY, removing our skills, and indoctrinating our children into dependency, Babylon built a generation of confused, disconnected laborers—cut off from their calling.

BUT THE MOST High never intended His people to be cogs in a machine.

WE WERE MEANT to be builders, creators, visionaries, and truth-bearers.

IT IS time to unlearn the lies, reclaim our trades, and rebuild education on righteousness and truth. Not with state-sanctioned curriculum, but with the eternal words of YAH.

. . .

WE ARE NOT HERE to fit into their system.

We are here to build our own.

THE IMPORTANCE OF
MARRIAGE & FAMILY

*M*arriage is not just a social contract; it is a covenant that mirrors YAH's relationship with Israel (us).

When YAH wanted to describe His love for His people, He spoke of marriage. When He rebuked them for idolatry, He called it adultery.

MARRIAGE STABILIZES NATIONS. It creates legacies, wealth, and generational wisdom.

Babylon knows this, which is why it wages war on marriage through:

•Pornography that warps reality and expectations and feeds lust.

•No-fault divorce laws that trivialize covenant.

• Marriage legislation that incentivizes women to leave

•Media that glamorizes single, hypersexual lifestyles.

•Government systems that reward single motherhood over intact families.

. . .

WHEN HEBREW MEN abandon their posts and Hebrew women reject divine order, families fracture.

Fractured families raise unstable children.

Unstable children become broken adults who repeat the cycle.

THE RESTORATION of the Hebrew nation begins in the home.

A righteous man, a virtuous woman, and children raised in the fear of YAH — that is how we rebuild what was lost.

COVENANT, Covering & Children — Restoring Hebrew Marriage

IN A WORLD of broken vows and fractured homes, the covenant of marriage has been mocked, abandoned, and replaced with temporary pleasures and long-term pain. But to the Most High, marriage has never been optional. It is sacred. It is a covenant — not just a contract.

HEBREWS, we must return to holy matrimony.

TOO MANY OF our people have come to believe that "the good life" exists outside the home. Hebrews chase club lights, corporate promotions, and social media illusions — all while their families crumble in the background.

HEBREW WOMEN, in particular, have been propagandized to pursue everything but the family:

•Give your best years to academic degrees.

•Give your best energy to corporations.

•Save your submission for your boss, not your husband.

•Raise your children alone, while blaming the absent father — all while the system cheers.

THIS IS NOT EMPOWERMENT. This is enslavement disguised as freedom.

MARRIAGE IS NOT THE GOAL — It Is the Foundation

THE WESTERN WORLD SAYS:

"GET YOUR EDUCATION FIRST. Build your career. Find yourself. Then, maybe, settle down at 30 or 40."

BUT THE MOST High never said that.

THE MOST HIGH designed a system where a woman is covered by her father until she is given to her husband — and then covered by him. This is not oppression. This is protection.

WHEN WE DELAY MARRIAGE, we create an open door for fornication. Lust fills the gap that should be covered by covenant.

THE TRUTH IS:

•A woman was made to be a helpmeet — not for a degree. Although there is nothing wrong with and no condemnation on an intelligent, educated, and degreed Hebrew women. In most cases it should not be the central goal of a Hebrew woman's life.

•A man was created to build legacy — not through casual encounters, but through covenant.

•Children are not meant to be born into confusion, but into structure — with a father and a mother under the authority of YAH.

"No More Baby Mamas — Reclaiming Biblical Marriage and Legacy"

IN BIBLICAL TIMES, the child belonged to the father — and so did the responsibility.

"HE SHALL NOT DIMINISH her food, her clothing, and her duty of marriage."

— Exodus 21:10

IF A MAN LAYS with a woman and brings forth a child, then he is responsible for that woman (unless she is lost to adultery and fornication and or rejects his covering) and that child — no exceptions.

IT IS NOT OPTIONAL.

It is not negotiable.

It is covenant.

HEBREW MEN MUST STOP ACTING like sperm donors and reclaim their roles as priests, providers, and protectors.

HEBREW WOMEN MUST STOP ACCEPTING government checks as replacements for the covenant of a man of YAH.

. . .

Marriage Is Ministry

MARRIAGE IS the first institution ever created — before nations, before temples, before the priesthood.

"FOR THIS CAUSE shall a man leave his father and mother, and cleave unto his wife: and they shall be one flesh."
— Genesis 2:24

MARRIAGE IS how we build nations.

It is how we reflect the image of Christ and His bride.

It is the soil from which righteous children spring forth.

IF WE DO NOT RESTORE marriage — we do not restore our people.

A DECLARATION to the Daughters of Zion:

ABSTAIN UNTIL MARRIAGE. Wait on YAH

TO EVERY HEBREW woman and girl: casual sex is NOT OK!

You are not a conquest. You are a crown. You spiritually degrade, emotionally scar, and mentally break yourself with every fornication, and new partner.

. . .

YOUR VALUE IS NOT in how many men desire you — it is in how holy you remain before YAH.

"Who can find a virtuous woman? For her price is far above rubies."
— Proverbs 31:10

WAIT FOR YOUR HUSBAND. Wait in righteousness. Wait in holiness. Let your womb be filled not by lust, but by love and legacy.

BE the treasure of one man, not a door knob for many.

THE IMPACT of multiple sexual partners on a woman's emotional, psychological, physical, spiritual, and marital health is real, measurable, and deeply sobering. Below is a brief breakdown of verified statistics and conclusions from psychological studies, sociological data, and biblical wisdom.

THE MORE PARTNERS, The Less Stability : Marriage and Satisfaction Decline with Partner Count

NATIONAL CENTER for Biotechnology Information (NCBI):

Women with more than 2 premarital sex partners were significantly less likely to report being very happy in their marriages.

WOMEN with 10+ partners had the lowest odds of marital satisfaction.

Institute for Family Studies (IFS) (2020):

· · ·

Women with 0–1 partners before marriage had the highest rates of marital stability and happiness.

Women with 5+ partners before marriage were over 3x more likely to divorce.

Journal of Marriage and Family (2016):

The likelihood of divorce increases sharply with each additional premarital partner, especially for women.

Mental and Emotional Consequences

American Psychological Association (APA):

• Multiple sexual partners are associated with higher rates of anxiety, depression, and substance abuse, especially in women.

• Women are more likely than men to report emotional pain and regret after casual sex.

Psychology Today:

• Women bond chemically to each sexual partner through the release of oxytocin, the same hormone used during childbirth and breast-feeding to bond mother to child.

• When this bond is repeatedly formed and broken, it creates a cycle of emotional detachment, trust issues, and loss of self-worth.

. . .

1 CORINTHIANS 6:16 (KJV):

"What? know ye not that he which is joined to a harlot is one body? for two, saith he, shall be one flesh."

EVERY SEXUAL ACT creates a spiritual soul tie. The more partners, the more fragmented the soul becomes. Instead of wholeness, the woman is left with emotional residue, spiritual confusion, and broken bonds.

ECCLESIASTICUS (SIRACH) 26:9-10 (Apocrypha):

"The whoredom of a woman may be known in her haughty looks and eyelids... Keep a sure watch over a shameless daughter, lest she make thee a laughingstock to thine enemies..."

PROVERBS 6:26:

"For by means of a whorish woman a man is brought to a piece of bread: and the adulteress will hunt for the precious life."

THE SCRIPTURES WARN NOT ONLY of the act, but of the character decay that often follows it.

PHYSICAL CONSEQUENCES of Multiple Sexual Partners in Women

WHILE THE EMOTIONAL and spiritual consequences of sexual promiscuity are deep and lasting, the physical consequences are just as real — and often irreversible.

. . .

1. Changes to the Female Body

THE HUMAN BODY is designed to respond to consistency.

REPEATED sexual encounters with different partners over time cause physical changes to the vaginal wall and reproductive system. While not often discussed publicly, medical professionals acknowledge:

•Reduced tightness and elasticity of vaginal muscles with repeated activity.

•Some gynecologists refer to this as "vaginal laxity," which can increase with multiple partners or overactive sexual behavior.

•This can affect marital intimacy and satisfaction for both spouses.

PROVERBS 5:18-19 (KJV):

"Let thy fountain be blessed: and rejoice with the wife of thy youth. Let her be as the loving hind and pleasant roe; let her breasts satisfy thee at all times..."

A HUSBAND IS MEANT to receive the first fruits, not the leftovers.

2. Sexually Transmitted Diseases (STDs)

THE MORE PARTNERS A WOMAN HAS, the higher the statistical risk of exposure to:

•Chlamydia

•Gonorrhea

•HPV (Human Papillomavirus)

•Herpes

•HIV/AIDS

•Pelvic Inflammatory Disease (PID) — which can lead to infertility

CDC (CENTERS for Disease Control and Prevention):

Women account for nearly 50% of all new STDs each year in the United States, despite being less than half the population — largely because *the female body is more biologically susceptible to infections during intercourse.*

HPV IN PARTICULAR CAN:

•Lead to cervical cancer.

•Remain dormant for years.

•Be incurable in many strains.

SIRACH (ECCLESIASTICUS) 9:9 (Apocrypha):

"Sit not at all with another man's wife, nor sit down with her in thine arms, and spend not thy money with her at the wine; lest thine heart incline unto her, and so through thy desire thou fall into destruction."

3. Decreased Fertility and Birth Complications

REPEATED STDs or abortions from casual sex often leave scar tissue in the womb or fallopian tubes. This:

•Reduces a woman's ability to conceive.

•Increases the chance of miscarriage or ectopic pregnancy.

•Can result in lifelong reproductive complications.

The False Doctrine of "Sexual Freedom"

Modern society calls it "liberation," but the fruit is devastation:

•Broken bodies.

•Diseases that cannot be undone.

•Marriages that begin with disappointment instead of purity.

•Wombs that were meant to bring forth nations — now barren by choice or by damage.

1 Corinthians 6:18 (KJV):

"Flee fornication. Every sin that a man doeth is without the body; but he that committeth fornication sinneth against his own body."

This applies even more intensely to the woman, whose body is designed for intimacy, motherhood, and sanctity.

Final Word

When a woman gives herself to many men, she gives away more than her body:

•She gives away her essence and exclusiveness.

•She gives away her bloom.

•She gives away the best of her beauty, the strength of her purity, and the honor due to her husband.

. . .

EVERY MAN WHO ENTERS HER, takes something with him and leaves something behind.

By the time she reaches the man she was meant to marry, she may have nothing sacred left to give. And too much of other men left behind.

BUT THERE IS redemption in Yahusha. He can restore what was broken, heal what was wounded, and purify what was defiled.

A WOMAN WAS NOT DESIGNED to carry the weight of multiple men's bodies, spirits, and emotional residue.

EACH ENCOUNTER LEAVES A MARK.

EACH SOUL TIE leaves a tear in her soul.

SHE WAS MEANT to be cherished, not passed around.

She was made to bond to one, not be broken by many.

TO THE HEBREW MAN: From Player to Priest

YOU WERE NOT BORN to be a player, pimp, to have a roster, or be a "baby daddy."

You were born to be a priest, a protector, and a patriarch.

. . .

BUT TOO MANY of our brothers trade their crown for carnality,

their birthright for bedposts,

their calling for conquest.

SIRACH (ECCLESIASTICUS) 23:17 (Apocrypha):

"All bread is sweet to a whoremonger, he will not leave off till he die."

SLEEPING with multiple women is not manhood — it is slavery to lust.

STOP LYING. Stop Manipulating. Stop Defiling Daughters of Zion.

YOU CLAIM TO "LOVE WOMEN," yet you wound them for sport.

You chase bodies and leave souls in ruins.

You whisper lies to get them into bed and leave them with children and shame.

THE BIBLE SAYS:

PROVERBS 6:32 (KJV):

"But whoso committeth adultery with a woman lacketh understanding: he that doeth it destroyeth his own soul."

EVERY WOMAN you lie with is someone's daughter, and possibly someone else's future wife.

.   .   .

AND IF SHE belongs to YAH, you will answer for it.

1 THESSALONIANS 4:4-6 (KJV):

"That every one of you should know how to possess his vessel in sanctification and honour... That no man go beyond and defraud his brother in any matter: because that the Lord is the avenger of all such."

YOU DEFILE Yourself with Every Whore You Enter

THE ACT of sex is not just physical — it is spiritual.

1 CORINTHIANS 6:15-16 (KJV):

"Know ye not that your bodies are the members of Christ? shall I then take the members of Christ, and make them the members of a harlot? God forbid... He that is joined to a harlot is one body."

WHEN YOU SLEEP WITH A WHORE, you don't just stain her — you stain yourself.

You carry her trauma, her spirits, her soul-ties — into your next relationship, into your future marriage, into your children.

PRAY. Fast. Flee Fornication. Practice Retention.

IT'S time to take back your self-control.

•Turn off the porn.

•Block the flings or "friends"

•Starve your lust and feed your spirit.

•Pray, fast, and get in the word of Yah until you are strong enough spiritually to defend against what is killing you.

SIRACH 19:2 (Apocrypha):

"Wine and women will make men of understanding to fall away: and he that cleaveth to harlots will become impudent."

ABSTAIN.

Don't waste your seed.

Don't waste your years.

Don't waste your crown.

WAIT UNTIL MARRIAGE — It's Not Weak, It's Warrior Discipline

YOU'RE NOT a man because you sleep with women.

You're a man when you learn to conquer yourself.

LET your loins be governed by your convictions, not your urges.

Let your love be proven by honor and commitment, not by hookups.

CONQUERING lust is one of the most critical battles for the Hebrew man. We must stop giving our essence, our time, and our energy to women we don't intend to marry and cover.

"Be the treasure of one man, not a door knob for many."

Here are some Bible verses that express this idea:

•Proverbs 5:18-19: "May your fountain be blessed, and may you rejoice in the wife of your youth. A loving doe, a graceful deer - may her breasts satisfy you always, may you ever be intoxicated with her love." This verse encourages faithfulness and finding joy within one's marriage.
•1 Corinthians 7:2: "But since sexual immorality is occurring, each man should have sexual relations with his own wife, and each woman with her own husband." This verse emphasizes the importance of marital intimacy as a way to avoid sexual sin.
•Hebrews 13:4: "Marriage should be honored by all, and the marriage bed kept pure, for God will judge the sexually immoral and adulterous." This verse underscores the sanctity

OF MARRIAGE and calls for fidelity within it.

These verses highlight the value placed on exclusive and dedicated love within a committed marriage relationship.

BIBLICAL FOUNDATIONS OF MARRIAGE, Faithfulness, and Sexual Purity

1. Marriage is a Covenant, Not a Contract

MALACHI 2:14 (KJV):

"Yet ye say, Wherefore? Because the Lord hath been witness between thee and the wife of thy youth... she is thy companion, and the wife of thy covenant."

. . .

MARRIAGE IS NOT A CASUAL AGREEMENT — it is a divine covenant made in the sight of YAH.

PROVERBS 18:22:

"Whoso findeth a wife findeth a good thing, and obtaineth favour of the Lord."

A WIFE — not a friend, girlfriend, or situationship — is a blessing and favor from YAH.

2. Sex is Sacred — Only Within Marriage

HEBREWS 13:4 (KJV):

"Marriage is honourable in all, and the bed undefiled: but whoremongers and adulterers God will judge."

SEX IS HOLY — but only inside the bounds of marriage. Outside of it, it brings judgment, not blessing.

1 CORINTHIANS 6:18-20:

"Flee fornication... He that committeth fornication sinneth against his own body... Therefore glorify God in your body."

THE LUSTFUL MAN devours women without care — but it leads only to his destruction. Women are not bread to be consumed — they are treasures to be honored.

. . .

3. The Hebrew Woman's Virtue is Her Glory

PROVERBS 31:10-12:

"Who can find a virtuous woman? for her price is far above rubies. The heart of her husband doth safely trust in her..."

1 TIMOTHY 2:9-10:

"In like manner also, that women adorn themselves in modest apparel, with shamefacedness and sobriety; not with broided hair, or gold, or pearls, or costly array; But (which becometh women professing godliness) with good works.

VIRTUE AND MODESTY are not weakness — they are the weapons of royalty.

4. Yahusha on Marriage and Divorce

MATTHEW 19:5-6:

"For this cause shall a man leave father and mother, and shall cleave to his wife: and they twain shall be one flesh... What therefore God hath joined together, let not man put asunder."

YAHUSHA AFFIRMS THE GENESIS DESIGN — one man, one woman, one flesh, one covenant.

<u>Biblical Couples Who Modeled Covenant and Faithfulnes</u>s

Abraham & Sarah – Genesis 12–21

Though flawed, they walked in covenant, trusting YAH even in barrenness. She called him "lord," and he defended her. YAH blessed their faith and made them the root of the promise.

Isaac & Rebekah – Genesis 24

Their union was arranged by YAH's divine providence, and Isaac loved Rebekah. A model of submission, prayerful choice,

AND LOVE.

Boaz & Ruth – Ruth 1–4

Boaz honored Ruth's virtue, protected her reputation, and redeemed her. Ruth, once a Moabitess, became an ancestor of David and Yahusha through faithful covenant love.

Tobias & Sarah – Book of Tobit (Apocrypha)

Tobit 8:7 (KJV-Apocrypha):

"And now, O Lord, I take not this my sister for lust, but uprightly: therefore mercifully ordain that we may become aged together."

A beautiful example of prayer, purity, and holy intentions in marriage.

.   .   .

OTHER SACRED TEXTS ON PURITY & Union

BOOK OF JUBILEES 30:17-18

"AND ALL ,who commit it shall be put to death; and ye shall stone them with stones: and do not ye any unrighteousness in your judgments…"

SEXUAL SIN WAS a capital offense under the law because it was considered a defilement of YAH's image.

A HEBREW WOMAN should never be common property.

— she is a garden enclosed, a fountain sealed (Song of Solomon 4:12).

SONG OF SOLOMON 4:7:

"Thou art all fair, my love; there is no spot in thee."

SHE IS TO BE TREASURED, not trampled.

THE HEBREW MAN, likewise, must return to honor.

He cannot sow chaos, abandon his seed, and still expect kingship.

TOGETHER, they are to walk in covenant, not confusion.

Holiness, not hormones.

Legacy, not lust.

. . .

DON'T GIVE your best years to Babylon. Give them to your King, your covenant, and your Creator.

LET the Families Rise Again

IT IS time for Hebrew homes to be whole again.

THE MAN IS THE HEAD.

The woman is the foundation.

The children are the heritage.

THIS IS the order of YAH.

And anything outside of this order is disorder — no matter how much it is polished, praised, protected or propagated by Babylon.

A COMMUNITY CANNOT RISE if its families are broken.

A nation cannot be restored if its households are in rebellion.

WE CANNOT PUT on a mask of holiness by day and fornicate in secret by night.

We cannot cry out for justice while we neglect the first ministry — our homes.

WE NEED COVENANT, not contracts.

We need husbands, not "situationships."

We need wives, not baby mamas.

We need fathers, not sperm donors.

We need mothers, not government dependents.

WE NEED the fire of YAH to fall upon our families again.

MARRIAGE IS NOT JUST a social contract — it is a divine covenant, a sacred mirror of YAH's relationship with Israel, His chosen people.

WHEN THE MOST High wanted to describe His love, He didn't compare it to friendship.

He didn't compare it to leadership.

He called it marriage.

"FOR YOUR MAKER is your husband — YAHUAH of Hosts is His name; the Holy One of Israel is your Redeemer."

— Isaiah 54:5

WHEN ISRAEL REBELLED, YAH didn't say they broke a treaty.

He said they committed adultery.

That's how seriously He takes covenant.

MARRIAGE Is the Foundation of Legacy

Marriage stabilizes entire nations. It is the seedbed of:
•Legacy — Generational wealth, faith, and honor.
•Wisdom — Passed down from father to son, mother to daughter.
•Discipline — Taught in love, enforced through order.
•Covenant — Demonstrated daily, not just taught in sermons.

Babylon knows this. That's why it doesn't just ignore marriage — it attacks it.

Babylon's War on the Family

THE ENEMY HAS SYSTEMATICALLY DISMANTLED the Hebrew household through:

•Pornography — A spirit of lust that replaces intimacy with fantasy and unrealistic expectations. It teaches men to devalue women and worship their flesh. Porn desensitizes the mind, objectifies the body, and warps your view of intimacy. It also has the tendency to change your sexual appetite because once your brain is desensitized to watching normal sexual behavior, the things that use to gave you great pleasure now feel boring and unstimulating and the only way to feed the lust monster is to explore new proclivities of sexual debauchery.

•No-fault divorce laws — That trivialize covenant and make marriage disposable.

•Family court systems — That incentivize Hebrew women to leave their husbands through financial gain, child support, and government backing.

•Media propaganda — That glamorizes "the single life", hypersexuality, and careers over covenant.

•Economic dependence — Government programs that reward women for removing men from the home while punishing intact families through taxes and reduced aid.

. . .

THIS IS NOT BY ACCIDENT. It is design.

The serpent still whispers, "Did YAH really say…?" — and too many Hebrew women have believed him.

DELAYED MARRIAGE = Increased Fornication

THE SYSTEM HAS CONVINCED us that biology is wrong.

HEBREW WOMEN ARE TOLD:

•Go to college.

•Build your career.

•Travel the world.

•Start a family after you've given your best years to corporations and hedonism.

BUT THIS MINDSET is not biblical — it's Babylonian.

DELAYING marriage until your 30s increases the likelihood of fornication, heartbreak, broken engagements, abortions, and single motherhood.

And you would not be offering your best to your future husband.

WAITING UNTIL "YOU FIND YOURSELF" or while you're "working on yourself" is just code for wasting years in rebellion and fornication.

. . .

"NEVERTHELESS, to avoid fornication, let every man have his own wife, and let every woman have her own husband."

— 1 Corinthians 7:2

YAH DESIGNED marriage as the solution to sexual sin, not the reward after it.

THE MAN MUST COVER — The Woman Must Honor

WE MUST RETURN to the divine order:

•The father covers the daughter until he gives her to a husband.

•The husband becomes her covering — spiritually, emotionally, physically, and financially.

•The children are raised in that covering — safe, guided, and protected.

BUT NOW, the government has replaced the father.

The woman has become both ruler and provider.

The man has become absent — or worse, emasculated.

THIS IS A CURSE.

IF A HEBREW MAN lays with a woman and produces a child — he is responsible for that woman and that child. That's not a suggestion. That's biblical order.

. . .

IN BIBLICAL TIMES, children belonged to the father.

The lineage, the inheritance, the responsibility — all went through him.

"THE CHILDREN GATHER WOOD, the fathers kindle the fire, and the women knead their dough."

— Jeremiah 7:18

THERE WAS ORDER. And with order came blessing.

DAUGHTERS OF ZION — Choose Purity Start Waiting For Marriage

TO EVERY HEBREW WOMAN: you are not a product for the market.

You are not an influencer for Babylon.

You are not a boss without a covering.

YOU ARE A DAUGHTER OF ZION, and your virtue is your power.

"FAVOR IS DECEITFUL, and beauty is vain: but a woman that feareth YAHUAH, she shall be praised."

— Proverbs 31:30

STOP ADVERTISING your body and calling it empowerment.

Stop seeking attention when you were made for covenant.

. . .

A RIGHTEOUS MAN **doesn't want a woman who belongs to the streets.**

He wants a woman who belongs to YAH.

CALL TO THE MEN — You Are the Priest of the House

TO EVERY HEBREW MAN: You are not a player. You are not a "baby daddy."

You are the priest of your home.

•Stop sowing seed without building altars.

•Stop laying with women you don't intend to cover.

•**Stop blaming the system when you abandon your post**.

IF YOU CREATE A CHILD, you are bound by heaven to cover both mother and child.

NO EXCUSES. No escape. No compromise.

THE RESTORATION BEGINS at the Table

IT IS at the dinner table where families are formed.

It is at the prayer altar where legacies are sealed.

It is in covenant where healing begins.

WE'VE TRIED every system but YAH's system.

Now it's time to return to what was holy from the beginning.

. . .

A RIGHTEOUS MAN.

A virtuous woman.

Children raised in the fear and instruction of YAH.

THIS IS how we rebuild the Hebrew nation.

THIS IS how we restore the Kingdom.

CONCLUSION: Return to the Ancient Paths

THE PATH forward is not new — it is ancient.

IT IS the path of Abraham and Sarah.

Of Isaac and Rebekah.

Of Ruth and Boaz.

Of Joseph and Mary.

THEY WERE NOT PERFECT — but they were covenant-bound.

They honored YAH above their own feelings and desires.

IT IS time for the Hebrew man to rise and lead again.

It is time for the Hebrew woman to return to virtue and honor.

It is time for our children to see healthy Hebrew marriage, fathers present, and mothers protected and loved.

THE RESTORATION BEGINS in the home.

The home begins in covenant.

And covenant begins with submission to the Most High.

If you live together get married. Forget the idea of boyfriend and girl-friend it doesn't exist. Courting, betrothal, marriage.

<u>PROPHETIC PRAYER for the Unity of Hebrew Marriage</u>

ABBA YAH,

WE COME before You not with empty words, but with repentant hearts.

WE HAVE BROKEN COVENANT.

We have mocked marriage.

We have exchanged Your divine order for the confusion of Babylon.

BUT NOW WE RETURN.

RESTORE the hearts of the fathers to their children.

Restore the hearts of the mothers to their husbands.

Restore the dignity of our daughters and the strength of our sons.

· · ·

LET the men rise as priests and protectors.

Let the women rise as nurturers and wise builders of the home.

Let every broken marriage be healed.

Let every broken vow be renewed.

Let every broken family be made whole.

MAY every Hebrew home become a tabernacle of Your presence.

May our marriages preach louder than pulpits.

May our love testify of Your Kingdom on Earth.

WE DECLARE war on every spirit of lust, division, rebellion, abandonment, and pride.

And we loose unity, fidelity, holiness, honor, and love.

LET THE COVENANT BE RESTORED.

Let the families rise again.

IN THE NAME OF YAHUSHA, our Redeemer and King,

So be it. Amein. HalleluYah.

PART III
CULTURAL HIJACKS AND SPIRITUAL COUNTERFEITS

Chapters 17-24

Cultural Confusion – Hijacked Identities, Counterfeit Movements, and the War on Truth

"Woe unto them that call evil good, and good evil; that put darkness for light, and light for darkness…"

— Isaiah 5:20

"For God is not the author of confusion, but of peace, as in all churches of the saints."

— 1 Corinthians 14:33

We are living in an age of engineered chaos—where identity is fluid, truth is subjective, and history is rewritten in real-time. This is no coincidence. This is spiritual warfare cloaked in social activism, psychology, and political correctness.

And at the center of this chaos is the most dangerous tactic of the enemy:

Cultural confusion.

I. The Great Switch – When the Imitator Becomes the Image

Let us begin with the most treacherous deception of all: the impersonation of the chosen people.

"I know the blasphemy of them which say they are Jews, and are not, but are the synagogue of Satan."

— Revelation 2:9

While the true Hebrews were taken into captivity, scattered, oppressed, and despised, another people stepped into their identity— cloaked in religious garb, political power, and global sympathy.

•They claim to be Jews.

•They occupy the land.

•They control the narrative.

•They dominate the media.

But they are not the bloodline of Abraham, Isaac, and Jacob.

They are Edomites, Khazars, Gentiles, and imposters—protected by lies, funded by empires, and hidden behind the Holocaust to avoid any scrutiny.

Meanwhile, the true children of Judah are still treated as criminals, or the entertainment.

This was the great switch.

The world unknowingly blesses the counterfeit and curses the authentic.

II. Hijacked Movements – When Justice Becomes a Trojan Horse

Let us speak plainly.

The cries for justice in the Hebrew community have often been hijacked by movements that do not serve us, that do not honor our God, and that only pretend to love our people.

1. Black Lives Matter: The Movement vs. The Agenda

Yes—Black lives do matter.

But the organization known as Black Lives Matter was never about Hebrew restoration.

Their own founders confessed they were trained Marxists. The movement:

•Promoted anti-family ideology.

•Marginalized the Hebrew man.

•Elevated sexual confusion.

•Accepted money from white liberal institutions and gave no meaningful resources to Black neighborhoods.

It was a social justice decoy—designed to draw in sincere hearts while pushing a godless agenda.

2. LGBTQ+ as a Weapon of Babylon

Make no mistake—every soul deserves dignity. No one should be harmed or hated.

But the LGBTQ+ movement, as a political force, is not neutral. It has become:

•A Trojan horse in civil rights conversations.

•A substitute for Hebrew identity, convincing young people to find belonging in gender confusion instead of cultural clarity.

•A movement that teaches our sons to reject masculinity, and our daughters to trade modesty for rebellion.

They wave rainbow flags while desecrating the rainbow's original meaning—a covenant sign of mercy.

This is not love. It is spiritual war.

III. The Modern Hebrew: Misidentified, Misled, and Misdirected

The average Hebrew does not know who he is.

He may identify as:
•Black
•African-American
•Moor
•Muslim
• Indian
•Atheist

•Pan-Africanist

•Nation of Islam

•5 Percenter

•Conscious but not biblical

•Or simply "spiritual"

Meanwhile, the culture bombards him with images of dysfunction and rebellion:

•He's told to "manifest" success but reject the Most High.

•He's taught Egyptian mythology but not Hebrew prophecy.

•He honors Pharaoh, not Moses.

•He loves America but ignores Zion.

This is intentional.

If Satan can keep the Hebrew from knowing who he is, he can keep him from returning to covenant—and thus keep the whole world in bondage.

IV. When Culture Becomes a Cage

Let's look closely at what our people call "culture."

•A music industry that glorifies death, violence, fornication, drugs, disrespect, ignorance, and destruction.

•A fashion industry that celebrates nudity, lust, and vanity.

•A social media system that rewards and promotes vanity, pride, materialism, lust, ignorance, rebellion, and "likes" over righteousness.

•A public school system that teaches everything except truth.

We have confused expression with oppression.

We don't need any more "culture".

We need deliverance.

V. The War on Truth: Who Controls the Narrative?

The truth isn't just hidden.

It's being replaced.

Those who speak truth are now:

•Called hateful.

•Labeled conspiracy theorists.

•Shadow-banned on platforms.

•Fired from jobs.

•Cancelled by society.

Why?

Because truth threatens the system.

Truth wakes up the captives.

Truth exposes the elite.

Truth restores identity.

That is why Babylon fights it so viciously.

VI. Returning to Clarity: What Must Be Done

To escape cultural confusion, the Hebrew must:

1.Unplug from the matrix of false identities.

2.Reject counterfeit movements that use his pain to push wicked agendas.

3.Embrace his true name—Hebrew, not Negro or African American.

4.Return to the commandments of the Most High—not for legalism, but for alignment because we are saved by the blood of our Savior alone.

5.Separate from Babylon's version of culture and build a holy, righteous one rooted in Scripture.

. . .

"Come out of her, my people, that ye be not partakers of her sins..."

— Revelation 18:4

This is not just a spiritual call. It's a cultural revolution.

Summary:

Cultural confusion is the battlefield of our generation. The enemy has replaced truth with lies, identity with ideology, and legacy with lifestyle. The Hebrew must awaken, discern, and reclaim the narrative—not through emotional reaction, but through spiritual restoration. The time for confusion is over. Clarity is here.

UNIVERSE BELIEVERS
— A RELIGION OF SELF

*I*n a world starving for truth, people now feast on delusion.

MODERN SPIRITUALITY TELLS people to "trust the universe" — but what is the universe? It's a created thing, not a Creator. To say the universe "has a plan" is like saying your shoes will guide your destiny.

NEW AGE BELIEVERS OFTEN CLAIM they are "spiritual, not religious." But what they really mean is they serve a god made in their own image — one who never rebukes, never convicts, and always agrees with their latest desire. Their gospel is made of:

•Crystals instead of Christ.

•Sage instead of the Spirit.

•Energy instead of repentance.

THEY READ horoscopes but never read Scripture.

They manifest money but never manifest discipline.

They believe in chakras but not in sin.

They chant affirmations while ignoring abominations.

THESE BELIEFS ARE NOT HARMLESS — they are gateways. Once you replace the Most High with "the universe," you no longer answer to anyone. You become your own god, and every desire is justified. Every sin is repackaged as "self-love." Every demon is renamed "energy." Every rebellion is baptized in the language of "healing."

BUT A LIE DRESSED *in positivity is still a lie.*

THIS IS NOT ENLIGHTENMENT — it's ancient deception in a modern outfit.

A RELIGION OF SELF :

"I BELIEVE IN THE UNIVERSE."

"Manifest your own destiny."

"Worship the ancestors."

"The universe will work it out."

THIS IS NOT SPIRITUALITY — this is idolatry and rebellion wearing a crystal necklace.

NEW AGE BELIEF is nothing more than a religion of self, built for people who want the illusion of depth without the accountability of truth. It promises false :

•Power without repentance.

•Blessing without obedience.

•Spirituality without submission.

•"Healing" without holiness.

THEY CHANT mantras and talk about "energy," but at the core of it all, they worship their own emotions. Their god changes with their mood. Their morality shifts with their desires.

THEY DON'T BELIEVE in the universe.

They believe in themselves — their lusts, their traumas, their opinions — all enthroned as sacred.

THE BIBLE WARNED us of this:

"Every man did that which was right in his own eyes."
— Judges 21:25

THEY CALL ON "THE UNIVERSE" because the universe doesn't talk back.

It makes no demands.

It requires no sacrifice.

It gives no commandments.

It issues no judgment.

. . .

IT LETS them sin in peace.

BUT TRUTH IS NOT BASED on your truth — it's based on YAH's truth.

And the truth is: you will not manifest your way into the Kingdom. You will not burn sage and scare off demons. You will not chant your trauma away without confronting sin. You will not ascend spiritually while denying the One who sits on the throne of Heaven.

"YE SHALL BE AS GODS…"

— The serpent's first lie, still being whispered today.

THIS IS NOT LIGHT. It is Lucifer's counterfeit light.

A "UNIVERSE" that demands no repentance is nothing more than a golden calf carved out of ego, built to make people feel righteous while they walk straight into hell smiling.

MENTALLY ILL OR DEMONIC?
— THE LGBTQ AGENDA

*I*nside priDE MONth is a DEMON

WE LIVE in a time where truth is seen as hate. What Babylon calls "love" is actually spiritual sabotage. The LGBTQ community suffers astronomical rates of depression, suicide, substance abuse, domestic violence, violence, and broken relationships. But instead of asking why, Babylon demands celebration. Instead of repentance, they demand parades. Instead of deliverance, they demand affirmation.

IT IS an agenda being cultivated through every possible avenue imaginable to corrupt your children, and it is demonic.

THESE ARE the same spirits that reigned in Sodom and Gomorrah — spirits of sexual confusion, rebellion, and violent rejection of righteousness.

They are unrepentant and spiritually tormented.

. . .

TRANSGENDER SURGERIES ARE SKYROCKETING, yet regret is common. Psychological trauma is not healed by mutilating the body. Hormones cannot cast out demons. Scalpels do not rewrite DNA. Many discover that altering their bodies did not heal their souls — only left them more fractured and spiritually disoriented.

AND YET SOME FIND YAHUSHA. Some turn from that life and testify boldly of deliverance. These voices are silenced by the media and the algorithms. Mainstream platforms only elevate rebellion, not redemption.

THE SCRIPTURES ARE NOT vague on this topic. "You shall not lie with a man as with a woman; it is an abomination" (Leviticus 18:22). "For this cause, God gave them up to vile affections..." (Romans 1:26–28). This is not about hate — this is about truth that saves. Telling someone drowning in deception that they are "perfect the way they are" is not love. It is cruelty wrapped in a rainbow-colored lie.

THE MEDIA HAS BECOME the mouthpiece of this demonic agenda. In every movie, every series, every commercial, every ad, every social media influencer, every podcast, every song— they normalize what God calls sin. Homosexual or trans characters are inserted even when the original characters were not that way. Cartoons now promote gender confusion to toddlers. Drag queens read books in elementary schools while dressed like demons. Children are being taught to question their gender before they can even spell the word "gender." This is not diversity — this is indoctrination. It is a propaganda campaign aimed at grooming a generation to rebel against their Creator.

. . .

BUT THE DECEPTION has gone even further. Political leaders, and now even churches ordain sin. Pulpits are occupied by open homosexuals. Choirs are led by flamboyant rebels. Bibles are rewritten to remove "offensive" scriptures. These are not churches — they are synagogues of Satan (Revelation 2:9).

NO SPIRIT that exalts pride and denies repentance is of YAH.

This agenda is not just social — it is demonic.

IT IS the spirit of Sodom in the sanctuary.

LET it be known clearly and unapologetically:

ON NO LEVEL — moral,emotional,mental,political, social, physical, or spiritual — is anything associated with this agenda acceptable.

Repent. Turn away from your sin.

- a contrite heart and broken spirit he will not despise.

THE SACRIFICES of God are a broken spirit: a broken and a contrite heart, O God, thou wilt not despise."Psalm 51:17

FOR MEN and for women

It is 100% wrong on every level. It is an abomination. It is confusion. It is rebellion. It is sin. And it must be repented of, not celebrated.

HEBREWS, of all people, should be know better.

We know what happens when a people turn from YAH:

•Our ancestors suffered captivity for rejecting His laws.

•National sin brought national judgment.

•Embracing these lifestyles will not bring liberation — it will bring ruin.

HOMOSEXUALITY, transgenderism, and the larger LGBTQ agenda are not "alternative lifestyles" — they are spiritual strongholds. They are demonic unions. According to Scripture, they are abominations (Leviticus 18:22; Romans 1:26–28), not identities. We are not wrestling against flesh and blood but against principalities, powers, rulers of darkness, and spiritual wickedness in high places (Ephesians 6:12).

WE ARE NOT CALLED to accommodate wickedness — we are called to cast it out.

And the only flag we wave is the blood-stained banner of Yahusha HaMashiach.

OPINIONS, PLATFORMS, FEELINGS & FOLLOWERS

*I*n this age, attention is currency.

Platforms are confused for pulpits.

Followers are mistaken for fruit.

And feelings have been enthroned as truth.

ESPECIALLY AMONG WOMEN, social media has become a place where women advertise themselves for sale. It has become a temple of vanity and emotional addiction. It is no longer just a place to share — it is a place to be desired and worshiped. A place to perform, to posture, and to worship oneself.

THE ALGORITHM IS NOT NEUTRAL — it is engineered. It feeds off of dopamine addiction, insecurity, lust, negativity, and pride. And while it may feel empowering in the moment, the system is devouring its users from the inside out.

. . .

VALIDATION HAS BECOME A DRUG — and for many women, it's the only high that matters:

• Filters that transform reality, *until even the mirror becomes offensive.*

• Posed photos masked as "confidence" that are really cries for attention. And yes, I am talking about the turn my body around so I can show my backside and tongue sticking out of my mouth pictures.

• Thirst traps labeled "self-love" that are really seeds of lust.

• Cryptic captions about "healing" and "energy" while constantly fornicating. Hearts remain broken and spirits remain lost.

THE BIBLE SAYS:

"HE THAT TRUSTETH in his own heart is a fool."

— Proverbs 28:26

SOCIAL MEDIA TRAINS women to build their identity on illusion and then protect that illusion at all costs — even if it means destroying their peace, their modesty, their family, or their walk with God. It says, "Worship yourself." It says, "If they don't love you, love yourself louder." It says, "You deserve it all" — even if you've sown nothing but confusion and chaos.

THIS IS NOT EMPOWERMENT. This is engineered idolatry.

AND MEN ARE NO BETTER. The ones who chase these digital mirages become hollow, lust-driven, emotionally crippled, and obsessed with chasing status instead of building legacy.

. . .

WE'VE RAISED a generation where the illusion of the digital world trump's the truth and reality of the real one.

But let this be made clear:

IF YOUR PLATFORM doesn't lead people to righteousness,

it is just a stage for your own destruction.

THE MOST HIGH does not care how many likes you get — He cares how much light you carry.

He is not impressed with your followers — He is looking for your fruit.

SOCIAL MEDIA MAY BE the loudest voice in the culture, but it is not the holiest.

And if you build your identity on its validation, you will collapse under its deception.

IN AN AGE where anyone with a phone can become a prophet, discernment is no longer optional — it is essential. Social media has become a temple of influence where false teachers dress like life coaches and demons disguise themselves as healers. Many speak well but walk in darkness. They stir your emotions, feed your ego, and validate your dysfunction — all while leading you away from truth. Be careful who you listen to. People naturally gravitate toward voices that echo their feelings or justify their sin. But the truth doesn't always feel good — it corrects, convicts, and calls you higher. Don't follow someone just because they're popular, poetic, or relatable. Test every spirit. If their words don't align with THE WORD, they are nothing more than digital demons and wolves with a ring light and good editing.

WHAT IS OUR CULTURE?

We love to say, "It's just our culture."

But we rarely ask:

•Who defined it?

•Who profits from it?

•Who does it actually benefit?

THE TRUTH IS, much of what we call Hebrew culture today was manufactured in corporate boardrooms.

Record executives — many tied to the same financial dynasties that owned slave ships — decide who becomes a star, what music is promoted, and what images flood our children's eyes.

THEY DO NOT PUSH conscious music, healthy families, or financial literacy.

They push violence, hypersexuality, drug use, and material worship.

Because that is profitable. And because it keeps us sheep, easy to shear.

LIKE JACOB'S flocks that conceived spotted when they looked at spotted rods, we become what we see.

Our young imitate what is on their screens, not realizing it was all designed to shape them into Babylon's image.

IF WE WANT to reclaim our culture, we must stop letting outsiders define it. We must reject the music, movies, and social media from without. And we must reject the mental, emotional, and spiritual mindset from within.

What we call our "culture" today is the culture of the modern slave. A lost people dancing and singing joyfully about their own destruction. A genre of music is not a culture. Hip Hop is not our culture. A genre of music can define and/or speak for a culture, which Hip Hop has done at different times in the past but it is not the culture.

CULTURE BEGINS WITH IDENTITY.

WE MUST ROOT our culture in Torah, in covenant, in truth.

POLITICAL PARTIES
& MILITARY SERVICE

For centuries, Hebrews have poured loyalty, votes, and blood into systems that never intended to elevate them.

We joined the armies of nations that enslaved us, hoping to prove ourselves worthy. We stood on battlefields from Gettysburg to Normandy, from Korea to Kandahar, returning home to second-class citizenship.

MEANWHILE, political parties campaign in our churches mimicking our lingo, and make hollow promises.

Once elected, they push agendas that dismantle families, encourage sexual immorality, and secure our dependency.

NO POLITICAL PARTY will deliver Hebrews. No earthly government will enact YAH's justice.

Yahusha alone is King. His Kingdom is not of this world.

Our hope is not in ballots or bullets — it is in Zion restored.

We are not Democrats. We are not Republicans. We are Hebrews. We're not conservative. We're not liberals. We are Hebrews.

There should be a Hebrew political party birthed from the Hebrew Assembly. We should elect our own Hebrew leaders.

NOT ONE MORE DROP OF Hebrew blood should be spilled for the wars of the synagogue of satan and its military industrial complex puppet.

HEBREWS IN THE MILITARY: A Call to Disengage from Babylon's Wars

HEBREWS HAVE SHED blood on every battlefield this nation has called a war — from the Revolutionary trenches to the deserts of the Middle East. We have fought valiantly for freedoms we were never fully granted and defended a flag that often refused to defend us. But now, we stand at a prophetic crossroads. The next war America fights will not be just against flesh and blood — it will be a spiritual war, a judgment from YAHUAH Himself. To raise a weapon in that battle is to raise it against the Most High. I call every Hebrew soldier, sailor, marine, and airman to lay down Babylon's armor. Come out of her ranks. Your true battle is not overseas — it is in your homes, in your communities, and in your covenant. Do not let your loyalty to a collapsing empire outweigh your loyalty to the King of Kings. It is time to fight for righteousness, for the souls of our children, and for the restoration of our nation — not for the pride and profit of Egypt.

THE EUROPEAN
AMERICAN GENTILE MAN

*T*he common European American Gentile has long believed Hebrews to be inherently inferior.

This was not born in his heart by nature — it was implanted by propaganda:

•Pseudoscientific claims of racial hierarchy.

•Sermons that misused Scripture to justify slavery.

•Newspapers and television news stations that exaggerated every crime by a Black man while excusing atrocities by whites.

YET MOST AMERICAN European Gentiles were not plantation owners.

They were manipulated by elites to see Hebrews as the threat, never realizing they were pawns themselves in a larger system orchestrated by powers far above them.

STILL, the Bible makes clear they will not be judged for slavery alone, but for how they treated the Hebrews during captivity.

Mercy was always an option. Too many chose cruelty.

THE MOST HIGH is not blind.

He saw the cruelty when mercy was an option.

He heard the mocking laughter when we cried out.

He recorded every lash, every theft, every lie passed down as gospel.

THEY SAID they were just following orders.

Just living in the times.

Just doing what everyone else did.

But the prophets say otherwise.

"AS THOU HAST DONE, it shall be done unto thee." (Obadiah 1:15)

YAH ALLOWED judgment to fall on His people because of our sin —
but the nations went too far.

They touched the apple of His eye with unclean hands.

And though they forgot, He did not.

THEY HELPED FORWARD THE AFFLICTION.

They scattered us.

They mocked us.

They spoiled us.

They preyed upon the weak, the aged, the children.

. . .

BUT THE CLOCK has struck a new hour.

Now, the Judge of all the earth will repay.

Not simply for chains and ships —

But for every choice made in the dark when light was still an option.

"ALL THEY THAT devour thee shall be devoured." (Jeremiah 30:16)

YET — even now — mercy is not cut off.

The Most High is not only a God of justice. He is a God of grace and mercy.

To the Gentile man who sees, repents, and turns from the wickedness of his heritage — we welcome you as believers in Christ.

"IF MY PEOPLE... shall humble themselves, and pray, and seek My face, and turn from their wicked ways..." (2 Chronicles 7:14)

THE CROSS OF Yahusha was not a monument to one nation —

It was a door for every nation.

But that door is narrow.

You cannot carry your pride, your prejudice, or your patriotism through it.

LET NOT your nation's sins drag your soul to ruin.

You were not born with hate — you were taught it.

But now you have seen the truth.

And truth demands a choice.

CHOOSE MERCY.

Choose righteousness.

Choose repentance.

And the same blood that washes the Hebrew clean… will wash you also.

JUDGMENT FOR CRUELTY Against the Hebrews

ZECHARIAH 1:14–15

"SO THE ANGEL that communed with me said unto me, Cry thou, saying,

Thus saith the Lord of hosts; I am jealous for Jerusalem and for Zion with a great jealousy.

And I am very sore displeased with the heathen that are at ease:

for I was but a little displeased, and they helped forward the affliction."

GOD WAS ANGRY WITH ISRAEL, and allowed our captivity, and you will be judged not by the captivity, but how you treated us in captivity. They abused His people beyond what He allowed — and for that, He promised judgment.

Joel 3:2–3

"I will also gather all nations, and will bring them down into the valley of Jehoshaphat,
and will plead with them there for my people and for my heritage Israel,
whom they have scattered among the nations, and parted my land.
And they have cast lots for my people; and have given a boy for an harlot,
and sold a girl for wine, that they might drink."

A PROPHECY of end-time judgment upon the nations who sold, scattered, and dehumanized Israel.

JEREMIAH 30:16–17

"THEREFORE ALL THEY that devour thee shall be devoured;

and all thine adversaries, every one of them, shall go into captivity;

and they that spoil thee shall be a spoil,

and all that prey upon thee will I give for a prey.

For I will restore health unto thee, and I will heal thee of thy wounds, saith the Lord;

because they called thee an Outcast, saying, This is Zion, whom no man seeketh after."

GOD PROMISES to reverse the curses and judge those who took advantage of Israel in her broken state.

·   ·   ·

OBADIAH 1:10–15

"FOR THY VIOLENCE against thy brother Jacob shame shall cover thee, and thou shalt be cut off for ever.

...Thou shouldest not have looked on the day of thy brother in the day that he became a stranger;

...Neither shouldest thou have stood in the crossway, to cut off those of his that did escape.

...For the day of the Lord is near upon all the heathen:

as thou hast done, it shall be done unto thee: thy reward shall return upon thine own head."

A DETAILED CONDEMNATION of Edom for rejoicing in Jacob's suffering and assisting in his destruction.

ISAIAH 47:6

"I WAS wroth with my people, I have polluted mine inheritance,

and given them into thine hand: thou didst shew them no mercy;

upon the ancient hast thou very heavily laid thy yoke."

THE GENTILE NATIONS were permitted to rule over Israel temporarily — but they showed no mercy and will be punished accordingly

Rebuke of the sins of your fathers and repent for your complicity in a system built on those sins.

Again I implore you to choose truth and rightness.

And the same blood that washes the Hebrew clean… will wash you also.

We are not now nor have we ever been your enemy. We do not hate you. The same salvation offered to us is also offered to you.

THE EUROPEAN AMERICAN
GENTILE WOMAN

*O*ften painted as delicate flowers or innocent bystanders, European American Gentile women were not silent spectators to the oppression of the Hebrews—they were active participants. Behind the façade of fragility lay a powerful social force that upheld white supremacy and helped maintain the captivity of the Hebrew people in America.

EUROPEAN GENTILE WOMEN were central to this system.

They shaped its morality, policed its boundaries, reinforced its lies, and ensured its survival across generations.

THESE WOMEN:

• Upheld social norms that barred Hebrews from humanity, liberty, and opportunity.

• Weaponized femininity to appear harmless while directing some of the most violent responses in American history.

• Encouraged, justified, or directly caused the lynching of Hebrew men under the false cry of "protecting white womanhood."

• Raised their children to view Hebrews as lesser, dangerous, or subhuman—training the next generation of oppressors.

THEIR TEARS at the slightest perceived offense fueled lynch mobs.

Their silence in the face of injustice strengthened segregation.

Their approval maintained racial hierarchies inside homes, churches, schools, and communities.

THEY WERE the guardians of white supremacy's social order.

AND YET, despite all of this, we hold no hatred.

VENGEANCE BELONGS TO YAH, not to us.

EUROPEAN AMERICAN GENTILES need not fear retribution from Hebrews — for our hearts do not burn with the same malice that burn against us.

But the truth must be spoken.

And repentance must be embraced.

WE ONLY PRAY you turn to righteousness and cling to the truth — lest you share in Babylon's judgment.

The Wives of the Confederacy — Protectors of Slavery in Silk and Lace

While Confederate men marched onto battlefields, their wives waged a quieter but equally destructive war from their homes, plantations, and churches.

These women:
• Encouraged their husbands and sons to fight for slavery as a "God-ordained duty."
• Framed the defense of bondage as a noble act of Southern honor.
• Ostracized any white man or woman who questioned slavery.
• Taught their households that Hebrew enslavement was righteous, natural, and necessary for "civilized" life.

CONFEDERATE wives held immense cultural and moral influence.

They shaped the values of their communities, and they enforced the racial hierarchy inside their own homes.

MANY OF THEM:

• Managed plantations during the war, punishing enslaved Hebrews without restraint.

• Joined churches that preached a twisted theology where Jesus sanctioned slavery.

• Pressured pastors, politicians, and neighbors to preserve the system that benefited them economically and socially.

THESE WOMEN WERE NOT victims of their husbands' beliefs—they were co-architects.

· · ·

THEIR HANDS STIRRED POTS, stitched uniforms, and rocked cradles…

But they also stirred hatred, stitched together a racial caste system, and rocked America into generations of lies.

THEIR INFLUENCE DID NOT END with the Confederacy's defeat.

They passed their worldview on to their daughters—who carried the torch of deception with pride.

THE DAUGHTERS OF THE CONFEDERACY — The Architects of Historical Lies

NO GROUP HAS DONE MORE to rewrite American history than the **United Daughters of the Confederacy (UDC)**.

Formed in 1894, these women launched one of the most powerful propaganda campaigns in American history—one that still affects school textbooks, monuments, and national memory today.

THEIR MISSION WAS SIMPLE:

Rewrite the Civil War. Protect white supremacy. Destroy the truth.

AND THEY SUCCEEDED.

THE DAUGHTERS OF THE CONFEDERACY:

• Created and spread the "**Lost Cause**" myth — claiming the Civil War wasn't about slavery but "states' rights."

• Published rewritten textbooks that erased slavery's brutality and sanitized the Confederacy.

• Threatened schools and teachers who taught the truth.

• Funded and erected over 700 Confederate statues to honor slave-holding men as "heroes."

• Promoted the image of the "noble Southern lady" and the "faithful slave," both complete fiction.

• Ensured that generations of white children grew up believing the Confederacy was righteous and slavery was benevolent.

THESE WOMEN WERE NOT SIMPLY PRESERVING history—they were manufacturing lies.

THEY WEAPONIZED MOTHERHOOD, education, culture, and memory, turning Southern womanhood into a tool of national deception.

Their influence reached every classroom, courthouse, and town square in the South—and much of the North.

AND THE DAMAGE REMAINS:

• Millions still believe the Civil War "wasn't really about slavery."

• Confederate statues still stand in American cities.

• Textbooks still downplay slavery's horrors.

• White Southerners still cling to myths created by the UDC rather than the truth.

THE DAUGHTERS of the Confederacy were not historians—they were propagandists for white supremacy.

They ensured that America forgot the truth so that injustice could continue long after the war ended.

YET — even now — mercy is not cut off.

The Most High is not only a God of justice. He is a God of grace and mercy.

To the Gentile woman who sees, repents, and turns from the wickedness of her heritage — we welcome you as believers in Christ.

The cross of Yahusha was not a monument to one nation —

It was a door for every nation.

But that door is narrow.

You cannot carry your pride, your prejudice, or your patriotism through it.

LET NOT your nation's sins drag your soul to ruin.

You were not born with hate — you were taught it.

But now you have seen the truth.

And truth demands a choice.

CHOOSE MERCY.

Choose righteousness.

Choose repentance.

And the same blood that washes the Hebrew clean... will wash you also.

THE STANDARD OF BLESSING
OR CURSING ISRAEL

" $\mathcal{I}$ will bless those who bless you, and curse those who curse you."

— Genesis 12:3

This is an immutable spiritual law.

NATIONS THAT HAVE BLESSED Israel prospered; those that cursed Israel collapsed.

But what if the world doesn't know who Israel is?

What if they bless imposters and scorn the true seed of Jacob?

THAT IS PRECISELY the deception the adversary desires.

Gentiles must humble themselves to learn who Israel truly is, so they can stand rightly before YAH.

Hebrews must awaken to who they are, so they can reclaim covenant.

. . .

IT IS NOT enough to love the idea of Israel — you must love and honor the actual descendants scattered in captivity.

BLESSING OR CURSING — Why Knowing True Israel Matters in the End Times

"AND I WILL BLESS them that bless thee, and curse him that curseth thee: and in thee shall all families of the earth be blessed."

— Genesis 12:3

"MY PEOPLE ARE DESTROYED for lack of knowledge: because thou hast rejected knowledge, I will also reject thee..."

— Hosea 4:6

I. THE COVENANT Still Stands

WHEN THE MOST High made His covenant with Abraham, Isaac, and Jacob, it was eternal, not conditional on human approval or historical rewriting. The promises of land, blessing, and global impact were to be fulfilled through their descendants.

AND YET...

•The world has replaced the true seed with a counterfeit.

•The modern church has taught that "the Church is spiritual Israel"— a doctrine of replacement theology with no biblical foundation.

•Meanwhile, the people who actually descend from Jacob—the Black American descendants of slaves, and others scattered through the diaspora—are forgotten, oppressed, and unrecognized.

. . .

THIS ISN'T JUST a historical error. It's a spiritual offense that comes with serious prophetic consequences.

II. Blessing the Impostor, Cursing the Real

TODAY, Gentile Christians send billions to the modern state of Israel, believing they are fulfilling Genesis 12:3. But if the people they are blessing are not the true seed, then what are they actually doing?

"IF THE FOUNDATION BE DESTROYED, what can the righteous do?"

— Psalm 11:3

THEY ARE:

•Blessing Zionism, not Zion.

•Supporting a secular political entity, not the people of Yah.

•Ignoring the oppressed true Judah in their own cities, while exalting the impostor in Palestine.

WHAT HAPPENS when you bless the synagogue of Satan, thinking you're blessing the chosen?

YOU INHERIT A CURSE, not a blessing.

THE JUDGMENT IS NOT ONLY COMING upon them—it will come upon

nations, churches, and governments that knowingly or ignorantly stand against the true sons and daughters of Zion.

III. End-Time Prophecy and the True Israel

TO UNDERSTAND THE LAST DAYS, one must understand Israel—but not the counterfeit. The Bible is not centered on Rome, America, or the United Nations. It is centered on Jerusalem, Zion, and the people of the covenant.

BIBLICAL PROPHECY IS RACIAL, national, and spiritual. You cannot remove the identity of the Hebrews and still rightly interpret the Scriptures.

HERE ARE JUST A FEW EXAMPLES:

1. Ezekiel 37: The Valley of Dry Bones

A PROPHECY of the resurrection of the scattered house of Israel.

Who is dry, broken, oppressed, and globally despised?

Who was stripped of identity, language, and culture?

It is not Europe. It is not Ashkenaz.

It is the children of the transatlantic slave trade.

2. Deuteronomy 30: The Return from Captivity

"Then YHWH thy God will turn thy captivity, and have compassion upon thee…"
This is not a call to modern converts. This is a promise to true descendants of Jacob.

3. Revelation 7: The 144,000

TWELVE THOUSAND FROM EACH TRIBE—LITERAL tribes, not metaphors.

How can you claim to understand the End Times prophecy and not know who these people really are?

IV. The Curse of Ignorance

TO IGNORE the true Israel is to participate in the blinding spirit of Babylon. It is to:

•Read prophecy backwards, favoring the impostor.

•Call evil good, and good evil.

•Preach about the "Second Coming" without understanding who Yahusha is coming for.

THE CURSES of Deuteronomy 28 still mark the children of Jacob. But those curses are ending—and as they end, the Most High will repay the nations for how they have treated His people.

"FOR HE THAT toucheth you toucheth the apple of his eye."

— Zechariah 2:8

. . .

"HE SHALL HAVE judgment without mercy, that hath shewed no mercy..."

— James 2:13

TO REJECT the awakening of the true Hebrews is to reject the timing of the Most High.

V. The Role of the Gentiles

THIS IS NOT JUST a Hebrew issue—it is a Gentile warning.

GENTILES WHO LOVE YAH MUST:

1.Renounce replacement theology

2.Acknowledge who true Israel is

3.Support—not exploit—Judah's awakening

4.Repent of inherited lies and pride

5.Humble themselves under the Most High's design

"AND THE GENTILES shall come to thy light, and kings to the brightness of thy rising."

— Isaiah 60:3

THE BIBLE, like the world, is not colorblind. It is not blind to blood, lineage, covenant, or restoration. The book of Revelation does not end with a church that replaced Israel. It ends with the restoration of Israel and the submission of the nations to the King of Zion.

VI. The Final Blessing or Final Curse

THE WORLD STANDS AT A CROSSROAD:

•Bless true Israel, and be blessed.

•Curse true Israel, and face judgment.

THIS IS NOT ABOUT FAVORITISM. It's about order, truth, and justice. The true Hebrews are not perfect—but they are chosen. Not because of race, but because of covenant.

THE AWAKENING of Judah is the last trumpet before the return of the King.

THE WORLD MUST NOW DECIDE:

WILL YOU BLESS ZION—OR Babylon?

SUMMARY:

GENESIS 12:3 STILL APPLIES. But it applies to the right people, not the politically powerful impostors. The world has been trained to bless the wrong "Israel" while ignoring the broken, abused, and scattered children of Jacob. This mistake has eternal consequences. Understanding who Israel truly is isn't optional—it's the key to end-time prophecy, divine blessing, and final judgment.

PART IV
THE RESTORATION AND
THE COMING KINGDOM

Chapters 25-32

DESTROYED BLACK CITIES — NOT COINCIDENCE, BUT STRATEGY

*L*et us revisit Tulsa's Black Wall Street.

In 1921, it was a thriving hub of Black-owned businesses, banks, theaters, and homes.

Jealous mobs burned it to the ground. Insurance refused to pay claims.

The survivors lived in tents on the ashes of what they built.

TULSA WAS NOT ALONE.

Rosewood in Florida.

Thriving Black communities in Atlanta, Chicago, and dozens more — all systematically sabotaged by mobs, by eminent domain, by redirection of infrastructure.

INTEGRATION FOLLOWED, not to elevate Hebrews, but to control us.

By merging our schools with theirs, they dictated what our children learned.

By merging our markets with theirs they decided our standard of living, they decided who got loans and who did not.

THIS WAS NOT RANDOM.

It was strategic — a new phase of captivity, ensuring we remained subjects of Babylon no matter how free we claimed to be.

OUR CONTRIBUTION TO AMERICA

There is a myth that Hebrews have done nothing but drain America's resources.

This lie is not only insulting — it is historically absurd.

WHO CLEARED the forests and laid the roads across the South?

Who picked the cotton that financed Wall Street, New York banks, and global textile empires?

Who laid bricks for the White House, Congress, state capitals, courthouses, and universities that to this day lecture us about equality?

HEBREWS HAVE FOUGHT and died in every American war, built entire economies out of sharecropping scraps, and turned spiritual suffering into gospel music, rock, country, jazz, blues, r&b and pop, and inventions that shaped the modern world.

. . .

Broken down group by group, no other single group of people have contributed more to America's wealth and culture while receiving so little.

Our Contribution to America — A Legacy Denied, A Nation Built

I. A Foundation of Blood and Bricks

Before America was ever called a "superpower," it was a plantation economy—fueled, built, and maintained by the unpaid labor of Hebrew hands.

It was Hebrews who cleared the forests of the Carolinas and Georgia.

Hebrews who laid the bricks that built the early Southern economy.

Hebrews who constructed the grand estates of Virginia planters, and the very Capitol in which lawmakers would later debate our "three-fifths" humanity.

•The White House and U.S. Capitol Building were built with the hands of enslaved Hebrews. Government records prove enslaved workers were rented from their "owners" for the construction of these national monuments.

•Georgetown University and many other prestigious institutions in the Ivy League financed themselves by selling Hebrew men, women, and children into bondage.

II. Cotton, Commerce, and Wall Street's Bloody Birth

•In 1860, cotton made up 59% of U.S. exports. That cotton was picked almost entirely by Hebrews under slavery.

•Banks such as J.P. Morgan Chase and New York Life Insurance have admitted they profited directly from slavery—insuring slave owners against "loss" of enslaved people.

•Wall Street itself was originally the site of a slave market. In fact, the name "Wall" Street comes from the wall built to keep out Native tribes, with enslaved Africans sold along its corridor.

AMERICA'S financial dominance began with Hebrew blood, sweat and tears. Every skyscraper in Manhattan is rooted in that foundation.

III. Inventors and Innovators They Tried to Erase

HEBREWS DIDN'T JUST LABOR—WE created. We invented tools and technologies still used today, often denied credit or hidden in obscurity.

•Lewis Latimer (1848–1928): A genius inventor who worked with Thomas Edison and Alexander Graham Bell. He created the carbon filament for the incandescent lightbulb, which made the bulb last longer and practical for use. Without Latimer, Edison's bulb would've burned out quickly and remained useless.

•Garrett Morgan (1877–1963): Inventor of the three-position traffic signal and the gas mask (used in World War I). His inventions saved countless lives but were initially sold under a white frontman because of racial discrimination.

•Madam C.J. Walker (1867–1919): First documented self-made female millionaire in America (of any race). She built a haircare empire that created jobs for thousands of Hebrew women.

•Dr. Charles Drew (1904–1950): Pioneered the process of separating and storing blood plasma, laying the foundation for modern blood banks. He saved lives during World War II—but was later denied treatment by a white hospital, leading to his untimely death.

•Otis Boykin: Improved the pacemaker and helped advance modern computing through electrical resistor designs.

•Marie Van Brittan Brown: Invented the home security system in 1966—a prototype for modern surveillance and police notification systems.

•Frederick McKinley Jones: Invented the first portable refrigeration system for trucks and trains, revolutionizing the food and medical industries.

AND THERE ARE THOUSANDS MORE.

MANY WERE ROBBED of their patents, or forced to sell them to white companies who then took the credit. A system designed to erase the Hebrew genius at every turn.

IV. Cultural Domination: Music, Style, and Soul

WHEN AMERICA LOOKS COOL, sounds cool, or moves with rhythm—it is moving with Hebrew spirit.

•Spirituals sung in fields became blues and gospel, then country, then r&b, then rock, soul, and hip-hop.

•Elvis Presley, the so-called "King of Rock and Roll," got his moves and sound from watching Hebrew performers in Memphis juke joints. The way he moved, danced, sung, and carried himself was all an imitation of Hebrew men. Like putting on a costume.

•Country music was birthed from Hebrew banjo rhythms and Southern field songs—yet our name is barely mentioned in its history.

•Hip-hop, now a global culture, started in the Bronx as a Hebrew youth movement. It now generates billions of dollars, but the creators of the culture are excluded from ownership and decision-making.

FASHION FOLLOWS US. Slang copies us. Sports showcase us. And still, we are portrayed as the problem, the threat, the burden. Even though we have never dropped a bomb or declared war on anyone. The truth is we have never actually done anything to any group of people ever. Let me say that again. There is no history of Hebrew violence towards any race, religion, country, or people. It simply doesn't exist.

V. A Nation in Captivity with the Power of a Nation

DESPITE SYSTEMIC SABOTAGE and generational trauma, Hebrews in America today wield immense financial and cultural power:

•As of 2023, "African-Americans" have a spending power exceeding $1.8 trillion—more than the GDP of Mexico, Saudi Arabia, or Australia.

•If the 46 million "African-Americans" formed their own country, it would be in the top 20 economies globally.

•Yet less than 2% of our wealth stays in our communities for more than 24 hours—a tragic legacy of economic dependence.

WE BUILT AMERICA. We shaped its sound. We wrote its style. We fought its wars. We created its wealth.

WE ARE NOT the burden of this nation.

We are its engine.

We are its mirror.

We are its judgment.

THE HEBREW INVENTORS Who Changed the World — But Were Never Given Credit

WHILE AMERICA TEACHES that Thomas Edison invented the lightbulb, the filament that made it viable was created by a Hebrew man: Lewis Howard Latimer. And let's be clear Thomas Edison never invented anything. He was not in inventor. He was a businessman.

LATIMER, born to formerly enslaved parents, not only invented the carbon filament that made the lightbulb last longer and be mass-produced — he also helped draft the drawings for Alexander Graham Bell's telephone patent and wrote the first book on electric lighting. But his name is rarely mentioned in schoolbooks.

HE WAS FAR FROM ALONE.

NAME-BY-NAME — Just a Glimpse of Our Inventive Genius

•Garrett Morgan – Invented the three-position traffic light and the gas mask used in World War I.

•Madam C.J. Walker – First female self-made millionaire in America; built an empire on hair products for Black women, employing thousands.

•George Washington Carver – Revolutionized agriculture in the South with over 300 products derived from peanuts and sweet potatoes. Yet he's often reduced to "the peanut man" instead of the genius chemist and botanist that he was.

•Granville T. Woods – Known as "the Black Edison," he held over 50 patents including for the induction telegraph, used by trains to communicate while in motion.

•Frederick McKinley Jones – Invented refrigerated trucks and rail-cars, making fresh food delivery and wartime supply chains possible.

•Otis Boykin – Created electrical resistors used in computers, televisions, and pacemakers — modern medicine and technology rely on his brilliance.

•Dr. Patricia Bath – Invented the Laserphaco Probe, a device used for treating cataracts and restoring sight.

•Mark Dean – Co-invented the IBM PC and developed the technology that allowed for color monitors and the modern computer.

EACH OF THESE men and women pushed civilization forward — but were either ignored, underpaid, or erased in the historical record.

HEBREW INVENTORS and Their Inventions

•Lewis Howard Latimer – Carbon filament for lightbulbs

•Granville T. Woods – Induction telegraph, third rail for electric trains

•Garrett Morgan – Three-position traffic signal, gas mask

•Frederick McKinley Jones – Refrigerated trucks and railcars

•Otis Boykin – Electrical resistor, components in pacemakers

•Madam C.J. Walker – Hair-straightening formula, beauty empire

•George Washington Carver – Crop rotation techniques, 300+ peanut-based products

•Dr. Patricia Bath – Laserphaco Probe (cataract treatment)

•Mark Dean – Co-inventor of the IBM PC, color monitor technology

•Lonnie G. Johnson – Super Soaker water gun

•Philip Emeagwali – Contributions to the development of the internet

•Marjorie Stewart Joyner – Permanent wave machine (for hair styling)

•Norbert Rillieux – Sugar refining evaporation system

•Henry Blair – Corn planter and cotton planter

•Sarah Boone – Improved ironing board

•Thomas L. Jennings – Dry cleaning process

•Benjamin Banneker – Wooden clock, early almanacs

•Andrew Jackson Beard – Rotary steam engine, automatic railroad car coupler

•David Crosthwait Jr. – Heating, ventilation, and air conditioning systems

•Elijah McCoy – Automatic lubricator for steam engines ("The Real McCoy")

•Jan Matzeliger – Shoe lasting machine

•Richard Spikes – Automatic gear shift, beer tap

•Charles Richard Drew – Blood plasma storage and blood bank system

•James E. West – Electret microphone

•Lloyd Ray – Dustpan

•Joseph Lee – Bread-making machine

•John Albert Burr – Rotary blade lawn mower

•Clatonia Joaquin Dorticus – Improved photographic print wash

•Jesse Ernest Wilkins Jr. – Nuclear physics, Manhattan Project contributor

- Valerie Thomas – Illusion transmitter (3D imaging)
- Marie Van Brittan Brown – First home security system
- Shirley Ann Jackson – Caller ID and call waiting (telecommunications)
- Dr. Daniel Hale Williams – Performed first successful open-heart surgery
- Alice H. Parker – Gas heating furnace
- James Forten – Sailmaking technology
- William Purvis – Fountain pen
- Sarah E. Goode – Folding cabinet bed (predecessor to Murphy bed)
- Ernest Just – Research in cell biology and marine biology
- George T. Sampson – Clothes dryer (early version)
- Walter Sammons – Hair straightening comb
- Robert Flemming Jr. – Guitar-like instrument called the "Euphonica"
- John Standard – Improved refrigerator design
- Benjamin Montgomery – Steam-operated propeller
- Nathaniel Alexander – Folding chair
- Dr. Charles Richard Drew – Mobile blood banks
- George Crum – Potato chips (credited)
- Clara Brown – Washing machine improvements
- Alice Augusta Ball – Cure for leprosy (chaulmoogra oil extract)
- Thomas Elkins – Improved toilet and refrigeration apparatus
- Lydia O. Newman – Hairbrush with ventilation for Black hair
- William Hinton – Test for diagnosing syphilis

•Henry Sampson – Gamma-electric cell (used in early mobile communication)

•Alexander Miles – Automatic elevator doors

•Virgie Ammons – Fire escape

•Benjamin Bradley – Steam engine for warships

•Lewis Temple – Harpoon toggle head for whaling

AND YET AND STILL, there are thousands more

LIST OF EARLY Hebrew Political and Social Leaders — The Silenced & Undermined

1. Hiram Rhodes Revels

First Black U.S. Senator (Mississippi, 1870). A highly educated minister and Civil War chaplain, he was known for his intellect and dignity. Despite being duly elected, many senators tried to block him from taking his seat, claiming Blacks weren't citizens.

2. Blanche K. Bruce

First Black man to serve a full term in the U.S. Senate (Mississippi, 1875–1881). A landowner and advocate for Black education. He was later pushed out of influence as Reconstruction ended and white supremacy violently reclaimed Southern politics.

3. Robert Smalls 1839-1915

Civil War hero turned Congressman from South Carolina. Born a slave, he once hijacked a Confederate ship and delivered it to Union forces. Served multiple terms in Congress but was eventually removed due to targeted redistricting and voter suppression.

4. Pinckney Benton Stewart Pinchback (P.B.S. Pinchback)

First Black governor in U.S. history (Louisiana, 1872). Though briefly governor, he was repeatedly blocked from receiving his U.S. Senate seat due to racism and political maneuvering.

5. John Mercer Langston

First Black person elected to public office in the U.S. (Town Clerk in Ohio, 1855) and one of the first Black Congressmen (Virginia, 1890). Founder of Howard Law School. His election to Congress was contested and delayed for over a year.

6. Oscar Dunn

Lieutenant Governor of Louisiana (1868–1871). A strong advocate for universal education and civil rights. Mysteriously died in office; many suspect poisoning. Had he lived, he likely would've become governor.

7. Jonathan Jasper Wright

First Black State Supreme Court Justice (South Carolina, 1870). A brilliant legal mind, fluent in Hebrew and Latin. Forced out when white supremacists regained control after Reconstruction.

8. James T. Rapier

U.S. Congressman from Alabama. Advocated for civil rights legislation and land reform. After just one term, he was removed by redistricting and Klan intimidation. Died young of tuberculosis, his legacy buried by Jim Crow history.

9. Charles Edmund Nash

Only Black U.S. Congressman from Louisiana during Reconstruction. Pushed out after a single term by racial violence and political suppression.

10. Thomas W. Cardozo

Mississippi State Superintendent of Education. A man of Jewish and Black heritage, he revolutionized education in Mississippi, expanding access to formerly enslaved children. Forced to resign under false charges.

11. George Washington Murray

South Carolina Congressman and farmer. Authored several bills advocating for Black farmers. His political career was cut short by rigged elections and voter suppression.

12. Richard Harvey Cain

U.S. Congressman from South Carolina, bishop in the African Methodist Episcopal Church, and founder of Paul Quinn College. Lost re-election after gerrymandering. A theological and intellectual powerhouse.

13. BENJAMIN "PAP" Singleton

Exodus leader and community organizer who led freedmen out of the South to Kansas to escape oppression. His movement was intentionally defunded and obstructed by Southern elites.

. . .

14. Henry McNeal Turner

One of the first Black chaplains in the U.S. Army and later a Georgia legislator. Removed from office by Georgia's white majority who declared Blacks had "no right to hold office." He became a fiery bishop and Pan-Africanist.

15. Rev. J.C. Price

Orator, minister, and founder of Livingstone College. Known as one of the greatest Black speakers of the 19th century. Died mysteriously young, with many suspecting foul play due to his rising political influence.

16. Thomas E. Miller

South Carolina Congressman during Reconstruction and later president of South Carolina State University. Removed from Congress by contested elections. Rebuilt his legacy through education.

17. Alexander Crummell

Theological scholar, African nationalist, and founder of the American Negro Academy. Blocked from many institutions because of his racial pride and scholarly independence.

18. Francis L. Cardozo

South Carolina Secretary of State and State Treasurer. Highly educated, and helped reform public finance. Falsely accused and imprisoned by white supremacists after Reconstruction.

. . .

19. Isaiah Montgomery

Founder of Mound Bayou, Mississippi — a self-sufficient, all-Black town. Though brilliant, he was undermined by Booker T. Washington-style compromise politics that many later regretted.

20. John R. Lynch

Youngest Congressman at the time (elected at 26). Chaired the Republican National Convention in 1884. Authored a vital book on Reconstruction. Eventually pushed out and relegated to obscurity by the Dunning School narrative.

THIS DOES NOT EVEN SCRATCH the surface. To even begin to do justice to Hebrew inventions and contributions I would have to write another entire book and probably one with several volumes. There is no other single group of people who have contributed more to the prosperity of America than the Hebrew. This is a fact that cannot be denied.

CULTURAL DOMINANCE — But Not Cultural Ownership

DESPITE BEING MARGINALIZED, Hebrews dominate American culture.

WE DON'T JUST PLAY sports — we are the faces of the NBA, NFL, track and field, and boxing. We don't just sing — we birthed jazz, blues, gospel, soul, R&B, funk, hip-hop, and the backbone of modern pop.

WE DON'T JUST WEAR fashion — we are the blueprint for what fashion tries to imitate. We are the style, the sound, the movement. From the Harlem Renaissance to hip-hop, from Michael Jackson to Michael

Jordan, from Erykah Badu to Kendrick Lamar — we set the tone, and the world follows.

YET, culturally, we are often treated like seasonal trends, not the eternal wellspring of creativity that we are.

ECONOMIC IMPACT — A Nation Within a Nation

THE MODERN SPENDING power of Hebrews in Americans is estimated at $1.8 trillion as of 2025 — placing us in the top 20 economies in the world if we were a nation.

YET WE OWN LESS than 2% of America's wealth, because our dollars rarely circulate within our own communities. According to economists:

•The dollar circulates in Asian communities for 30 days.

•In Jewish communities, for 20 days.

•In white communities, 17 days.

•In the Black community? 6 hours.

WHY? Because we've been conditioned to consume, not to build.

WE WERE THE FOUNDATION — And the Fuel

THIS IS NOT a plea for validation.

It is a record for the judgment seat.

. . .

AMERICA CANNOT SAY it blessed the Hebrews when it:

•Used our bodies to build its wealth.

•Used our minds to fuel its innovation.

•Used our culture to entertain the world.

•And used our pain for profit.

WE ARE the cornerstone that was rejected.

THE DAHOMEY TRIBE
AND SELLING HEBREWS

1. The Role of Dahomey in the Slave Trade:

The Kingdom of Dahomey (located in present-day Benin) was a prominent West African kingdom from the 17th to the 19th century. Dahomey became notorious for its militaristic society and its central role in capturing and selling other African peoples—including Hebrew Israelites who had fled into West Africa after the destruction of Jerusalem in 70 A.D.

Dahomey raided surrounding regions and sold captives to European slave traders at coastal ports like Ouidah. The victims of these raids were often members of the Kingdom of Judah—many identifiable through oral histories and colonial documentation referring to the "Kingdom of Juda" along the Slave Coast.

2. Who Supplied Dahomey with Gunpowder and Weapons?

- European Nations: Primarily Spain, the Portuguese, Dutch, French, and British were involved in supplying gunpowder, muskets, and other arms in exchange for enslaved people.

. . .

- The Portuguese were among the earliest and most aggressive in establishing trading posts and relationships along the West African coast, particularly in the 15th and 16th centuries.

- The British Royal African Company and the Dutch West India Company also played key roles in this exchange.

- Guns-for-Slaves Economy: The cycle was simple—European traders provided firearms, cloth, and alcohol to the Dahomey in exchange for slaves. This further empowered Dahomey to expand its conquests and continue capturing Hebrews and other indigenous groups.

3. Complicity of Other Powers:

- Many Ashkenazi Jews, particularly those involved in European colonial trade, played prominent roles as slave ship owners, financiers, and traders (especially under the Dutch and Portuguese empires).

- Ouidah, a major slave port under Dahomey control, had direct connections with Jewish and European merchant networks.

KEY SOURCES FOR FURTHER STUDY:

- The Slave Coast of West Africa 1550–1750 by Robin Law

- Hebrewisms of West Africa by Joseph J. Williams

- The Jewish Role in the African Slave Trade by Dr. Tony Martin

- Oral accounts and maps that label West Africa as "The Kingdom of Juda" (see 1747 map by Emmanuel Bowen)

AFRICANS DID NOT SELL AFRICANS. Africans sold us. Hebrews.

THE DAHOMEY, a fierce kingdom in West Africa, captured and sold Hebrews.

They were not of the same lineage or covenant.

The Hebrews were a distinct people, even among melanin nations, recognized by cultural practices, circumcision, and oral traditions that traced them back to Israel.

EUROPEANS UNDERSTAND DISTINCTIONS.

They know the difference between a Frenchman and a Russian.

But when it comes to dark skin, they erase all nuance. This allowed them to justify an indiscriminate trade that was, in truth, laser-focused on one seed line: Judah.

THE SALE of Hebrews by non-Hebrews fulfilled the prophecy that we would be handed over to our enemies.

It was not tribal war — it was the orchestration of spiritual forces using willing human agents.

THE GANGSTER MENTALITY
IS NOT HEBREW

*B*abylonian Programming: The Rise of Cultural Confusion

The enemy has always used Babylon to confuse, seduce, and indoctrinate. In today's context, Babylon is not just a city or nation—it is a global system. This system teaches the Hebrew to glorify everything the Most High hates: pride, greed, lust, violence, and rebellion. It packages dysfunction as entertainment and rebellion as freedom.

Hollywood, pop culture, and mass media have become the prophets of this new Babylon. And what do they prophesy? That the Hebrew is only valuable if he is violent, vulgar, hypersexual, or foolish. That the Hebrew woman is only powerful if she is independent, naked, loud, promiscuous, and defiant. That family, holiness, and repentance are outdated relics.

The Hebrew child is now taught by screens, not by Scripture. The reverence is for rappers, not prophets. The altars are award shows, not altars of prayer. Babylon has modernized, but the game remains the same:

"Come out of her, My people, so that you will not share in her sins." –
Revelation 18:4

The Hebrew soul has been hijacked, and the result is visible: broken
homes, confused identities, and a generation in crisis.

Gangsterism: An Imported Identity

Contrary to popular belief, the "gangster" mentality did not originate
in the Hebrew community. It was learned—imported from American
society's glorification of organized crime. Italians had the Mafia. Irish
had the Mob. White America cheered on Al Capone and John
Dillinger in black-and-white films, decades before N.W.A. ever
recorded a track.

When the Hebrew people were deliberately placed at the bottom of
society, shut out of economic systems, told they were nothing, and
bombarded with violent media, they imitated what they were shown:
power through crime, respect through fear, freedom through rebellion. But this was never our culture—it was a borrowed mask. And
wearing that mask has cost us dearly.

The true Hebrew culture is built on covenant, not chaos. On family,
not factions. On righteousness, not rebellion. We were never meant to
imitate Babylon—we were meant to call it to repentance.

America has always loved criminals — as long as they weren't
Hebrews.

•Westerns romanticized outlaws.

•Newspapers mythologized bank robbers.

•Hollywood glamorized mafia dons.

Long before there were Hebrew street gangs there were real life documented Italian, Jewish, and Irish street gangs. America cheered for
violent men, romanticized their lives, and lined up to watch their
films.

When Hebrews mimicked what Babylon exalted — Bravado, organized crews, gratuitous violence, codes of silence — we were branded as thugs and super-predators.

Yet who owned the studios that made Scarface iconic? Who decided the Sopranos deserved prime time?

Hebrews did not invent this culture of crime.

We were infected by it, rewarded for embracing it, and then punished for living out the roles Babylon wrote for us.

KNOWING WHO ISRAEL IS
— THE KEY TO PROPHECY

S o much of end-time prophecy revolves around Israel:

•Jerusalem as a burdensome stone.

•Nations gathering against her.

•The remnant being saved out of tribulation.

BUT WHAT IF the world blesses the wrong Israel?

What if they fund regimes that oppress true Hebrews while scorning the scattered children of Jacob still living under curses?

THAT IS EXACTLY the confusion the enemy engineered.

By hiding the true identity of Israel, Satan has nations blessing imposters and cursing the real heirs of the covenant.

This ensures judgment falls not just on Babylon, but on those Gentiles who unknowingly stood against YAH's people.

. . .

IDENTIFYING Israel rightly is not racism or superiority.

It is obedience to the Most High's order. And it is essential in understanding eschatology, which is end time prophecy.

"I WILL BLESS those who bless you, and curse those who curse you."

ISRAEL IS — The Key to Prophecy

LUKE 21:24 (KJV):

"And they shall fall by the edge of the sword, and shall be led away captive into all nations: and Jerusalem shall be trodden down of the Gentiles, until the times of the Gentiles be fulfilled."

THIS VERSE GIVEN by Yahusha is one of the clearest prophetic markers in all of Scripture. It sets a timeline: Israel will be scattered into captivity, Jerusalem will be dominated by Gentiles, and only *after* the "times of the Gentiles" are fulfilled will Israel be restored.

FROM THIS FOUNDATION, three truths become evident:

1. The time of the Gentiles must be fulfilled.

2. The Hebrews will repent and be converted.

3. Only then will they return to their land.

THE ASHKENAZI CONTRADICTION

IF THE ASHKENAZI Jews in modern Israel were truly the covenant people, then prophecy would already be fulfilled. They returned to the land in 1947 through the Balfour Declaration, political maneuvering, and war. Yet Yahusha said that the Gentile era must be complete *before* Israel's restoration.

THE TIME OF THE GENTILES — Defined and Fulfilled

WHEN THE HEBREW people rejected the Messiah, Yahusha (Jesus), the Most High allowed salvation to be offered to the Gentile nations. This fulfilled prophetic warnings (Deuteronomy 28) and ushered in what Yahusha called *"the times of the Gentiles"* (Luke 21:24). The Apostle Paul echoed this transition, saying, *"through their fall salvation is come unto the Gentiles, for to provoke them to jealousy"* (Romans 11:11). This period, marked by Gentile evangelism, church growth, and global influence, coincided with the Hebrews enduring curses, captivity, and loss of identity as foretold by Moses.

BUT THE TIME of the Gentiles has a limit. Once the Gospel has reached the ends of the earth (Matthew 24:14), and the Gentile nations begin to fall into apostasy and rebellion (2 Thessalonians 2:3), the spiritual authority will shift back to Israel. Paul declares, *"Blindness in part is happened to Israel, until the fullness of the Gentiles be come in"* (Romans 11:25). That "fullness" signals a prophetic turning point—when the Hebrews awaken, return to covenant, and reclaim their spiritual inheritance. As this dispensation ends, the anointing returns to Israel, and the Messiah prepares to restore the Kingdom. The time of the Gentiles being fulfilled means the shift is here—*Judah is rising*, and with it, the reign of the true Kingdom.

And what does the evidence show. Since 1947, the Gentiles have continued to experience revival. Great preachers such as **Billy Graham, John MacArthur, Paul Washer, Adrian Rogers, Martin Lloyd-Jones, R.C. Sproul, and Charles Stanley** rose up long after 1947. Countless Gentiles have continued to come to Christ. This proves that even though now apostasy has already consumed the

Gentile church the time of the Gentiles has still been ongoing since 1947.

HOW THEN CAN MODERN Israel claim covenantal restoration when the Gentiles are still being gathered? According to prophecy, you cannot have both simultaneously — either the Gentile era is fulfilled and Israel is restored, or we are still in the Gentile era. The contradiction unmasks the false claim.

THE BIBLICAL PATTERN of Return

DEUTERONOMY 30:1–5 (KJV):

"And it shall come to pass, when all these things are come upon thee, the blessing and the curse... and shalt return unto the Lord thy God... Then the Lord thy God will turn thy captivity, and have compassion upon thee... And the Lord thy God will bring thee into the land which thy fathers possessed, and thou shalt possess it..."

THE COVENANT RETURN of Israel does not happen through deceit, warfare, or man-made declarations. It happens through **repentance**. Only when the true Hebrews repent as a people will the Most High gather them back into the land. The counterfeit return of 1947 does not fit the scriptural pattern. Instead of repentance, the land became marked by pornography, homosexuality, and child trafficking — a direct contradiction of Torah.

THE ROOT of Jesse and the Second Gathering

Isaiah 11:10–12 (KJV):

"And in that day there shall be a root of Jesse, which shall stand for an ensign of the people; to it shall the Gentiles seek... And it shall come to pass in that day, that the Lord shall set his hand again the second time to recover the remnant of his people..."

The Root of Jesse is Yahusha. First, the Gentiles seek Him. And then they fall away from Him. Then, the Most High moves "a second time" to gather His remnant people. Notice the sequence: the Gentile apostasy precedes the Hebrew restoration. We are living in that time right now, where most

GENTILES, and indeed entire Gentile nations are falling away from The Most High Yahuah and lack morality, wisdom, and discernment. The second gathering — the return of the true Hebrews from across the earth — is now at hand

YAH's COVENANT of Peace

ISAIAH 54:4–17 is a chapter of promises. The Most High Yahuah (YHWY), identifies Himself as the **"Holy One of Israel"** — not the god of political Zionism or of America, but the Elohim of Abraham, Isaac, and Jacob and there descendants. He promises to regather His people, to cover their shame, and to reestablish His covenant of peace.

AT THE CLIMAX of this chapter YAH declares:

"This is the heritage of the servants of the Lord, and their righteousness is of me, saith the Lord." (v. 17)

THE MOST HIGH makes it clear: our righteousness is not of ourselves, but of Him through Yahusha. His righteousness is imputed upon us when we believe. It is through this covenant, sealed at the cross, that the true Hebrews — scattered across the nations — will rise again.

THE REAL ESCHATOLOGY

THE MODERN CLAIM of restoration in 1947 is not the fulfillment of prophecy. It is a counterfeit, an early attempt to seize what only Yah can give. The true restoration will not come by Balfour or war, but by repentance and divine intervention.

KNOWING who Israel is becomes the key to prophecy. Without recognizing the true people of the covenant, eschatology collapses into confusion. But when we align the Word with history, the truth becomes undeniable: the Hebrews scattered through slavery and captivity — particularly the descendants of Judah in the Americas — are the people who will return when the time of the Gentiles is complete.

Only then will Jerusalem be redeemed, and only then will prophecy reach its final fulfillment.

Isaiah 54:4-17 KJV —

4 Fear not; for thou shalt not be ashamed: neither be thou confounded; for thou shalt not be put to shame: for thou shalt forget the shame of thy youth, and shalt not remember the reproach of thy widowhood any more.
5 For thy Maker is thine husband; the Lord of hosts is his name; and thy Redeemer the Holy One of Israel; The God of the whole earth shall he be called.
6 For the Lord hath called thee as a woman forsaken and grieved in spirit, and a wife of youth, when thou wast refused, saith thy God.

7 For a small moment have I forsaken thee; but with great mercies will I gather thee.

8 In a little wrath I hid my face from thee for a moment; but with everlasting kindness will I have mercy on thee, saith the Lord thy Redeemer.

9 For this is as the waters of Noah unto me: for as I have sworn that the waters of Noah should no more go over the earth; so have I sworn that I would not be wroth with thee, nor rebuke thee.

10 For the mountains shall depart, and the hills be removed; but my kindness shall not depart from thee, neither shall the covenant of my peace be removed, saith the Lord that hath mercy on thee.

11 O thou afflicted, tossed with tempest, and not comforted, behold, I will lay thy stones with fair colours, and lay thy foundations with sapphires.

12 And I will make thy windows of agates, and thy gates of carbuncles, and all thy borders of pleasant stones.

13 And all thy children shall be taught of the Lord; and great shall be the peace of thy children.

14 In righteousness shalt thou be established: thou shalt be far from oppression; for thou shalt not fear: and from terror; for it shall not come near thee.

15 Behold, they shall surely gather together, but not by me: whosoever shall gather together against thee shall fall for thy sake.

16 Behold, I have created the smith that bloweth the coals in the fire, and that bringeth forth an instrument for his work; and I have created the waster to destroy.

17 No weapon that is formed against thee shall prosper; and every tongue that shall rise against thee in judgment thou shalt condemn. This is the heritage of the servants of the Lord, and their righteousness is of me, saith the Lord.

Summary: Isaiah 54:4–17 – A Prophetic Word to the Scattered Hebrews

This passage of Isaiah is often misapplied to the church at large or to Gentile believers. But when read in proper **context**, it becomes clear: **this message is not universal—it is targeted. It is addressed to the covenant people of Israel**, specifically the **scattered and afflicted remnant of Zion**, who endured shame, captivity, and violence across generations.

VERSES 4–6 speak to a woman (Zion) who was forsaken, barren, and grieved in spirit—**a widow once rejected by her husband (YHWH)**. This language perfectly mirrors the history of the true Hebrew people: sold into slavery, stripped of heritage, and exiled from their spiritual inheritance.

VERSES 7–10 promise mercy and a renewed covenant, echoing the covenant promises made to Abraham and David. These promises were not made to Gentiles but to the **biological descendants of Israel** —those who endured generational judgment and are now being restored.

VERSES 11–12 DESCRIBE AFFLICTION, storms, and being "not comforted"—yet now being rebuilt with sapphires, jewels, and right-eousness. What other people group can claim **centuries of slavery, trauma, and oppression**, followed by a prophetic awakening in the end times?

VERSES 13–17 culminate in a promise of divine protection, justice, and restoration. "No weapon formed against thee shall prosper" is not a random Christian slogan—it is a prophetic declaration **to the oppressed remnant of Jacob**, whose suffering has always had a spiritual root.

. . .

Only One Group Fits This Prophecy

Let's be plain:

This was not written to Rome. Not to Europe. Not to America. Not to the institutional Church.

It was written to:

• A people beloved but forsaken because of sin and rejecting Yahusha.

• A nation scattered to the four corners.

• A generation who lost language, culture, and covenant.

• A remnant who would rise again in the last days with identity, power, and righteousness.

Who else fits that description but the descendants of the transatlantic slave trade—those sold, stripped, and scattered, yet awakening today with divine fire?

Isaiah 54 is not poetic comfort for all mankind. It is the scroll of **restoration for Zion.**

THE GREAT FALLING AWAY
OF THE GENTILE CHURCH

*P*aul warned of a great falling away before Yahusha returns.

We are living it.

GENTILE CHURCHES that once preached repentance now celebrate pride parades.

They replace biblical holiness with positive thinking and motivational speeches.

Mega-pastors amass fortunes while their congregants starve for truth.

MEANWHILE, the awakening among Hebrews grows.

We rediscover the Torah, the feasts and lunar Sabbath, the name of our Elohim, Yahuah, and the testimony of our king and Savior Yahusha.

This is not arrogance — it is prophecy unfolding.

. . .

As GENTILE CHURCH systems crumble into apostasy, the true Hebrew Assembly rises.

This is not division by skin; it is a separation by obedience.

Whoever clings to Zion and walks in covenant, Hebrew or Gentile, will stand together and praise and serve Yahuah in righteousness under our Savior and King Yahusha.

The Great Falling Away

THE APOSTLE PAUL'S warnings on the "Great Falling Away" are found predominantly in the books of **Romans and 2 Thessalonians**. He describes an end-times rebellion—a large-scale apostasy—that must occur before the return of the Messiah. These warnings were directed not only to Hebrew believers but mostly to the **Gentile church**, urging them to remain humble and steadfast as Israel experiences a temporary spiritual hardening.

The Apostasy Foretold — 2 Thessalonians 2

IN **2 THESSALONIANS**, Paul cautions believers not to be deceived into thinking the "Day of the Lord" has already come. He outlines the sequence of events leading up to Messiah's return:

1. **The Great Rebellion**

Paul declares that the return of Christ "will not happen unless the falling away comes first, and the man of lawlessness is revealed, the son of destruction" (**2 Thessalonians 2:3**).

The Greek term **apostasia** means a widespread **defection from the faith**—a rebellion against both YAH's authority and His covenant.

2. The Rise of the Man of Sin

This global departure from truth sets the stage for the emergence of the **Antichrist**—"the man of sin"—who will exalt himself above God and even take a seat in the temple, demanding worship.

The Warning to the Gentiles — Romans 11

IN ROMANS 11, Paul uses the metaphor of an **olive tree** to explain Israel's unique covenant and to caution Gentile believers against arrogance:

• Grafted Branches

Paul reminds Gentiles that they are like **wild olive branches** grafted into the cultivated olive tree of Israel. They now share in the **richness of Israel's root**—its covenant, promises, and heritage—but they do not replace the natural branches.

• A Call to Humility

Paul warns sharply:

"Do not be arrogant, but fear; for if God did not spare the natural branches, He will not spare you either."

(Romans 11:20–21)

Gentiles are saved by **faith**, not by superiority, and should remain humble toward the Hebrews.

• The Mystery of Israel's Hardening

Paul reveals a divine mystery: Israel has experienced a **partial hardening** until the "**fullness of the Gentiles**" has come in (**Romans 11:25**). But this hardening is temporary—God has not abandoned His people.

Paul's Unified Warning

Paul's message to the Gentile church is urgent and clear:
• A massive **apostasy** is coming, where many will abandon sound doctrine and follow deception.
• Gentiles must not grow prideful or dismissive of Israel's role in YAH's covenant plan.
• Standing in faith is the only safeguard; unbelief leads to being **cut off** from the root entirely.

THE GREAT FALLING Away is not only a prophetic sign of the end—it's a **warning to remain grounded in truth** as deception increases and spiritual darkness is amplified.

THE WHITE-WASHED
HEBREW MIND

*P*erhaps the most tragic victory of captivity is the Hebrew who desperately tries to prove he is not like his own people.

WE'VE SEEN THEM:

•The brother who ridicules Hebrew women for their hair, skin, and speech, chasing validation from Gentiles.

•The sister who shames Hebrew men as broke and ghetto, boasts that her children are "mixed," and looks down on her own mother's features.

RIGHTEOUS UNION vs. Rejection of Identity

THIS IS NOT a condemnation of interracial marriage. Scripture gives us multiple examples of righteous unions between Hebrews and Gentiles who served the Most High. Moses, the great deliverer of

Israel, married Zipporah, a Midianite woman — and YAH was not displeased. Boaz, a noble Hebrew man, married Ruth the Moabitess, and from their union came King David, and ultimately, Yahusha the Messiah. Even Rahab the Canaanite prostitute, by faith, was grafted into Israel and became part of the Messianic lineage.

THE MOST HIGH never forbade marrying foreigners simply because they were from another nation — He forbade marrying those who worship other gods. His concern has always been spiritual allegiance, not skin color or tribe. As it is written, "Be ye not unequally yoked together with unbelievers" (2 Corinthians 6:14). This includes unbelieving Gentiles and unbelieving Hebrews alike.

SOLOMON, a man blessed with divine wisdom and favor, was not condemned for marrying foreign women alone — he was judged because those women turned his heart toward other gods. In his old age, he built altars to their deities, defiling the covenant of Israel. That is why YAH was angry — not because of race, but because of idolatry.

IT MUST BE SAID: marrying a believing Gentile who walks in righteousness and honors the Messiah is your prerogative. But abandoning your people, your heritage, your history, and your reflection in the mirror just to gain Gentile approval — that is spiritual sickness. It is self-rejection masquerading as love. It is assimilation, not covenant.

YAH NEVER ASKED you to stop loving others. But He does require you to remember who you are.

I AM NOT ADVOCATING for interracial marriage — **I firmly believe the healing of our nation begins when Hebrew men and Hebrew** women come together to build strong, righteous families. That is our highest calling. I believe Hebrew Men Should marry Hebrew Women and vice versa. But let it also be clear: there is no law against marrying a righteous Gentile, and such a union is not sin in the eyes of YAH. The standard is faith, not flesh.

YAH NEVER TOLD Israel to become Egyptians, Assyrians, Greeks, or Romans or American.

He told them to be set apart, holy unto Him.

The ultimate psychological conquest is when a man denies his own lineage and scorns the people of his own covenant.

THE WHITEWASHED HEBREW: Disassociation and Self-Rejection

ONE OF THE most effective strategies of cultural domination is assimilation through identity erasure. Many Hebrews—stripped of their heritage, language, land, and spiritual authority—have unknowingly adopted the culture and values of the very empire that enslaved them. This condition is not natural; it is programmed. It is the fruit of centuries of psychological engineering designed to convince the Hebrew that his only way to survive is to disassociate from his own people.

THIS IS why many Hebrew men and women recoil at being called Israelites. They have been taught—by schoolbooks, pulpits, screens, and society—that this identity is either irrelevant, extremist, or fictional. The trauma runs so deep that many choose assimilation over authenticity, even when it costs them their soul.

"THEY THAT HATE you shall rule over you." – Leviticus 26:17

. . .

EVEN IN INTERRACIAL UNIONS, the problem is not the diversity of melanin or ethnicity—Scripture is clear that salvation is available to all who believe. But when one partner abandons their heritage to appease the other, or when love becomes a cloak for cultural erasure, then spiritual confusion is birthed. The issue isn't about color—it's about covenant.

THE HEBREW who refuses to love their own reflection has already lost the war within.

THE WHITE-WASHED HEBREW: A Case Study in Psychological Captivity

THE MOST INSIDIOUS form of slavery is not physical bondage—it is mental captivity. The man who is chained in his mind will remain obedient to his oppressor long after the shackles have been removed from his wrists. And in the case of the Hebrew people in America and across the diaspora, this captivity has taken the form of self-rejection, cultural amnesia, and spiritual assimilation.

THE TERM "WHITE-WASHED" Hebrew does not speak to skin tone or mixed heritage. It speaks to the brother or sister who, having been so deeply conditioned by centuries of Eurocentric indoctrination, has come to despise their own people, their history, their appearance, their struggle—and ultimately, their calling.

THESE ARE the Hebrews who believe their deliverance is found in full assimilation into Gentile power structures. They wear the robes of false inclusion and acceptance while crucifying their own identity.

They deny the suffering of their ancestors and the truth of the Scriptures that affirm their chosenness. They adopt a worldview that celebrates their conquerors and mocks their own prophets. They kneel at the altars of universities, governments, and religious institutions that were built to erase them. They speak with polished diction but have no voice in matters of liberation.

ONCE AGAIN,: this is not a critique of interracial fellowship or marriage. This is about something deeper—a spiritual divorce from one's people. When a Hebrew man or woman forsakes their own community, abandons their prophetic heritage, and treats the struggle of their people with contempt or detachment, they are operating under a spell—a Babylonian enchantment that whispers, "If you just act like them, dress like them, talk like them... you will be free."

BUT IT IS A LIE. Because even in the boardroom, the Ivy League classroom, or the gated community, the Hebrew man is still a stranger. He is applauded for his excellence as long as it doesn't awaken his people. He is tolerated as long as he remains spiritually neutered and culturally detached.

THIS IS what James Baldwin once warned us about when he said, "To be a Negro in this country and to be relatively conscious is to be in a rage almost all the time." But many Hebrews have chosen unconsciousness over rage. It is more comfortable. It is more convenient. It feels safer to pretend that history no longer matters. But this false comfort is the narcotic of the colonized soul.

THE SHIFT OF DISPENSATION
AND THE 400-YEAR PROPHECY

"*K*now of a surety that thy seed shall be a stranger in a land that is not theirs, and shall serve them; and they shall afflict them four hundred years."

Genesis 15:13

FROM 1619 TO MODERN TIMES, Hebrews in America have lived this prophecy line by line.

Slavery, sharecropping, Jim Crow, redlining, mass incarceration — all while the churches of America grew wealthy off their tithes yet stayed silent on their suffering.

BUT SOMETHING IS CHANGING.

Gentile dominion is waning.

European church systems are collapsing into humanism and outright apostasy.

Meanwhile, the true Hebrews are awakening, fulfilling Ezekiel's vision of dry bones standing up.

THIS IS *the shift of dispensations.*

THE AGE of Gentile rule over the things of YAH is drawing to a close.

Jacob's time is returning, and the nations tremble because they sense it even if they cannot name it.

BREAKING THE CURSE – Repentance, Restoration, and the Return to Covenant

"IF MY PEOPLE, which are called by my name, shall humble themselves, and pray, and seek my face, and turn from their wicked ways; then will I hear from heaven, and will forgive their sin, and will heal their land."

— 2 Chronicles 7:14

"AND IT SHALL COME to pass, when all these things are come upon thee, the blessing and the curse... and shalt return unto the Lord thy God... then the Lord thy God will turn thy captivity, and have compassion upon thee."

— Deuteronomy 30:1–3

I. THE CURSE Was Not Permanent – It Had an Expiration Date

THE CURSES of Deuteronomy 28 were severe—but they were never intended to be permanent. Yah is a righteous judge, but He is also abundant in mercy. He did not forsake His people; He allowed judgment to bring remembrance.

CAPTIVITY IS NOT THE END.

Repentance is the beginning of return.

WHEN YAH SCATTERED ISRAEL, He also left behind a prophetic key:

"BUT IF FROM thence thou shalt seek the Lord thy God, thou shalt find him…"
— Deuteronomy 4:29

THE TIME of remembrance is now. The awakening has begun. The dry bones are shaking in the valley (Ezekiel 37), and Judah is rising—not in revenge, but in restoration.

II. Repentance: The Key That Unlocks the Promise

THE MOST HIGH does not desire burnt offerings, temple rituals, or vain repetitions. He desires a broken spirit and a contrite heart.

REPENTANCE ISN'T MERELY about turning from sin—it's about returning to covenant.

TRUE REPENTANCE REQUIRES:

•Confession of identity: "We are the children of Israel."

•Confession of sins: personal and national, including idolatry, sexual immorality, hatred, and rebellion.

•Renunciation of false gods and false culture: rejecting Egypt (America/Babylon), celebrity worship, materialism, and lust.

•Obedience to the commandments: including the Sabbath, dietary laws, and love for one another, not for salvation because we are saved by the blood of our Messiah alone but for cohesion and structure. For obedience and holiness.

•Faith in Yahusha the Messiah: the doorway back to the Father and the final sacrifice that sealed the covenant.

"IN RETURNING and rest shall ye be saved; in quietness and in confidence shall be your strength..."

— Isaiah 30:15

THE DOOR to Yah's presence is open—not because we deserve it, but because His mercy endures forever.

III. The Remnant and the Road Back to Zion

NOT ALL WILL REPENT. Not all will believe.

BUT A REMNANT WILL. And that remnant will spark a nationwide revival.

"THOUGH ISRAEL BE as the sand of the sea, a remnant shall return..."

— Isaiah 10:22

·   ·   ·

THE RETURN to Zion is not about boarding planes to modern-day Israel.

It's about boarding the ark of obedience and spiritual alignment.

THE TRUE RETURN INCLUDES:

•Regathering in faith, not by passports.

•Renewed understanding of Torah and The Gospel through grace.

•Restored family order: Hebrew men reclaiming leadership, Hebrew women returning to virtue.

•Rejecting Babylon's programming: entertainment, sexual confusion, materialism and greed.

THE TRUE ISRAEL will be revealed not by geography, but by righteousness.

"AND THEY SHALL KNOW that I am the Lord, when I have gathered them into their own land... and have left none of them any more there."

— Ezekiel 39:28

IV. Yahusha: The Bridge Back to the Father

NO REPENTANCE IS real without Yahusha the Messiah.

HE IS NOT a white European man.

He is not the face on Catholic cathedrals.

He is not the slave-master's Jesus.

He is:
•A Hebrew man born from the tribe of Judah,
•The Lion and the Lamb,
•The living Torah,
•The only path to salvation.

"No man cometh unto the Father, but by me."

— John 14:6

Without Yahusha, there is no redemption. Without His blood, the covenant cannot be renewed.

He is not just a prophet. He is the Son of Yah, the Messiah, the Door, the Light, the Way, the Shepherd, the Resurrection, and the King.

V. The Restoration of the Covenant – What That Looks Like

As the Hebrew people awaken and return to Yah:

•Their minds are renewed

•Their families are healed

•Their communities are revived

•Their enemies are confused

•And the nations take notice

. . .

"IN THOSE DAYS it shall come to pass... that ten men shall take hold... of him that is a Jew, saying, We will go with you: for we have heard that God is with you."

— Zechariah 8:23

THE WORLD HAS SEEN ENOUGH of churchianity. It has seen enough hypocrisy. Now it will see the real Israel—set-apart, holy, wise, and anointed.

This is not religion.

THIS IS RESTORATION.

VI. The Breaking of the Yoke

AS WE RETURN, Yah breaks the curses.

"FOR I WILL BREAK his yoke from off thy neck, and will burst thy bonds, and strangers shall no more serve themselves of him."

— Jeremiah 30:8

WHAT ONCE BOUND US:

•Systemic oppression,

•Mis-education,

•Gang mentality,

•Fatherlessness,

•Addiction,

•Hopelessness...

...WILL NOW BE BROKEN in Yahusha's name.

BUT ONLY THROUGH OBEDIENCE.

Only through surrender.

Only through truth.

VII. What the Gentiles Must Do

THIS RETURN DOES NOT LEAVE Gentiles hopeless—it calls them to humility and alignment.

THE GENTILES (European and other nations) must:

•Recognize and repent for the atrocities of slavery, colonization, and religious deception.

•Reject the synagogue of Satan and its false Israel.

•Support the awakening of the true Hebrews—not through charity, (although reparations should be discussed in some form) but through truth and justice.

•Join the covenant through Yahusha—not by replacing Israel, but by being grafted in (Romans 11).

"BLESSED BE EGYPT MY PEOPLE, and Assyria the work of my hands, and Israel mine inheritance."

— Isaiah 19:25

Summary:

The curse is being broken, not by power or politics, but by repentance. The scattered and enslaved people of the Most High are returning—not to a man-made religion, but to a living covenant. This chapter is a call to every Hebrew: It is time to return home. Your Father waits with open arms. Your identity has been restored. Your land will follow. And the world will witness the rebirth of Zion.

PART V
THE END-TIME AWAKENING AND ETERNAL JOY

Chapters 33-45

RESTORING THE SABBATH: UNDERSTANDING THE LUNAR CYCLE

Restoring the Sabbath: Understanding the Lunar Cycle

In ancient Hebrew culture, there were no names for the days of the week like "Monday" or "Saturday." Instead, time was tracked using the moon's phases, as ordained in creation:

"He made the moon to mark the seasons…"

— Psalm 104:19

The Sabbath was not observed every "Saturday" as we understand it today, but rather on a seven-day cycle tied to the new moon — this is known as the Lunar Sabbath. Here's how it worked:

How the Lunar Sabbath Works:

1.New Moon = Day 1 of the Month

The sighting of the new moon marked the beginning of a new month. This day was celebrated and set apart (Numbers 10:10, 1 Samuel 20).

2.Sabbaths followed on the 8th, 15th, 22nd, and 29th days of the lunar month.

These are seven-day intervals following the New Moon day.

3.After the 29th day, the cycle would reset with the next New Moon, and the count restarted.

There Were No Named Days Like "Saturday"

•Ancient Hebrews counted "day one, day two, day three…" leading up to the seventh day.

•The concept of "Saturday" and "Sunday" comes from pagan Roman and Babylonian calendars, each day named after a deity (e.g., Sun-day for the Sun god, Satur-day for Saturn).

Scriptural Support:

•Exodus 16 shows the Sabbath counted after the New Moon in the wilderness.

•Isaiah 66:23 speaks of future worship "from one New Moon to another, and from one Sabbath to another."

•1 Samuel 20 shows David observing both New Moons and Sabbaths as distinct but connected.

Context of 1 Samuel 20:

David is hiding from King Saul, who is trying to kill him. David speaks to Saul's son, Jonathan, and they devise a plan to test Saul's intentions. The plan centers around David's absence during the New Moon festival — a significant appointed time when attendance was expected, especially at the royal table.

Key Verses:

1 Samuel 20:5 (KJV)

"And David said unto Jonathan, Behold, to morrow is the new moon, and I should not fail to sit with the king at meat: but let me go, that I may hide myself in the field unto the third day at even."

•This shows that the New Moon was a special feast day, and David was expected to be present.
•It also implies it was a known and pre-calculated appointed time.

1 Samuel 20:18 (KJV)

"Then Jonathan said to David, To morrow is the new moon: and thou shalt be missed, because thy seat will be empty."

•The New Moon was such an expected gathering, that David's absence would be notable.

•This shows its ceremonial importance — likely involving both feasting and sacrifices (see Numbers 10:10, Numbers 28:11–15).

1 Samuel 20:24–27

"So David hid in the field: and when the new moon was come, the king sat him down to eat meat... Nevertheless Saul spake not any thing that day: for he thought, Something hath befallen him, he is not clean; surely he is not clean. And it came to pass on the morrow, which was the second day of the month, that David's place was empty..."

•This confirms the New Moon celebration lasted more than one day.

•Saul noticed David's absence and assumed ceremonial uncleanness, meaning it was a sacred observance.

Implication: Connection to the Sabbath Cycle

•New Moon Days were not counted as regular workdays or part of the weekly seven-day count,

•After the New Moon, Sabbaths would fall on the 8th, 15th, 22nd, and 29th — aligning with the lunar cycle.

•David's hiding "until the third day at even" (v.5) suggests a count connected to both the New Moon day and the weekly cycle.

Modern Challenges

Today's Gregorian calendar, created by Pope Gregory XIII in 1582, detached the weekly cycle from the lunar cycle — making it very difficult for most people to follow the true biblical Sabbath.

•Work schedules, school calendars, and societal systems are built around fixed seven-day weeks, not lunar months.

•As a result, many believers honor the Sabbath as best they can, typically from Friday evening to Saturday evening or from any evening that they are free until the next evening, in remembrance — though this is not the exact biblical pattern, it reflects the intent of obedience.

The true Sabbath was never about a "Saturday" — it was a heavenly appointment tied to the moon, marking rest and worship on the 8th, 15th, 22nd, and 29th days of each month.

Understanding the Lunar Sabbath isn't about legalism -it's not about being saved or going to heaven, belief in Yahusha is the one and only thing you need for that— it's about returning to the rhythm of creation and honoring the Most High in spirit and in truth.

Exodus 20:8

"Remember the sabbath day, to keep it holy."

This is part of the Ten Commandments, specifically the fourth commandment. The passage goes on to explain that six days are for labor, but the seventh day is a Sabbath to Yahuah, and no work should be done on it.

Again:

The ONLY thing we need for salvation is belief in the Most High Yahuah and belief in His Son, our Lord and Savior. The Christ, the Messiah, the King Yahusha.

THE FALSE CHRISTS
OF THE LAST DAYS

*Y*ahusha warned us plainly:

"MANY SHALL COME in my name, saying, I am Christ; and shall deceive many."

— Matthew 24:5

WE THINK of obvious cult leaders, but deception is far subtler.

False Christs today come as:

•Politicians promising salvation through policies.

•Mega-pastors preaching prosperity without holiness.

•New Age gurus offering "Christ consciousness" apart from repentance.

•Even movements that merge Yahusha's name with lawlessness, stripping Him of His commandments.

. . .

IN THE LAST DAYS, the spirit of Antichrist does not always deny Christ's name — it redefines it to fit rebellion.

Only those grounded in the Word of Yah and filled with the Ruach will discern the true from the counterfeit.

THE RISE of False Messiahs and the Deception of the Last Days

"FOR MANY SHALL COME in My name, saying, 'I am Christ,' and shall deceive many."

— Matthew 24:5

"EVEN HIM, whose coming is after the working of Satan with all power and signs and lying wonders…"

— 2 Thessalonians 2:9

I. SATAN'S LAST STAND: A Kingdom Built on Deceit

THE ENEMY of our souls knows his time is short.

FROM THE GARDEN of Eden to modern geopolitics, his weapon has never changed — deception.

•He lied to Eve: "You shall not surely die."

•He was able offer Yahusha the kingdoms of this fallen world, for satan was — and is — the prince of its systems and the *"father of lies"* (*Jonh 8:44)*.

•He has lied to the world: creating false saviors, false religions, false science, false world systems, and false hopes.

THE WORLD we live in is not neutral.

It is a spiritual battlefield camouflaged in entertainment, religion, technology, and politics.

IF WE ARE to be a people of truth, we must expose every lie — no matter how sacred or sentimental it has become.

II. The White Jesus: The Greatest Religious Hoax in History

LET'S start with the most obvious yet most protected deception — the so-called image of "Jesus Christ":

•Caesar Borgia, son of Pope Alexander VI, was the face of the European Christ painted by Michelangelo and Leonardo da Vinci during the Renaissance.

•Scripture clearly describes a Hebrew man with skin like bronze and hair like wool (Revelation 1:14–15), not a pale European with blue eyes and straight hair.

•This image was used during slavery to pacify, to intimidate, and to replace the real Messiah with a false, Eurocentric idol.

THIS IS NOT JUST a case of mistaken ethnicity — it's spiritual identity theft.

THE WHITE JESUS became a weapon of colonization.

A god of Rome, not Zion.

A Christ of conquest, not covenant.

AND MANY ARE STILL BOWING to Caesar Borgia in their hearts, thinking they are worshipping YAHUSHUA.

III. The False Christs of the Modern Age

THE DECEPTION DIDN'T STOP with white Jesus. The enemy has multiplied false messiahs in every generation:

1. Political Saviors

•Charismatic leaders rising as "saviors" of oppressed people — but leading them into compromise, corruption, or deeper captivity.

•Presidents, dictators, or activists worshipped like messiahs.

•They offer hope without holiness, change without repentance, and progress without righteousness.

2. Economic Christs

•The god of money and capitalism promising salvation through materialism.

•The lie that wealth is deliverance, and poverty is sin.

•Mega-preachers claiming the kingdom is "seed money" away — turning the temple into a marketplace of manipulation.

3. New Age & Spiritual Christs

•The rise of the "universe" movement, crystals, manifesting, and chakra healing.

•The lie that you are your own god, removing the need for the Most High.

•Many Hebrews, in rejecting Christianity, are falling into Egyptian mysticism, African ancestral worship, and occult practices disguised as "liberation."

"I'M SPIRITUAL BUT NOT RELIGIOUS"

"The ancestors are guiding me."

"Christ consciousness is within us all"

These are not harmless philosophies — they are open doors to demonic influence.

4. Technological Messiahs

•Artificial intelligence, transhumanism, and the push for man to become his own god.

•The worship of data, surveillance, and control.

•Digital "immortality" offered as a replacement for eternal life in YAH.

THIS IS the beast system rising — not with horns and fire — but with algorithms and convenience.

IV. The Coming Global Deceiver: The Anti-Messiah

SCRIPTURE WARNS of one who will come:

•With miracles and lying wonders (2 Thessalonians 2:9)

•Exalting himself above all gods (Daniel 11:36–37)

ASAPH MACCABEE

•Sitting in the temple of God, declaring himself to be god (2 Thessalonians 2:4)

This Anti-Messiah, or Beast, will unite the world in false peace — but behind his charm will be the spirit of Satan himself.

The deception will be so powerful that even the elect could be fooled, if not for YAH's mercy (Matthew 24:24).

He will appeal to all religions.

He will unite nations under one currency, one voice, one law.

He will persecute the remnant who keep the commandments of YAH and the testimony of YAHUSHA (Revelation 12:17).

The Hebrew awakening is not just inconvenient for the powers that be — it is a direct threat to the plans of the Beast.

V. Guard Your Crown: Discerning the True Messiah

"Take heed that no man deceive you."

— Matthew 24:4

How do we know the real Messiah when He returns?

•He comes from the sky with power and glory, not through elections or media (Matthew 24:30).

•He gathers His people from the four corners of the earth, not just Israel (Matthew 24:31).

•He will restore Zion, judge the nations, and rule with righteousness — not campaign slogans or global treaties (Isaiah 11, Revelation 19).

THE TRUE MESSIAH cannot be imitated by flesh and blood.

WHEN HE RETURNS, the earth will tremble.

VI. The Call to Discernment in These Last Days

WE MUST SHARPEN OUR DISCERNMENT.

"BELOVED, believe not every spirit, but try the spirits whether they are of God: because many false prophets are gone out into the world."

— 1 John 4:1

THIS IS THE TIME TO:

•Test everything by Scripture

•Seek the guidance of the Ruach Ha'Qodesh

•Cut ties with counterfeit gospels, idols, and distractions and indeed people, places and things.

•Walk boldly in obedience and humility

•Teach your children truth — before the system teaches them lies

THE WAR for your mind is real.

The war for your soul is eternal.

Summary:

In these last days, deception is the enemy's masterstroke. From false Christs to false systems of salvation, the devil has crafted a thousand masks to lead YAH's people astray. But the remnant must not be fooled. We must walk with discernment, cling to the true Messiah, and reject every idol — no matter how beautiful, intelligent, rich, or popular it appears. This is not just about avoiding deception — it's about preparing for the return of the King.

THE WHITE JESUS — HISTORY'S MOST POWERFUL DECEPTION

*P*erhaps no image has done more damage than the white Jesus.

Modeled after Cesare Borgia, the son of a pope and known homosexual murderer, this portrait became the face of divinity worldwide.

THE BIBLE DESCRIBES Yahusha as having skin like burnished bronze and hair like wool — features familiar to Hebrews, not Europeans.

THIS WAS NOT ACCIDENTAL.

Colonizers needed a god who looked like them to justify ruling over darker nations.

A white Jesus made them saviors and Hebrews eternal slaves, even in the spiritual imagination.

WHEN WE PRAY to this image, we subconsciously bow to the oppressor.

When we worship the man on their stained glass, we internalize our own inferiority.

KNOWING YAHUSHA as the Lion of Judah — a man who resembled the very people shipped in chains — is not about race pride.

It is about truth.

Truth that breaks psychological bondage and returns dignity to Zion.

BLACK SKIN, White Jesus — How Christianity Was Hijacked and Weaponized

"FOR IF HE that cometh preacheth another Yeshua, whom we have not preached, or if ye receive another spirit, which ye have not received... ye might well bear with him."

— 2 Corinthians 11:4

"WOE UNTO YOU, scribes and Pharisees, hypocrites! For ye shut up the kingdom of heaven against men: for ye neither go in yourselves..."

— Matthew 23:13

I. THE IDENTITY Theft of the Century

THE MESSIAH of the Scriptures was:

•Born in Bethlehem,

•Raised in Nazareth,

•A descendant of David and Judah,

•A man "with hair like wool and feet like burnt bronze" (Revelation 1:14–15).

YET THE WORLD was given a different image:

•Pale skin,

•Flowing golden hair,

•Blue eyes,

•Passive gaze,

•And a European robe.

THE SON of Man was remade into the son of Caesar.

THIS WAS no innocent artistic error.

It was the most effective psychological warfare ever deployed—a calculated effort to:

•Erase the Hebrew identity of the Messiah,

•Justify white supremacy under the banner of the cross,

•And sever the spiritual connection between Black descendants of slaves and their true Redeemer.

II. The Roman Church and the Great Switch

THE EARLY FOLLOWERS of Yeshua (Jesus) were:

•Hebrew,

•Torah-observant,

•Spirit-filled,

•Persecuted by the Roman state.

BUT IN THE 4TH CENTURY, Emperor Constantine merged Christianity with Roman politics at the Council of Nicaea (325 A.D.), birthing what would become the Roman Catholic Church.

THIS WAS the turning point when:

•Biblical truth became state religion,

•Hebrew roots were replaced with pagan rituals,

•And Messiah Yahusha was transformed into Jesus the Christ of Europe.

FROM THERE:

•The Sabbath was changed from the lunar Sabbath (which is the only real Sabbath) to the 7th day (Saturday) to the 1st day (Sunday),

•Pagan holidays like Saturnalia became "Christmas,"

•The feast days of YHWH were outlawed,

•And statues of Zeus and Apollo were renamed "Jesus" and "Peter."

THE CHURCH no longer preached the gospel of the Kingdom.

It preached control—using fear, ritual, and state power.

III. The Cross and the Sword: Colonial Christianity

During the transatlantic slave trade, missionaries came with Bibles in one hand and chains in the other.
They told the enslaved:
•"Obey your masters" (twisting Ephesians 6:5),
•"Turn the other cheek" (Matthew 5:39),
•"God made you inferior,"
•"Your suffering is the will of God,"
•"You will be rewarded in heaven, not on earth."

THIS WASN'T CHRISTIANITY.

It was colonial indoctrination—designed to:

•Pacify rebellion,

•Sanction injustice,

•And divorce the Hebrew from his divine heritage.

SLAVE BIBLES WERE DISTRIBUTED WITH:

•Exodus removed,

•Psalms of deliverance omitted,

•No mention of Hebrew identity.

WHAT REMAINED WAS a gospel of white supremacy—where the savior looked like the oppressor and the victims were told to submit in silence.

IV. White Jesus: The Trojan Horse in the Hebrew Soul

The image of "White Jesus" is more than inaccurate—it is idolatrous.

"Thou shalt not make unto thee any graven image…" — Exodus 20:4

Yet every Black church for generations was forced to look up at a man who:

•LOOKED NOTHING LIKE THEM,

•Came from no Hebrew tribe,

•And embodied the face of their captivity.

THIS WAS INTENTIONAL PSYCHOLOGICAL WARFARE.

TO BELIEVE in a white messiah meant:

•Associating divinity with whiteness,

•Associating blackness with sin and shame,

•Worshiping the oppressor's image,

•While rejecting the reflection of the true Savior in the mirror.

THIS SPIRITUAL DECEPTION caused generations to:

•Love Caesar and call him Christ,

•Serve the church and not the Kingdom,

•And unknowingly deny the bloodline of the Lion of Judah.

V. The Real Yeshua: The Hebrew Messiah

The true Messiah:
•Kept Torah,
•Observed the feasts of YHWH,
•Called out religious hypocrisy,
•Taught in parables,
•Was rejected by religious elites,
•Was betrayed by one of His own,
•And was ultimately crucified by Rome.

HE DID NOT COME to start a religion.

He came to fulfill prophecy, to gather the lost sheep of the house of Israel (Matthew 15:24), and to establish a Kingdom.

HE WAS HATED because He spoke truth, walked in righteousness, and threatened the empire.

AND TODAY, His true followers are awakening.

"AND YE SHALL KNOW the truth, and the truth shall make you free." — John 8:32

VI. The Return of the Hebrew Church

WE ARE LIVING in the days of restoration.

The true Hebrew church:
- •Is arising from the ashes,
- •Casting off false doctrine,
- •Returning to biblical commandments,
- •Embracing Yahusha as the Hebrew Messiah,
- •And preaching the gospel of repentance.

This church is not Black or white—it is righteous.
It is not Baptist, Pentecostal, or Catholic—it is Kingdom.
It is not submissive to Babylon—it is loyal to Zion.

THE BRIDE IS AWAKENING, the veil is being torn, and the Messiah is coming back—not as a European, not as a Roman priest, but as a warrior King from the tribe of Judah.

SUMMARY:

CHRISTIANITY WAS HIJACKED, whitewashed, and weaponized to oppress the very people it was meant to liberate. The image of white Jesus has been used to distort Scripture, justify colonialism, and spiritually enslave the Hebrew people. But the real Yahusha is being revealed, and the true church is being restored—bold, righteous, and unapologetically Hebrew.

THE COMING ANTI-MESSIAH

*S*cripture warns of a coming man of sin who will perform wonders, unite religions, and demand worship.

• He will solve crises that plague the world, earning trust.

• He will speak of unity, love, and global harmony — yet require absolute allegiance.

• He will desecrate holy places and wage war on the remnant who keep YAH's commandments.

He will unite the whole world under on currency, one law one rule. He will fool the world into believing he is the savior. He will subjugate the world and persecute the remnant.

The world is being groomed for this figure:

• Through tolerance that tolerates everything except holiness.

• Through technology that tracks and molds behavior.

• Through economic systems poised to punish those who refuse the mark of compliance. (Mark of the beast)

. . .

THE TRUE HEBREWS and the grafted-in Gentiles who cling to them will · stand apart — hated by all nations for Yahusha's sake.

But we will not bow.

And the Lamb who was slain will return to destroy the beast with the breath of His mouth.

——THE ANTI-MESSIAH (Antichrist) in Scripture

1. The Spirit of Anti-Messiah

• **1 John 2:18** — "Little children, it is the last time: and as ye have heard that **antichrist shall come,** even now are there many antichrists; whereby we know that it is the last time."

• There is both a **spirit of deception** already at work and a future **singular figure** to come.

• **1 John 4:3** — "Every spirit that confesseth not that Yahusha Ha'Mashiach is come in the flesh is not of Elohim: and this is that spirit of antichrist."

• Any teaching that denies Yahusha's true identity, His divinity, or His incarnation carries the spirit of Anti-Messiah.

2. The Man of Lawlessness

• **2 Thessalonians 2:3–4**

"Let no man deceive you by any means: for that day shall not come, except there come a **falling away first,** and that man of sin be revealed, the son of perdition;

Who opposeth and exalteth himself above all that is called Elohim… so that he as Elohim sitteth in the temple of Elohim, showing himself that he is Elohim."

· · ·

312

- PAUL WARNS OF A FUTURE FIGURE — **the Man of Sin** — who will:

- Arise **after a great apostasy** (falling away).

- Exalt himself as divine.

- Desecrate something holy (links to Daniel 9:27 & Matthew 24:15).

3. The Beast Power

- **Revelation 13:1–8**

A beast rises out of the sea with ten horns and seven heads, receiving power from the dragon (Satan).

- REPRESENTS an **end-time global empire** led by a blasphemous ruler.

- All nations marvel and follow him.

- He makes war against the set-apart ones (saints).

- **Verse 7:** "It was given unto him to make war with the saints, and to overcome them: and power was given him over all kindreds, tongues, and nations."

- This is the **political dimension** of the Anti-Messiah.

- **Revelation 13:11–18**

A second beast arises — "the false prophet."

- PERFORMS MIRACLES.

- Deceives the world.

- Forces all to take the **Mark of the Beast** (v.16–17).

- This is the **religious dimension** — uniting worship, politics, and economics under one authority.

. . .

4. The Abomination of Desolation

• **Daniel 9:27** — The "prince that shall come" makes a **seven-year covenant** but breaks it halfway, desecrating the sanctuary.

• **Daniel 11:36–37** — "The king shall do according to his will... exalt himself above every god... and regard no god of his fathers."

• **Matthew 24:15** — Yahusha refers back to Daniel, saying:

"When ye therefore shall see the **abomination of desolation**, spoken of by Daniel the prophet, stand in the holy place..."

• THE ANTI-MESSIAH WILL DESECRATE something holy in Jerusalem, triggering the Great Tribulation.

5. The Deception of Signs and Wonders

• **Matthew 24:24** — "For there shall arise false messiahs, and false prophets, and shall show **great signs and wonders**; insomuch that, if it were possible, they shall deceive the very elect."

• The Anti-Messiah's power will involve supernatural deception.

• **Revelation 13:13** — Calls fire down from heaven to convince the world of his authority.

• **2 Thessalonians 2:9–10** — "Even him, whose coming is after the working of Satan with all power and signs and lying wonders..."

6. Final Judgment

• **Revelation 19:19–20**

• At Yahusha's return, the beast and the false prophet are captured and thrown into the lake of fire.

- **Revelation 20:10**
- Satan, who empowered the Anti-Messiah, is also cast into the lake of fire forever

BABYLON HAS FALLEN — AMERICA IN PROPHECY

$\mathcal{B}$abylon and Egypt: The Twin Towers of Oppression

THOUGH SEPARATED by geography and time, Egypt and Babylon were spiritual twins—empires of bondage.

•Egypt represents physical slavery—chains, forced labor, and visible oppression.

•Babylon represents spiritual and psychological slavery—indoctrination, assimilation, manipulation, materialism and confusion.

TODAY, the Hebrew people dwell in modern-day Egypt and Babylon combined—a nation that enslaved them with iron yokes, and now enslaves them with mental chains.

THEY ARE NO LONGER WHIPPED with leather.

They are whipped with lies, bound by debt, distracted by screens, and drugged with cultural toxins.

THE WHIP BECAME THE WAGE.

The plantation became the project.

Pharaoh became the politician.

And the golden calf became the television, computer, and phone screen.

II. Psychological Pharaohs: Mind Control in the Modern Age

TODAY'S SLAVE master doesn't ride a horse or carry a whip—he controls systems.

• EDUCATION: misleads and deprives us — teaching Hebrews they were slaves, not kings, prophets, or priests or even leaders, inventors, and innovators.

•Entertainment: celebrates chaos, normalizes perversion, mocks truth, and shames those who pursue holiness.

•Politics: gives the illusion of choice while offering the same poison in different-colored bottles.

•Religion: keeps the people pacified, emotional, and uninformed.

•Media: ensures that anything holy looks foolish, and everything vile looks glamorous.......and keeps the people pacified, emotional, and uninformed.

IT IS mind control through media.

Witchcraft through words.

Spells through songs.

The result? A people with no memory of Zion—marching in circles in a wilderness of confusion.

"THEY KNOW NOT, neither will they understand; they walk on in darkness…"

— Psalm 82:5

III. The Hebrew-American Dream: A False Inheritance

AMERICA PROMISED the descendants of slaves a dream—but gave them a nightmare wrapped in glitter.

•You can be rich—if you sell your soul.

•You can be free—if you submit to the system.

•You can be accepted—if you conform and erase your identity.

MANY HAVE TRADED their inheritance as Hebrews for a bowl of Babylonian stew.

JUST AS ESAU sold his birthright for a moment of hunger, so too have many Hebrews today sold their covenant for:

•Fame,

•Comfort,

•Compromise,

•Or fear of rejection.

. . .

EVEN WORSE, most have sold it for nothing except for a life of perpetual poverty, dysfunction, and pain. Most people who have bought into the Babylonian American dream have only bought an inheritance of slavery. For the vast majority there is no fame. There is no riches. There is no comfort. Only sin, poverty, dysfunction, and pain. Only the Mirage of Babylons lies. And they are left happily chasing after something that never really existed.

BUT YAH IS NOT MOCKED.

He is calling His people back—not to the American dream, but to the Kingdom vision.

IV. False Gods, New Names

Egypt had Ra, Osiris, and Isis.
Babylon had Marduk, Ishtar, and Baal.

TODAY, the idols are different, but the worship is the same.

•Money is the new golden calf.

•Celebrities are the new false gods.

•The self is the new altar.

•Social media is the new temple.

AND THE PEOPLE BOW DAILY:

•Offering time,

•Attention,

•Obedience,

•And even their children...

...TO DIGITAL PHARAOHS and Babylonian priests in business suits.

"THEY PROVOKED him to jealousy with strange gods, with abominations provoked they him to anger." — Deuteronomy 32:16

V. What Babylon Offers—and What It Takes

BABYLON IS SEDUCTIVE. It offers:

•Riches,

•Pleasure,

•Platforms,

•Influence,

•Protection...

...BUT ONLY IF you remain silent about truth.

IT OFFERS a platform if you'll preach tolerance, not repentance.

It offers wealth if you'll rap about murder, not mercy.

It offers influence if you go along with the demonic agendas that have become mainstream.

BUT MAKE NO MISTAKE: Babylon comes to collect.

. . .

IT DEVOURS the souls of artists and influencers, the anointing of pastors, the strength of men, and the innocence of women and children.

IT TAKES EVERYTHING—AND gives nothing eternal in return.

VI. The Call to Come Out

YAH IS NOT WAITING on America to repent.

He is calling His people to come out of spiritual Egypt and Babylon—mentally, emotionally, economically, and spiritually.

•Come out of false identity.

•Come out of toxic culture.

•Come out of these corrupted institutions.

•Come out of trusting Pharaoh more than the Most High.

RETURN TO:

•The covenant,

•The commandments,

•The community of the righteous,

•And the true Messiah—Yahusha HaMashiach, not the whitewashed imposter of Rome.

"AND YE SHALL KNOW the truth, and the truth shall make you free." — John 8:32

. . .

SUMMARY

THE HEBREW PEOPLE are still in Egypt—only now the chains are invisible. Babylon has not fallen—it has evolved. The systems of America echo the spiritual oppression of ancient empires, deceiving Hebrews into loving their own bondage. But YAH is raising a remnant who will come out—who will renounce the golden calves of this culture and walk boldly in covenant, identity, and truth. The Red Sea is opening—but only for those who refuse to bow to Pharaoh.

REVELATION 18 SPEAKS of **Babylon the Great**, a global superpower clothed in luxury, enriching merchants and spreading sorceries. It says she trafficked in the souls of men and was drunk on the blood of saints.

AMERICA FITS THIS PORTRAIT PRECISELY.

•Built on the backs of Hebrew slaves.

•Spreading sexual immorality, violence, and material worship through movies, music, and markets.

•Invading nations, toppling governments, yet calling itself a beacon of freedom.

BABYLON'S JUDGMENT IS CERTAIN.

Her sins have reached unto heaven, and YAH remembers her iniquities.

In one hour, her wealth will be destroyed. Her merchants will weep.

And those who trusted in her systems — military, economic, political, or religious — will share her fate.

Mystery Babylon and the Fall of America — Judgment for a Nation That Oppressed Zion

"COME OUT OF HER, My people, that ye be not partakers of her sins, and that ye receive not of her plagues."

— Revelation 18:4

"BABYLON THE GREAT IS FALLEN, is fallen… for all nations have drunk of the wine of the wrath of her fornication."

— Revelation 18:2-3

I. THE IDENTITY of Mystery Babylon: Not Just Ancient, but Prophetic

WHEN JOHN the Revelator penned the words of Revelation, he wasn't merely chronicling events from the Roman Empire. He was shown a mystery—a prophetic image of a future empire:

• An empire full of wealth, luxury, and blasphemy.

• A global power that made "merchants of the earth rich."

• A nation drunk with the blood of the saints and prophets.

THAT EMPIRE IS NOT ROME.

That empire is not Iraq.

That empire is not metaphorical.

. . .

THAT EMPIRE—MYSTERY Babylon—is America.

LET THE READER UNDERSTAND:

"FOR SHE SAITH in her heart, I sit a queen, and am no widow, and shall see no sorrow." (Rev. 18:7)

— Who else boasts of being "number one"?

— Who else proclaims to be "the greatest nation on earth"?

II. The Sins of Babylon: Sexual Perversion, Idolatry, and Bloodshed

AMERICA IS NOT JUST guilty of slavery.

Her iniquity is deeper than racial injustice.

SHE HAS FILLED the earth with spiritual filth:

•Pornography and sexual perversion exported across the globe.

•Pedophilia and child trafficking hidden behind elite institutions.

•Abortion clinics lining impoverished Hebrew neighborhoods.

•Idols of fame, wealth, and entertainment replacing the Most High.

•Churches preaching prosperity, not repentance.

SHE HAS BLASPHEMED HIS NAME, persecuted His people, and mocked His commandments.

AND THE BLOOD cries out from the ground.

. . .

III. The Blood of the Saints: America's Greatest Hidden Crime

"AND IN HER was found the blood of prophets, and of saints, and of all that were slain upon the earth."

— Revelation 18:24

WHAT IS the blood that cries out?

•The millions of Hebrew babies aborted in the womb. (20 million)

•The lives of enslaved Hebrews who died in the Middle Passage.

•The voices of lynched men, raped women, and silenced prophets.

•The spiritual death of entire generations, robbed of truth.

AMERICA HAS BUILT her empire on the backs of Judah, and the Most High has kept the record.

AS SHE CELEBRATES independence every July, the heavens record her crimes.

Her freedom was our captivity.

IV. Why Judgment Must Come: Divine Justice Cannot Be Delayed

THE MOST HIGH is not mocked.

HIS PATIENCE IS NOT WEAKNESS.

. . .

EVERY EMPIRE that touched His covenant people—Assyria, Babylon, Egypt, Rome—was judged.

AND NOW, Mystery Babylon is ripe for destruction.

"REWARD her even as she rewarded you, and double unto her double..."
— Revelation 18:6

THIS IS NOT a message of hatred.

This is a warning from the throne of heaven.

AMERICA HAD A CHANCE TO REPENT.

She built churches, but not righteousness.

She sent missionaries, but withheld justice.

She quoted Scripture, while she lynched the saints.

AND NOW: judgment is inevitable.

V. The Fall Will Be Sudden: Economic Collapse, War, and Fire

"IN ONE HOUR so great riches is come to nought."
— Revelation 18:17

. . .

THE SCRIPTURES SAY her fall will be swift:

•Her economy will collapse, leaving merchants weeping.

•Her cities will burn, consumed by internal chaos and foreign fire.

•Her military power will fail, overrun by enemies she once mocked.

•Her political system will fracture, unable to contain the wrath of YAH.

NATIONS WILL LOOK on in horror, crying "Alas! Babylon is fallen!"

BUT THOSE WHO know the Most High will not be shocked—they have seen the writing on the wall. They will be prepared.

VI. "Come Out of Her, My People": A Call to the Remnant

THE MOST HIGH gives one command to His people in Babylon:

"COME OUT OF HER, MY PEOPLE..."
— Revelation 18:4

THIS IS NOT JUST about physical departure (though that may come).
It is primarily a call to spiritual, mental, and emotional separation.

The remnant must:
•Reject Babylon's lack of morality—no more compromise.
•Refuse her food, entertainment, and idols—no more gluttony and eating fake food that literally harm, not nourish the body.
•Reclaim their identity—no more "Black" or "African American" confusion.
•Return to Torah, study The Gospel—walk in the covenant once more.

To "COME OUT" means to leave her systems even if your body is still in her borders...... Until it's time to physically leave.

IT MEANS TO SAY:

"I am Judah. I am Hebrew. I will no longer serve Babylon's gods." In Yahusha's name.

VII. Babylon's End, Zion's Rise: A Prophetic Exchange

As BABYLON FALLS, Zion rises.

THIS IS NOT JUST about judgment.

It's about redemption.

THE MOST HIGH WILL:

•Regather His people (Isaiah 11:12, Jeremiah 30:3).

•Restore His covenant (Ezekiel 36:24–28).

•Establish His kingdom with Yahusha Ha'Mashiach as King.

•Exalt those once despised (Zephaniah 3:19).

"FOR THE LORD will have mercy on Jacob, and will yet choose Israel, and set them in their own land."

— Isaiah 14:1

BABYLON'S ASHES will become Zion's foundation.

AND THE WORLD WILL KNOW:

The God of Israel is not a myth.

He has remembered His people.

SUMMARY:

AMERICA IS NOT MERELY A NATION—IT is Mystery Babylon, the great harlot described in Revelation. Her sins have reached heaven. Her judgment is sealed. The Most High is calling His remnant to come out of her spiritually and prepare for the fall. This is not about fear—it is about prophecy. As Babylon crumbles, Zion will rise, and the true people of YAH will be restored.

Babylon Has Fallen — The Fall of America and the Final Exodus

"Babylon the great is fallen, is fallen, and is become the habitation of devils…"
— Revelation 18:2

"Come out of her, my people, that ye be not partakers of her sins, and that ye receive not of her plagues."

— Revelation 18:4

I. The Modern Babylon Is Not in the Middle East — It's in the West

For centuries, Bible scholars argued over who the "Mystery Babylon" of Revelation was.

Some pointed to ancient Iraq.

Some to Rome.

Others to a symbolic spiritual system.

But those with spiritual eyes and historical discernment

understand what the prophets saw:

Babylon is America and America is a manifestation of Rome.

A land clothed in wealth,

drunk with blood,

boasting in pride,

and warring against the saints of the Most High.

She enslaved a chosen people.

She corrupted the nations with her culture.

She placed herself above God.

And now — her judgment is near.

.   .   .

II. Why America Matches Every Description of Mystery Babylon

AMERICA'S national symbol is the eagle — a creature repeatedly associated in Scripture with destructive, invading powers.

DEUTERONOMY 28:49 (KJV)

"THE LORD SHALL BRING a nation against thee from far, from the end of the earth, as swift as the eagle flieth; a nation whose tongue thou shalt not understand."

THIS IS from the curses upon Israel — clearly identifying an oppressive, foreign power descending like an eagle.

OBADIAH 1:4 (KJV)

"THOUGH THOU EXALT thyself as the eagle, and though thou set thy nest among the stars, thence will I bring thee down, saith the Lord."

THE TERM "CONFEDERATE" is not only historical — it is biblical, referring to alliances made against the people of YAH.

PSALM 83:3–5 (KJV)

"THEY HAVE TAKEN crafty counsel against thy people, and consulted against thy hidden ones. They have said, Come, and let us cut them off from being a nation... For they have consulted together with one consent: they are confederate against thee."

THIS SPEAKS of a spiritual and political alliance to erase the identity and legacy of the true Hebrews.

ISAIAH 8:12 (KJV)

"SAY YE NOT, A confederacy, to all them to whom this people shall say, A confederacy; neither fear ye their fear, nor be afraid."

THIS WARNS the people of YAH not to join or fear confederacies that operate in rebellion against Him.

•THE CONFEDERATE STATES OF AMERICA — which defended slavery and waged war to preserve it — embodied this very spirit of being "confederate against" YAH's chosen.

•More broadly, modern political, financial, and religious alliances are still forming "confederacies" — not to uplift the Hebrews but to keep them shut out, asleep, lost and scattered.

SO THE BIBLE says a nation from far away, whose language they would not understand, and is represented by a eagle is prophesied to put the children of the Most High (Judah) in bondage and be "confederate" against them to cut them off from being a nation and erase their memory and history —— this along with other scriptures about the Hebrews being taken in bondage in ships and many other obvious biblical parallels, all paint a very clear picture of not only who the Hebrews are but also who Mystery Babylon is.

· · ·

REVELATION 17–18 outlines characteristics of Babylon.

Let's line them up:

"SHE SITS UPON MANY WATERS" (Rev 17:1):

America controls global commerce, politics, and culture — from sea to shining sea.

"WITH WHOM THE kings of the earth have committed fornication" (Rev 17:2):

Every nation has adopted her capitalism, music, sexual immorality, and rebellion.

"FULL OF NAMES OF BLASPHEMY" (Rev 17:3):

She mixes faith with greed — preachers sell salvation, and churches bow to political idols.

"DRUNKEN WITH THE blood of the saints" (Rev 17:6):

From slavery to police violence to sterilization campaigns — the blood of Hebrews cries out from American soil.

"DECKED IN GOLD AND PRECIOUS STONES" (Rev 18:16):

The richest empire in human history, while her poor are left in ghettos and impoverished inner cities.

"FOR IN ONE hour is thy judgment come" (Rev 18:10):

America's fall will be sudden. Economic collapse. War. Fire. Famine. Pestilence.

. . .

THERE IS no other nation that fits the prophetic profile more precisely than the United States of America.

III. America's Founding Was Always Rooted in Rebellion

"WOE TO THE BLOODY CITY! It is all full of lies and robbery…"
— Nahum 3:1

AMERICA WAS NEVER the "land of the free."

It was a land built on:

•The genocide of Indigenous

•The enslavement of Hebrews

•The theft of Mexican lands

•The lie of Christian liberty while upholding white supremacy

THE SO-CALLED "FOUNDING FATHERS" were slaveholders and Freemasons.

They declared "In God We Trust" while funding human trafficking.

They drafted a Constitution that called us three-fifths of a man.

MAKE NO MISTAKE: Babylon was not born righteous — she was born in rebellion.

IV. The Plagues Are Already Being Loosed

Revelation 18:8 says her plagues will come in one day:
"death, mourning, and famine."

Look around:
•Plagues: COVID-19 was just the beginning. The judgment of pestilence is coming.
•Famine: Supply chains are breaking. Food insecurity grows in the richest country on earth.

•DEATH: Suicides, overdoses, shootings, and societal decay are claiming millions.

•Mourning: Depression, divorce, gender confusion, and lawlessness are surging.

AND MOST DANGEROUSLY — the war has already started

AMERICA THROUGH PROXY (SOS) is provoking global conflict.

Alliances are shifting.

Economic collapse is coming.

The Most High will use the very enemies she armed to burn her with fire (Rev 17:16).

V. The Final Exodus Is Coming — But This Time Not on Boats

"HE WILL GATHER the outcasts of Israel... from the four corners of the earth."

— Isaiah 11:12

. . .

THIS WILL NOT BE the exodus of Moses.

It will be greater.

THE HEBREWS ARE AWAKENING across the globe.

And just as YAH brought our ancestors out of Egypt,

He will now bring His children out of Egypt, a second time. Out of Babylon.

THIS IS NOT FANTASY.

This is prophetic fulfillment.

A second exodus is coming.

JEREMIAH 16:14–15 declares that the day will come when people will no longer remember the Red Sea crossing,

but they will speak of how YAH brought His people out of all the nations.

WE ARE THAT GENERATION.

VI. Come Out of Her, My People — A Call to Separation

"BE YE SEPARATE, saith the Lord, and touch not the unclean thing."
— 2 Corinthians 6:17

IF YOU REMAIN TIED to America's sins, you will share in her plagues.

This is not the time to blend in.

This is not the time to chase the bag, the fame, or the platform.

THE MOST HIGH IS SEPARATING:

•Wheat from tares

•Remnant from rebels

•Daughters of Zion from daughters of Babylon and men of the Most High from the boys of Babylon

NOW IS THE TIME TO:

•Repent

•Detach

•Prepare

•Preach

•Warn

•Pray & Watch

WE ARE NOT JUST CALLED to survive the fall of Babylon —

we are called to usher in the rise of Zion.

Summary:
America — the modern-day Babylon — matches every prophetic description in Revelation. Its sins have reached heaven, and its judgment is near. The Hebrews must not cling to a collapsing empire. The time has come to prepare for the second exodus, where the Most High will gather His people from the ends of the earth. We must come out, be set apart, and prepare to reign in the Kingdom.

. . .

America, the New Egypt — The Land of Bondage and Judgment

"I am Yahuah thy Elohim, which have brought thee out of the land of Egypt, out of the house of bondage."
— Exodus 20:2

"And it shall come to pass... that Yahuah shall set His hand again the second time to recover the remnant of His people... and shall assemble the outcasts of Israel."
— Isaiah 11:11–12

I. A Second Egypt for a Stiff-Necked People

When YAH delivers a people and they turn their back on Him, judgment returns in layers.

Ancient Egypt was the first captivity — but not the last.
America is the modern Egypt — and far more cunning.

"I will bring you into Egypt again with ships..." (Deuteronomy 28:68)
The Most High was not referring to a return to the physical land of Egypt.
No — this was a prophetic metaphor.

The ships symbolized something new:
A second bondage. A transatlantic judgment. A prophetic reenactment.

In biblical Egypt:
•The Hebrews built cities for Pharaoh.
•Their male children were targeted for extermination.
•They were enslaved.
•They were delivered by a prophet with power.

In modern America:
•The Hebrews built the wealth of the Western empire.
•Their sons were lynched, imprisoned, aborted, and shot in the street.
•Their enslavement and captivity has spanned over 400 years.
•And a new deliverance is now underway.

America is the new Egypt.
And just like Pharaoh, she is hardening her heart.

II. The Evidence: America's Egyptian Blueprint

"OH, you mean other than the giant egyptian obelisks in the middle of Washington DC?"

1. Systematic Enslavement

•Cotton plantations = Ancient brick-making fields.

•Whips, overseers, chains, and forced labor = Replicas of Pharaoh's taskmasters.

•Chattel slavery in America lasted over 250 years, followed by 100 more years of legal apartheid.

2. Infanticide and Eugenics

•Pharaoh killed Hebrew boys (Exodus 1:16).

•America legalized abortion and targeted Black communities.

•Margaret Sanger, founder of Planned Parenthood, said:

"We do not want word to go out that we want to exterminate the Negro population…"

— Letter to Dr. C.J. Gamble, 1939

. . .

3. Cultural Erasure

•Egypt changed Hebrew names (Daniel, Mishael, Azariah, Hananiah).

•America did the same: stripped names, languages, and identity.

•Even the religion was replaced — Yah became Jesus, Torah became traditions, and Sabbath became Sunday.

4. Generational Trauma

•Egypt crushed the spirit of the Hebrews.

•America created a system that normalized:

•Generational poverty

•Fatherlessness

•Criminalization

•Psychological despair

III. The Pharaohs of the Modern Era

WHO ARE THE MODERN PHARAOHS?

•Presidents who signed civil rights bills with one hand and signed war orders with the other.

•Corporations that profit off the prison industrial complex.

•Media moguls who glorify violence, perversion, and blasphemy.

•Elite financial families who funded both sides of wars and own your labor through debt.

AMERICA DID NOT FREE the slave — it simply evolved the plantation.

Chains became laws.

Whips became policies.

Auction blocks became courtrooms.

Cotton fields became street corners.

AND JUST LIKE EGYPT, this nation refuses to let YAH's people go.

IV. Why Did YAH Allow This?

THIS IS the question many Hebrews ask:

"IF WE ARE the chosen people, why did this happen to us?"

BECAUSE COVENANT DISOBEDIENCE brings covenant consequences.

"YOU ONLY HAVE I known of all the families of the earth: therefore I will punish you for all your iniquities."
— Amos 3:2

WE REJECTED the laws of our Elohim.

We served idols.

We profaned His Sabbaths.

We made covenants with death (Isaiah 28:15).

SO HE KEPT HIS WORD — both blessing and curse (Deuteronomy 28).

He scattered us among the nations.

He allowed us to be sold.

He let us forget our identity.

But the punishment was never to destroy — only to correct.

And just like He judged Egypt for their cruelty,

He will now judge modern Egypt — America — for the blood she has shed.

V. Plagues Are Coming Again

"As in the days of Egypt, I will show wonders in the heavens and in the earth."
— Joel 2:30

The plagues are already beginning:

•Environmental disasters

•Economic instability

•Civil unrest

•Pestilence and famine

•Increasing natural catastrophes

Just like ancient Egypt, modern America will be brought low.

And once again, the true Hebrews will be called to come out.

. . .

"COME OUT OF HER, MY PEOPLE…" (Revelation 18:4)

YAH IS NOT JUST TALKING about geography.

He's talking about spiritual separation:

•Come out of her lies.

•Come out of her churches.

•Come out of her mindset.

•Come out of her sin.

THE BRIDE MUST DETACH from Egypt before she can enter the Promised Land.

VI. The Second Exodus Is at Hand

"AND THERE SHALL BE a highway for the remnant of his people… like as it was to Israel in the day that he came up out of the land of Egypt."

— Isaiah 11:16

THERE WILL BE A GREATER EXODUS — this time not just out of a country, but out of a system.

THE NATIONS WILL SEE the power of YAH again.

The sky will shake.

The sea will part — metaphorically or literally.

And His people will rise.

BUT THE MESSAGE is the same:

LET MY PEOPLE GO.

AND PHARAOH — modern Babylon, Rome, America —
will refuse.

SO JUDGMENT WILL FALL.

SUMMARY:

AMERICA IS NOT JUST another nation. It is the spiritual and prophetic
twin of Egypt — a land of bondage, exploitation, and rebellion against
YAH. The transatlantic slave trade was the fulfillment of
Deuteronomy 28:68. The oppression of the Hebrews in America
mirrors that of Egypt. And just as YAH judged Pharaoh, He will judge
this modern empire. But the remnant must be ready. The second
Exodus is already in motion.

THE CUP OF BABYLON — Wine, Whoredom, and Wrath

"BABYLON THE GREAT IS FALLEN, is fallen… she made all nations drink
of the wine of the wrath of her fornication."

— Revelation 14:8

. . .

"COME OUT OF HER, My people, that you be not partakers of her sins, and that you receive not of her plagues."

— Revelation 18:4

I. THE MYSTERY WOMAN: Who Is Babylon?

SHE IS NOT A LITERAL WOMAN —

She is a system. A city. A spiritual empire that sits upon many waters.

"AND THE WOMAN… is that great city, which reigneth over the kings of the earth."

— Revelation 17:18

THIS WOMAN IS DECKED in purple and scarlet — the colors of royalty and religion.

She holds a golden cup — not with water, not with wine — but filled with the filthiness of her fornication.

She is drunk on blood — the blood of saints, prophets, and the innocent.

THIS IS MYSTERY BABYLON.

She is not just Rome.

She is not just America.

She is the global harlot system of false worship, elite rule, sexual immorality, and spiritual rebellion —

A counterfeit kingdom that imitates the Kingdom of YAH but serves Satan.

. . .

SHE IS the mother of harlots — because she births systems of deception.

II. The Wine of Her Fornication

"THE INHABITANTS of the earth have been made drunk with the wine of her fornication."

— Revelation 17:2

WHAT IS THIS WINE?

IT IS the ideology and spiritual seduction of Babylon:

•Humanism — "You are your own god."

•Materialism — "Money is your salvation."

•Sexual perversion — "Do what ever you feel."

•Occult mysticism — "Truth is relative. All paths lead to god."

•Ecumenism — "Let's unite every religion… except the truth."

THIS WINE INTOXICATES THE WORLD,

Nations are drunk.

Churches are drunk.

Even Hebrews — once sober — now sip from her cup on Sundays, in pulpits, and in politics.

. . .

SHE HAS TURNED the nations into adulterers,

Cheating on the Most High for comfort, power, and pleasure.

III. America: The Daughter of Babylon

LET'S BE CLEAR:

BABYLON IS ANCIENT. It goes back to Nimrod and the Tower.

But America is a daughter of this system — a hybrid of Roman, Grecian, Egyptian, and Babylonian influence.

JUST LIKE ANCIENT BABYLON:

•She worships idols — Hollywood, celebrities, money.

•She promotes fornication — from billboard to algorithms.

•She enslaves nations through debt and war.

•She traffics souls — through pornography, prisons, and pharmakeia (Revelation 18:23).

AND JUST LIKE BABYLON, her end is written.

"BABYLON IS FALLEN... for her sins have reached unto heaven."

— Revelation 18:2–5

IV. The Merchants and the Murderers

"The merchants of the earth are waxed rich through the abundance of her delicacies."
— Revelation 18:3

Babylon is an economic beast.

Her tentacles reach:
•Wall Street
•Big Tech

•BIG Pharma

•Oil

•Media empires

•Fashion industries that use child labor

•Food conglomerates that poison for profit

AND WHO SUFFERS?

THE POOR GENTILE. The black. The indigenous. The Hebrew.

Because Babylon was never built for righteousness — only riches.

AND WHAT MAKES IT WORSE?

"IN HER WAS FOUND the blood of prophets, and of saints, and of all that were slain upon the earth."

— Revelation 18:24

. . .

SHE DOES NOT JUST DECEIVE — she kills.

•Through war

•Through prisons

•Through sterilization

•Through spiritual deceit

HER PASTORS PREACH prosperity but ignore prophecy.

Her politicians quote Scripture but legalize sin.

Her systems smile while they destroy you.

V. The Warning Cry: Come Out of Her

YAH DOES NOT STUTTER.

"COME OUT OF HER, My people, that ye be not partakers of her sins..."
— Revelation 18:4

THIS IS NOT OPTIONAL.

YOU CANNOT KNOW your Hebrew identity and drink from Babylon's cup.

You cannot walk in covenant and walk in compromise.

TO "COME OUT" means:

•Detach your heart from her values

•Unplug your mind from her media

•Refuse her feast of immorality

•Reject her ideologies — feminism that hates men, capitalism that crushes the poor, religion that silences truth.

THIS IS SPIRITUAL WAR.

You cannot serve YAH and Babylon.

VI. Judgment Is Coming

"THEREFORE SHALL her plagues come in one day: death, and mourning, and famine; and she shall be utterly burned with fire."

— Revelation 18:8

BABYLON WILL FALL.

THIS IS NOT A POLITICAL PREDICTION — it is a prophetic certainty.

•Her cities will burn.

•Her dollar will collapse.

•Her churches will be empty.

•Her idols will be useless.

•Her leaders will flee— but there will be nowhere to hide.

YAH WILL AVENGE the blood of His people.

And when He does, the world will weep — but the remnant will rejoice.

"REJOICE OVER HER, thou heaven, and ye holy apostles and prophets; for Elohim hath avenged you on her."

— Revelation 18:20

SUMMARY:

BABYLON IS NOT JUST A PLACE — it is a system, a seduction, and a sentence of death. America is her daughter, feeding the world the wine of confusion, rebellion, and idolatry. But the judgment is written. The call is urgent. "Come out of her, My people." The Hebrew must detox, disengage, and prepare. For Babylon will fall, but Zion will rise.

BABYLON HAS FALLEN — America's Role in Prophecy and Her Final Judgment

"FLEE out of the midst of Babylon, and deliver every man his soul: be not cut off in her iniquity; for this is the time of YAHUAH's vengeance; He will render unto her a recompense."

— Jeremiah 51:6

"BABYLON THE GREAT IS FALLEN, is fallen... and is become the habitation of devils, and the hold of every foul spirit."

— Revelation 18:2

. . .

I. Who — or What — Is Mystery Babylon?

THE SCRIPTURES SPEAK REPEATEDLY of a mysterious end-time empire called Babylon — a wicked, wealthy, and seductive global power that corrupts nations and is ultimately destroyed by divine judgment.

MANY HAVE WRONGLY ASSUMED this is ancient Babylon in Iraq. But Revelation makes it clear: this Babylon is a future kingdom, marked by:

•Global influence and trade dominance (Rev. 18:3)

•Great wealth and luxury (Rev. 18:11–13)

•Religious idolatry and spiritual fornication (Rev. 17:4–5)

•Blood on her hands — especially the blood of the saints and prophets (Rev. 18:24)

THERE IS ONLY one modern nation that fits every prophetic detail:

The United States of America.

II. The Daughter of Babylon: A Modern Superpower Built on Slavery and Sorcery

"YOU ARE the daughter of Babylon... who will be destroyed suddenly."

— Isaiah 47:1–9 (paraphrased)

AMERICA IS NOT JUST A NATION — it is the spiritual and economic stronghold of the beast system. Let us examine the prophetic parallels:

· · ·

1. Built on the Blood of the Hebrews

AMERICA'S WEALTH and global dominance were built on the backs of the true children of Israel — the descendants of the transatlantic slave trade.

•Cotton, sugar, and tobacco became America's economic engine because of Hebrew slave labor.

•Wall Street itself began as a slave market — a literal "street" for selling human stock.

•The Constitution defined our ancestors as three-fifths of a man, legally dehumanizing the chosen people.

AMERICA HAS NEVER REPENTED. Instead, she has sanitized her crimes with statues, textbooks, and distorted curriculum.

BABYLON IS DRUNK WITH BLOOD — and she will drink the cup of wrath.

2. The Queen of Idolatry and Abominations

LIKE ANCIENT BABYLON, America is a land of idols:

•It is said the Statue of Liberty is modeled after Semiramis, the Babylonian "Queen of Heaven" and it also "coincidentally" bears striking resemblance if not an exact match to various depictions of Lucifer.

•Egyptian Obelisks (phallic Baal symbols) are erected in Washington D.C. and mirrored in Vatican City and London, England. The three headed monster of the beast, the military, spiritual and financial arms of Babylon.

•Her entertainment industry glorifies witchcraft, rebellion, homosexuality, fornication, and greed

•Her churches preach prosperity but not repentance — false doctrine in Jesus' name

AMERICA HAS BAPTIZED paganism and called it "freedom."

BUT FREEDOM without righteousness is simply lawlessness.

3. A Global Merchant Power

REVELATION 18 SAYS the kings and merchants of the earth weep over Babylon's fall because their "merchandise" can no longer flow.

AMERICA IS the world's largest importer, cultural exporter, and media empire. Every corner of the globe consumes:

•Her music

•Her fashion

•Her food

•Her moral filth

AMERICA IS NOT JUST A NATION — she is a global system of seduction.

III. America's Hidden Covenant With Satan

While America proclaims "In God We Trust," her foundation reveals a different allegiance:
•Freemasonry, which heavily influenced the Constitution and architecture of Washington D.C., is rooted in Luciferian symbolism.
•The dollar bill features the Eye of Horus (the "all-seeing eye") and an unfinished pyramid — both occult symbols.
•Presidents, judges, and elites swear oaths not just on Bibles, but in secret societies like Skull & Bones and Bohemian Grove.

AMERICA'S true god is not YAH — it is power, control, and the prince of this world.

SHE MADE a covenant to prosper by oppression. And now, her cup is full.

IV. The Coming Judgment of Babylon

"IN ONE HOUR your judgment has come."

— Revelation 18:10

SCRIPTURE IS CLEAR: Babylon will not be reformed — she will be destroyed.

•Her fall will be sudden, not gradual.

•Her cities will burn.

•Her merchants will mourn.

•Her people will flee in terror.

. . .

No political movement can stop it. No protest can delay it.

This is not a warning — it is a prophetic certainty.

America's sins have reached heaven, and her judgment is written.

V. Come Out of Her, My People

"Come out of her, my people, that ye be not partakers of her sins, and that ye receive not of her plagues."
— Revelation 18:4

This is the call to the Hebrews in America — both spiritual and physical:

1.Come out spiritually

•Reject her idols, systems, and compromises.

•Do not place your trust in Babylon's money, entertainment, or religion.

2.Come out mentally

•Deprogram your mind from white supremacy, false Christianity, and the American dream.

•Renew your mind in the Scriptures and embrace your identity as YAH's covenant people.

3.Prepare to come out physically

•Many will be called to flee. Some already are.

•This will be a second Exodus — but led by the Ruach, not fear.

WE ARE NOT citizens of Babylon — we are children of Zion.

VI. The Remnant Shall Be Saved

THOUGH BABYLON FALLS, the remnant will rise.

•Just as YAH called Lot out of Sodom, He is calling the Hebrews out of America.

•Just as He parted the Red Sea, He will make a way again.

•Just as He judged Egypt, He will crush Babylon — and it will be our vindication, not our destruction.

THIS IS NOT JUST about judgment. It is about deliverance.

SUMMARY:

AMERICA IS the Daughter of Babylon — the end-time empire foretold by prophets and revealed in Revelation. Her sins are many, her judgment is near, and her influence has corrupted the world. Yet within her borders are the chosen people of YAH — asleep, scattered, and suffering. But YAH is waking them up. The call is urgent: come out of her, spiritually and physically. For Babylon will fall, but Zion shall be redeemed with justice, and her converts with righteousness (Isaiah 1:27).

COME OUT OF HER, MY PEOPLE

*Y*AH's call is clear:

"COME OUT OF HER, my people, that ye be not partakers of her sins, and that ye receive not of her plagues."

— Revelation 18:4

THIS IS MORE THAN GEOGRAPHIC. It is spiritual.

•Come out of her philosophies that normalize sin.

•Come out of her educational systems that erase your history and dumb down your brilliance.

•Come out of her economic traps that keep you in perpetual debt and dependence.

•Come out of her religious institutions that preach another gospel.

. . .

LIKE LOT'S WIFE, many Hebrews look back longingly at Babylon.

-AND YES, she was looking back because some of her daughters were still there, but this is also a powerful message that you are going to have to leave some people you love behind. And even just a look back at them could mean your destruction.

THEY MISS ITS COMFORTS, luxuries, and foods, its entertainments, its false sense of security.

But Babylon is marked for destruction.

Clinging to it means sharing in its plagues.

REPENTANCE OR RUIN – The Final Choice for the Hebrew and the Gentile

"IF MY PEOPLE, which are called by My name, shall humble themselves, and pray, and seek My face, and turn from their wicked ways; then will I hear from heaven, and will forgive their sin, and will heal their land."

— 2 Chronicles 7:14

"NOW THEREFORE FEAR THE LORD, and serve Him in sincerity and in truth... choose you this day whom ye will serve."

— Joshua 24:14–15

ASAPH MACCABEE

I. A Line Drawn in the Sand

This world is not drifting toward peace. It is sprinting toward judgment.

Every empire that touched the apple of God's eye has fallen or will fall. Egypt, Assyria, Babylon, Rome, Spain, Portugal, Britain —and yes, America—is now trembling under the weight of its sins.

You cannot build nations on stolen land, enslaved people, and

SYSTEMIC REBELLION without reaping the whirlwind.

WE ARE NO LONGER in an age of warning. We are in the age of decision.

II. To the Hebrew: Repent, Return, Reclaim

HEBREW MAN AND WOMAN, this is your wake-up call.

YOU HAVE BEEN:

•Miseducated by Babylon.

•Manipulated by media.

•Milked by capitalism.

•Muzzled by religion.

•Marked by the enemy.

BUT THE MOST High is calling you back.

. . .

THIS IS NOT ABOUT:

•Being "pro-Black"

•Becoming "woke"

•Posting memes

•hatred or violence to anyone or any group of people

THIS IS ABOUT REPENTANCE.

REPENTANCE IS NOT JUST AN APOLOGY.

It is a spiritual U-turn—a rejection of rebellion and a return to right-eousness.

RETURN TO:

•The commandments.

•The Gospel.

•The character of Yah.

•Belief in the death, burial, and resurrection of Messiah.

THERE IS A CALLING on your nation and it is time for the Hebrew man to return to acting worthy of that calling

YOU WERE NEVER JUST MEANT to survive—you were called to lead the world back to truth.

"YOU ARE the light of the world. A city set on a hill cannot be hidden." (Matthew 5:14)

. . .

III. To the Gentile: Humble, Honor, and Help

GENTILE READER, this is your chance—not to be erased, but to be aligned.

THIS MESSAGE IS NOT about hate. It's about truth and accountability.

THE TRUE HEBREWS WERE ENSLAVED, lied to, and scattered. But you were lied to also.

You were taught a counterfeit gospel—one that erased the original church, ignored prophecy, and replaced righteousness with religion.

BUT YOU HAVE a role in the restoration:

IF YOU'RE a Gentile who believes in Christ (Yahusha):

1.Honor the true children of Israel—not by worshiping them, but by acknowledging the truth.

2.Uproot replacement theology from your churches.

3.Reject antisemitism—not the fake definition, but the real hatred aimed at true Hebrews.

4.Support the awakening—through justice, truth-telling, and standing with the oppressed.

5.Repent of your nation's complicity, even if you personally didn't enslave anyone.

. . .

THIS IS the time to decide who you really are as a nation who you really are as a Christian, who you really are as a person.

"I WILL BLESS those who bless you, and curse those who curse you..." (Genesis 12:3)

YOU MUST DECIDE if you will stand with the Most High or with the kingdoms of men.

There is no neutral ground.

IV. Two Choices, One Outcome

LET US BE CLEAR.

EVERY PERSON—HEBREW or Gentile—must choose between:

1.Repentance

→ Humility, truth, salvation, and restoration.

2.Ruin

→ Pride, rebellion, deception, and judgment.

"HE THAT COVERETH his sins shall not prosper: but whoso confesseth and forsaketh them shall have mercy." (Proverbs 28:13)

THE MOST HIGH is not looking for performance. He's looking for a broken and contrite heart.

. . .

What Does National Repentance Look Like?

WE ARE NOT SAVED as a people simply by calling ourselves "Hebrews."

Identity without obedience means nothing.

REAL NATIONAL REPENTANCE INCLUDES:

•Confessing the sins of our ancestors (Nehemiah 1:6).

•Tearing down idols—whether they be celebrities, traditions, or false doctrines.

•Restoring the family: Hebrew men covering, Hebrew women nurturing, Hebrew children respecting.

•Refusing to imitate Babylon: in daily life, music, fashion, politics, and priorities.

•Returning to Yah—not just with words, but with lifestyle.

THE POWER of the Hebrew people is not in numbers, marches, or hashtags.

It's in covenant obedience.

VI. The Final Warning

WE ARE WATCHING the fall of Western civilization in real-time:

•Economic collapse.

•Political chaos.

•Natural disasters.

•Cultural insanity.

•Moral decay.

THIS IS NOT RANDOM.

BABYLON IS FALLING—AND the Most High is calling His people to come out of her before the collapse is complete.

"WATCH THEREFORE, for ye know neither the day nor the hour wherein the Son of man cometh." (Matthew 25:13)

THERE IS no time to waste.

This is not the season for debate.

This is the season for decision and action.

Summary:

The entire purpose of this book, this awakening, this journey—boils down to this: repentance or ruin. The Hebrew must remember. The Gentile must reckon. And the world must prepare. Because whether we like it or not, judgment is coming—and only those who align with the truth will be spared.

Come Out of Her, My People — Leaving Babylon and Embracing the Covenant

"And I heard another voice from heaven, saying, Come out of her, my people, that ye be not partakers of her sins, and that ye receive not of her plagues."
— Revelation 18:4

I. WHAT IS BABYLON?

BABYLON IS NOT JUST A CITY—IT is a spiritual system. It is a kingdom of:

•Confusion (Babel),

•Idolatry,

•Witchcraft,

•Sexual perversion,

•Greed and economic enslavement,

•Political and religious corruption.

IT IS AMERICA.

It is the Vatican.

It is Hollywood.

It is Wall Street.

It is the United Nations.

It is every system that exalts itself against the knowledge of the Most High.

BABYLON HAS MANY DAUGHTERS—BUT only one mother. She rides the beast, drunk with the blood of the saints (Revelation 17:6). She holds a golden cup, full of abominations. She preaches freedom, but delivers chains.

II. Hebrews in Babylonian Captivity—Again

THE TRANSATLANTIC SLAVE trade was not just physical—it was spiritual. The Hebrews didn't just lose their homeland—they lost their:

•Names,

•Language,

•Culture,

•Scriptures,

•Covenant identity.

Along with losing their humanity, liberty, dignity, and families.

IN RETURN, Babylon gave them:

• A church without conviction,

• Worship without holiness,

- Salvation without sanctification.

- Praise without purity,

- Religion without the Ruach.

- A Sunday show with no substance,

- A religion that serves the state, not the Kingdom.

IT WAS a new form of slavery—a mental and spiritual plantation with no visible chains.

"THEY THAT CARRIED us away captive required of us a song…"
— Psalm 137:3

THEY MADE mockery of the sons and daughters of Zion, turning their suffering into entertainment, and their struggle into profit.

III. The Voice from Heaven

BUT NOW THE heavens thunder with a command:

"COME OUT OF HER, MY PEOPLE!"

THIS IS NOT OPTIONAL. This is not a suggestion. This is life or death.

TO REMAIN in Babylon is to:

•Drink from her cup of wrath,

•Participate in her judgments,

•Be swept away in her collapse.

YOU CANNOT SERVE Yah and Mammon. You cannot walk in the Spirit and still be yoked to Babylon-Egypt-Rome-America.

IV. WHAT DOES "COMING OUT" Mean?

COMING out of Babylon does not mean merely leaving a country—it means leaving a mindset.

YOU MUST COME OUT OF:

•Religious confusion: Reject the false doctrines of Rome, the prosperity gospel, and Christian Zionism.

•Cultural compromise: Stop celebrating pagan holidays, stop mimicking Gentile sexual immorality, stop consuming entertainment that defiles the soul.

•Economic idolatry: Babylon thrives on exploitation, debt, and greed. You must stop chasing money and start chasing righteousness.

•Racial inferiority: Babylon trained you to hate yourself. To see your Hebrew identity as a burden. Come out from under the curse of shame and walk in the dignity of your calling.

COMING OUT MEANS:

•Restoring the Sabbath,

•Keeping the Hebrew holidays, celebrations and Feasts,

•Walking in Torah by the Ruach Ha'Qodesh (Holy Spirit),

•Living in covenant holiness under Yahusha.

•Discipling your children in truth—not public school lies.

YOU ARE NOT AMERICAN.

You are not African-American.

You are not Black by Babylon's definition.

You are Hebrew.

V. Judgment Is Coming

THE PLAGUES ARE NOT JUST poetic—they are prophetic:

•Economic collapse,

•Famine and pestilence,

•Political instability,

•Natural disasters,

•War and rumors of war,

•Mass deception and delusion.

THESE ARE BIRTH PANGS.

THE SYSTEMS of this world are crumbling. Hollywood is being exposed. The Vatican is unraveling. American democracy is descending into chaos. The global economy is on the brink.

BABYLON WILL FALL. It's not a matter of if, but when.

. . .

THE MOST HIGH is shaking the nations so that only His Kingdom remains.

VI. A Call to the Gentiles, Too

"COME OUT OF HER, MY PEOPLE…"

THAT INCLUDES Gentiles who fear Yah and love the truth. Good people who don't have hate in their hearts. I do not want this to be a condemnation on Gentiles in any way, because if you do not repent, you are already condemned. I urge you to choose life and truth. I implore you to choose Yahusha.

TO OUR GENTILE brothers and sisters:

•Stop worshiping Rome.

•Stop spiritualizing fake Israel.

•Stop ignoring the true people of the Book.

•Humble yourself. Join Judah, not replace Judah.

"TEN MEN of the nations shall take hold of the skirt of him that is a Jew, saying, We will go with you: for we have heard that God is with you."

— Zechariah 8:23

THIS IS the hour of alignment. If you bless Israel, bless the right one.

. . .

VII. The Wilderness and the Remnant

COMING out of Babylon isn't the end—it's the beginning.

JUST AS THE Hebrews left Egypt and entered the wilderness, so must this generation. The wilderness is:

•A place of cleansing,

•A place of testing,

•A place of preparation.

The Remnant will be purified. Not all who awaken will endure. But those who do will be:
•Kings and priests,
•Witnesses and warriors,
•The Bride and the Army.

THE NEW JERUSALEM is not for Babylon's children. It is for those who overcame Babylon with their testimony and by the blood of the Lamb.

Summary:
Babylon is collapsing. The call to come out is echoing from heaven. To remain in her is to share her fate. This is the hour for the true Hebrews—and the faithful Gentiles who believe in and love Yah—to break the chains of confusion, paganism, and spiritual slavery. The wilderness awaits, but so does the Kingdom. The Most High is calling His people home.

THE SECOND EXODUS

The Second Exodus — Deliverance from the Land of Our Captivity

"THEREFORE, behold, the days come, saith YAHUAH, that it shall no more be said, 'YAH liveth, that brought up the children of Israel out of the land of Egypt';

But, 'YAH liveth, that brought up the children of Israel from the land of the north, and from all the lands whither He had driven them.'"

— Jeremiah 16:14–15

"HE WILL SET up an ensign for the nations, and will assemble the outcasts of Israel, and gather together the dispersed of Judah from the four corners of the earth."

— Isaiah 11:12

I. The First Exodus: A Prophetic Blueprint

To understand the Second Exodus, we must look back at the first.

The children of Israel were enslaved in Egypt. Forced to build the empire that oppressed them. Pharaoh grew rich on Hebrew labor, just as America did. When the cries of Israel rose up, YAH heard and remembered His covenant with Abraham.

HE SENT PLAGUES — economic, environmental, social.

He crippled Egypt's idols — their crops, their Nile, even their firstborn.

And then He led His people out by a mighty hand, through parted waters, with gold stripped from Egypt, on a journey back to their inheritance.

THIS WAS NOT JUST HISTORY — it was prophecy in pattern, a shadow of something far greater.

II. The Prophetic Promise of a Second Exodus

The prophets spoke consistently of a final, global gathering of Israel, so dramatic that the original Exodus would pale by comparison.

"Behold, I will bring them from the north country, and gather them from the coasts of the earth... a great company shall return thither."
— Jeremiah 31:8

THIS SECOND EXODUS is not merely spiritual — it is literal, global, undeniable.

•From America's inner cities and rural communities

•From the Caribbean islands where sugar and slaves were traded

•From the favelas of Brazil and the shantytowns of Colombia to Hebrew communities scattered all over Central and South America in practically every country.

•From Britain, France, Germany, Spain and throughout Europe where scattered Hebrews live as minorities along with the Afro Middle Easterners scattered throughout all of the Arab countries.

•From Ghana, Nigeria, and South Africa and only a few other parts of Africa— still home to many tribes of Israel hidden under new names

THIS IS why the awakening matters.

Identity precedes exodus.

YAH is not gathering Baptists, Methodists, or generic "Christians."

He is gathering the house of Israel and the house of Judah, plus the grafted-in Gentiles who cling to the covenant.

III. Why This Exodus Must Happen

"AS I LIVE, saith the Lord GOD, surely with a mighty hand, and with a stretched out arm, and with fury poured out, will I rule over you."

— Ezekiel 20:33

BECAUSE AMERICA IS EGYPT.

Because Europe is spiritual Rome.

Because Babylon has no inheritance for the children of Zion.

THIS SECOND EXODUS is judgment on the nations that enslaved us and vindication for the people they oppressed.

•We cannot build forever in a foreign land under foreign gods.

•We cannot remain captives to a system that profits off our confusion.

•We must be led out to be ruled by our King — Yahusha — under His Torah, not under man's broken systems.

IV. The Wilderness Purge: Only the Faithful Will Cross Over

THERE IS a sobering truth that parallels the first Exodus.

"AND I WILL BRING you into the wilderness of the people, and there will I plead with you face to face… And I will purge out from among you the rebels."

— Ezekiel 20:35–38

NOT ALL WHO wake up will walk in.

Not all who know they are Hebrews will inherit Zion.

MANY WILL STILL CLING to Babylon in their hearts —

to her money, her idols, her sexual immorality, her feminism, her gangster mentalities, her false doctrines.

. . .

So YAH says there will be a wilderness again, a place of testing and refining.

Rebels will fall. Only the humble, obedient remnant will pass through to the land promised to Abraham.

This is why we must prepare now.

We must purify our hearts, our homes, our marriages, and our communities.

Because the journey is not just out of Egypt — it is into covenant.

V. The Role of Yahusha in the Second Exodus

Just as Moses led the first Exodus, Yahusha Ha'Mashiach leads the second.

•He is our Passover Lamb — covering us so judgment passes over.

•He is our pillar of fire by night and cloud by day — guiding us through chaos.

•He is the rock that gives water in the desert — spiritual sustenance for the faithful.

•And He will return to gather His elect with His mighty angels (Matthew 24:31).

"He that scattered Israel will gather him, and keep him, as a shepherd doth his flock."

— Jeremiah 31:10

VI. Signs the Exodus Is Near

The world's current shakings are not random — they are birth pains:
•Economic instability — Pharaoh's wealth is being threatened.
•Environmental disasters — the plagues are ascending.
•Racial tensions and violence — Egypt grows hostile when it fears losing its slaves.
•Global awakening of Hebrews — the bones are rattling, coming together.

AND SOON…

YAH will say once again:

"LET MY PEOPLE GO."

AND THIS TIME, there is no Pharaoh who can stand against Him.

VII. Prepare for the Journey

WE MUST PREPARE — not by stockpiling Babylon's goods, but by:
•Storing up faith.

•Training our children in Torah and truth.

•Strengthening community ties.

•Living lives of holiness and obedience.

SO WHEN THE TRUMPET SOUNDS, we are ready to move — spiritually first, physically when He commands.

. . .

SUMMARY:

THE SECOND EXODUS is not allegory — it is prophecy. The same Elohim who brought our ancestors out of Egypt with signs and wonders will do it again on a global scale. America, the new Egypt, will lose its slaves. The scattered Hebrews will be regathered, purified, and returned to covenant under their true King. Only the faithful remnant will cross over. The preparation must begin now.

WHEN JUDAH AWAKENS – Signs, Power, and the Rise of the Remnant

"JUDAH, thou art he whom thy brethren shall praise... thy hand shall be in the neck of thine enemies... The sceptre shall not depart from Judah, nor a lawgiver from between his feet, until Shiloh come."

— Genesis 49:8–10

"IN THE PLACE where it was said unto them, Ye are not my people, there shall they be called the children of the living God."

— Romans 9:26

I. THE AWAKENING Begins

FOR CENTURIES, Judah slept.

•Beaten down by slavery.

•Conditioned through propaganda.

•Drugged by religion.

379

•Distracted by entertainment.

•Divided by design.

BUT SOMETHING IS HAPPENING in this generation.

ACROSS THE WORLD—FROM the streets of Atlanta to Eritrea, from Santiago Cuba to the beaches of Belize and the island of Roatán, Honduras. From Haiti to the Dominican Republican to the prisons of America—the tribe of Judah is stirring. They are beginning to question, to search, to study, to weep, to repent, and to rise.

THE VALLEY of dry bones (Ezekiel 37) is shaking.

The bones are finding each other.

The breath is returning.

And the Most High is restoring His army.

THIS IS NOT A MOVEMENT.

This is prophecy fulfilled.

THE GREAT AWAKENING — Dry Bones and the Breath of YAH

"SON OF MAN, can these bones live?"

— Ezekiel 37:3

"Then He said unto me, 'Prophesy upon these bones… Behold, I will cause breath to enter into you, and ye shall live.'" — Ezekiel 37:4–5

. . .

I. THE VALLEY OF DEATH: Scattered, Silenced, and Forgotten

WHEN EZEKIEL RECEIVED THIS VISION, he was not looking at literal corpses. He was staring at the spiritual condition of YAH's people — broken, lifeless, scattered among the nations.

THESE BONES WERE:

•Dry — long disconnected from life

•Many — a multitude without identity

•In a valley — symbolizing captivity, exile, and humiliation

THIS WAS the state of the House of Israel and the House of Judah — especially Judah — who had been scattered by the sword, captured by empires, and cut off from their inheritance.

"OUR BONES ARE DRIED, and our hope is lost: we are cut off for our parts."

— Ezekiel 37:11

DOES that not sound like us?

•Our names erased.

•Our land stolen.

•Our history revised.

•Our language lost.

•Our God replaced.

•Our families shattered.

•Our dignity buried.

BUT EVEN IN the valley of despair — YAH sent a word.

II. Prophesy to the Bones: Identity Before Breath

BEFORE BREATH CAME, the bones had to hear the word.

"PROPHESY UPON THESE BONES, and say unto them, O ye dry bones, hear the word of YAH!"
— Ezekiel 37:4

THIS IS the awakening message being shouted across the earth today:

"YOU ARE NOT SLAVES — you are Hebrews.

You are not cursed — you are covenant.

You are not Black by accident — you are Judah by blood.

You are not a product of Africa — you are exiles from Zion."

WE WERE NEVER GENTILES. We were never African-American. These were names given to us in Babylon.

AND NOW, the Word is being spoken over us — and bones are starting to move.

. . .

III. Bone to Bone: Identity Leads to Unity

"AND THE BONES CAME TOGETHER, bone to his bone."
— Ezekiel 37:7

AS WE AWAKEN, there is a divine realignment happening:

•The disjointed Black man is reconnecting with his spiritual lineage.

•The scattered Hebrew woman is reclaiming her crown.

•Tribal families, once separated by slave ships and borders, are beginning to recognize one another.

WE ARE NOT JUST WAKING up individually — we are being knit back together.

JUDAH IS FINDING ISSACHAR.

Levi is linking arms with Benjamin.

The two sticks of Judah and Ephraim are being readied for reunification (Ezekiel 37:16–17).

THE MOST HIGH is restoring His nation — piece by piece, name by name, truth by truth.

IV. Sinews, Flesh, and Skin: Cultural Restoration

"And I beheld, lo, the sinews and the flesh came up upon them, and the skin covered them above..."
— Ezekiel 37:8

. . .

WHAT DOES THIS MEAN SPIRITUALLY?

ONCE THE BONES (identity) come together, YAH begins to restore our culture:

•Language (Hebrew tongues once silenced by slave traders now revived in worship and song)

•Customs (Shabbat, Feasts, Torah, modesty, honor)

•Order (patriarchy restored, women respected as queens, children protected from Babylon)

•Music (no longer poisoned with violence and perversion but saturated with praise)

•Purpose (a chosen nation rising, rejecting confusion and walking in covenant)

BUT THERE'S A PAUSE HERE...

THE BODY STANDS — whole, visible, beautiful —

Yet something is missing.

V. No Breath — A Nation Without the Ruach

"...BUT there was no breath in them."

— Ezekiel 37:8

. . .

HERE LIES the danger of waking up ethnically but remaining dead spiritually.

MANY HEBREWS TODAY are learning who they are but not returning to who He is.

Some know identity, but walk in pride.

Some preach laws, but lack love.

Some cry "we are Judah!" — but ignore the Ruach Ha'Qodesh (the Holy Spirit).

WE MUST NOT STOP at identity — we must receive the breath of YAH.

VI. Prophesy to the Wind: The Breath of Life Returns

"THEN SAID HE UNTO ME, Prophesy unto the wind… and say, Thus saith YAH: Come from the four winds, O breath, and breathe upon these slain, that they may live."

— Ezekiel 37:9

THIS IS what's happening right now across the world:

•In America

•In the Caribbean

•In the UK

•In Jamaica and Brazil

•In Ghana, Nigeria, South Africa

•In Israel, France, even in prisons and projects

. . .

THE RUACH IS BREATHING AGAIN.

THE BREATH OF YAH IS:

•Filling Hebrew men with courage and righteousness

•Restoring Hebrew women with dignity and strength

•Awakening children with purity and purpose

•Reviving a people left for dead

AND THEY ARE STANDING UP...

VII. An Exceeding Great Army

"AND THEY LIVED, and stood up upon their feet, an exceeding great army."

— Ezekiel 37:10

MAKE NO MISTAKE:

THIS IS NOT JUST a religious movement — this is a resurrection.

Not a physical war — but a spiritual uprising.

NO BULLETS. No bombs.

Just truth, repentance, worship, obedience, and fire.

. . .

THIS ARMY WEARS NO UNIFORMS, yet it marches with purpose.

It has no generals, yet it moves with unity.

It has no land, yet it knows its kingdom is near.

THIS IS THE REMNANT.

The dry bones have awakened.

The breath of YAH is moving.

SUMMARY:

THE PROPHECY of dry bones was never just about ancient Israel. It is about us — the scattered Hebrews of the transatlantic slave trade, now rising from the valley of death. We are being restored in identity, unity, culture, and spirit. The Most High is breathing life back into His people, and we are standing as a great army — ready for the return of our King.

I. WHO IS JUDAH? The Foretold People

JUDAH IS NOT SIMPLY a tribe of Israel. Judah is the spiritual and prophetic head of the twelve tribes. When Judah rises, Israel rises. When Judah is lost, so is the covenant.

THROUGHOUT HISTORY, Judah has:

•Led worship – King David was Judah.

•Produced kings – Solomon was Judah.

•Carried the bloodline of the Messiah – Yahusha is the Lion of Judah.

•Endured captivity first – Babylon.

•Been targeted most in the last days – America, Caribbean, South America.

"For the Lord hath chosen Zion… This is My rest forever: here will I dwell; for I have desired it." (Psalm 132:13–14)

Judah's role is not to dominate, but to demonstrate the righteousness of Yah to the world.

This awakening is not about arrogance. It's about alignment.

II. How the Remnant Is Rising

You won't see it in the mainstream.

The rise of Judah is not televised, because the world's systems know that if the real Judah rises, their control collapses.

But the signs are everywhere:

•Young men refusing gang life and turning to Scripture.

•Women rejecting hypersexuality and walking in modesty and spiritual authority.

•Entire families reclaiming Sabbath, feast days, and covenant living.

•Thousands studying the Torah, learning Hebrew, and renouncing pagan religion.

•Music, art, and literature glorifying Yah instead of the flesh.

THIS IS NOT church as usual. This is restoration.

III. Spiritual Signs: Prophetic Confirmation

THIS AWAKENING IS NOT HAPPENING in a vacuum. The Scriptures foretold it:

"IN THE LAST DAYS, I will pour out My Spirit on all flesh…" (Joel 2:28)

"THOUGH ISRAEL BE as the sand of the sea, only a remnant shall be saved." (Romans 9:27)

WE ARE WITNESSING:

•Dreams and visions among Hebrew youth.

•Supernatural boldness to speak truth against corruption.

•A hunger for righteousness deeper than tradition.

•A tearing down of idols, even within the "church."

•Deliverance from generational curses, trauma, and bondage.

THE AWAKENING IS NOT JUST intellectual—it's spiritual.

IV. The World Responds with Fear and Distraction

Why are algorithms suppressing Hebrew awakening content?

Why are mainstream pastors silent?

Why do celebrities face backlash the moment they question historical narratives?

Because truth terrifies Babylon.

THEY CAN NO LONGER CONTROL a people who know who they are.

SO THE SYSTEM RESPONDS WITH:

•Distractions: entertainment, sports, scandals.

•Disinformation: calling truth "hate speech" or "conspiracy."

•Division: pitting awakened Hebrews against each other in camps and doctrine wars.

•Demonic pushback: from media, music, fashion, and legislation.

BUT THE REMNANT does not fear.

"NO WEAPON FORMED against thee shall prosper." (Isaiah 54:17)

V. What the Rise of Judah Means for the World

THE REAWAKENING of Judah isn't just for Judah.

· · ·

IT SIGNALS A GLOBAL SHIFT:

•The reign of false religious authority is ending.

•The veil is being lifted from prophecy.

•The true gospel is going forth.

•The curses of Deuteronomy 28 are being broken.

•The Most High is preparing to restore the kingdom.

"HE THAT SCATTERED Israel will gather him, and keep him as a shepherd doth his flock." (Jeremiah 31:10)

THE RESTORATION of Judah will lead to the regathering of all the tribes.

AND THIS TIME, they will not be slaves. They will be priests, rulers, and lights to the nations.

SUMMARY:

JUDAH IS NO LONGER ASLEEP. A remnant is rising—stronger, wiser, holier. This is not the end of the story—it's the beginning of the redemption. The world is shifting, prophecy is unfolding, and every soul must decide whether to resist or return. Because once Judah awakens, nothing can remain the same.

SCRIPTURE SAYS there will come a time when people no longer say,

· · ·

"YAH LIVES who brought up the children of Israel out of Egypt,"

but rather,

"YAH lives who brought up the seed of Israel from all the lands where He scattered them."

This is the second exodus — greater than the first.
•YAH will gather the Hebrews from every continent.
•This regathering will confound nations, proving who His people are.

BUT JUST LIKE the first exodus, not all who leave Egypt make it to the Promised Land.

Rebellion, murmuring, and hidden sin will disqualify many.

THE SECOND EXODUS will separate the faithful from the false.

It will be the ultimate act of restoration for Zion.

THE RISE of Zion and the Restoration of the Kingdom — The Final Regathering of the Twelve Tribes

"AND IT SHALL COME to pass in that day, that the Lord shall set His hand again the second time to recover the remnant of His people…"

— Isaiah 11:11

"AND THEY SHALL BE NO MORE two nations, neither shall they be divided into two kingdoms any more at all."

— Ezekiel 37:22

. . .

I. THE LOST Tribes Were Never Lost to YAH

THE SCATTERING OF Israel was not abandonment—it was discipline. The Most High said plainly:

"I WILL SCATTER you among the heathen, and disperse you in the countries... but I will not make a full end of you." (Jeremiah 30:11)

THE ASSYRIAN CONQUEST took ten tribes (Israel) to the east. Eventually they went across the Bering Strait into Alaska, down through Canada, and on to populate the Americas all the way down to the bottom of south America.

The Babylonian captivity took Judah into exile.

The Roman siege of 70 A.D. scattered the remainder into Africa and eventually across the seas.

BUT YAH never lost sight of His people.

WHILE THE WORLD DECLARED THEM "LOST"...

He kept them marked, preserved, and prophesied.

THE SO-CALLED "AFRICAN AMERICANS," Afro-Caribbeans, Afro-Brazilians, and Black Latinos are not strangers to Scripture—they are its central characters. These make up the majority but not all of dispersed Judah. While in Ghana and Nigeria you will find the majority of Judah whom were never dispersed from West Africa.

Including Hebrew tribes such the Ashanti, Limba, Igbo, Lemba, Falasha, Yoruba, Songhai & Mandé and a scattered a few others.

THEY ARE NOT Gentiles pretending to be holy—they are Hebrews reawakening to their inheritance.

II. The Two Sticks Become One: Judah and Ephraim Reunited

"SON OF MAN, take thee one stick, and write upon it, For Judah... then take another stick, and write upon it, For Joseph... and join them into one stick."

— Ezekiel 37:16–17

THE MOST HIGH'S plan is not to just awaken Judah.

He will reunite the whole house of Israel—Judah and Ephraim, the southern and northern kingdoms.

THIS IS why you're seeing awakenings among:

•The Igbo of Nigeria (descendants of Gad and Levi)

•The Lemba of South Africa (priestly Kohanim lineage)

•The Pashtun of Afghanistan and Pakistan (possibly from Ephraim)

•Native and Indigenous American tribes (possibly fragments of Issachar, Reuben, and others)

YAH WILL UNITE them by Spirit, not by politics.

By blood, not by denominations.

By covenant, not by colonization.

NO CHURCH CAN STOP THIS.

No government can prevent this.

This is the work of the Most High Himself.

III. What Will This Restoration Look Like?

1. A Spiritual Awakening:

Millions of Hebrews will begin rejecting the false names, pagan holidays, and church traditions of Babylon.

They will return to Torah, accept Yahusha as Messiah, and proclaim the true Gospel of the Kingdom.

2. A Geographic Regathering:

According to Isaiah, Jeremiah, and Ezekiel, the remnant will be brought "from the four corners of the earth" back to the Land of Promise.

"AND I WILL BRING them again into their land that I gave unto their fathers." (Jer. 30:3)

NOT BY ZIONISM.

Not by United Nations approval.

Not by military might.

By the mighty hand of the Most High.

. . .

3. A Government Under YAH:

Yahusha Ha'Mashiach will reign as King over the whole earth from Jerusalem.

THERE WILL BE NO ELECTIONS.

There will be no political parties.

There will be no compromise.

THE LAW SHALL GO FORTH from Zion, and the Word of YAH from Jerusalem (Isaiah 2:3).

IV. The Gentiles Will Acknowledge Israel's True Identity

"AND THE GENTILES shall come to thy light... and kings to the brightness of thy rising."

— Isaiah 60:3

IN THE DAY of Zion's rise, the deception will end.

THE WORLD WILL REALIZE:

•The people who were called "niggers" are actually kings and priests.

•The slaves of America were the children of Jacob.

•The despised are the beloved of YAH.

. . .

AND THE GENTILES—THOSE who humble themselves—will cleave to the house of Israel (Isaiah 14:1).

Not as masters.

But as fellow servants under the reign of Yahusha.

THIS WILL NOT BE a reign of revenge, but of righteousness.

V. The Rebirth of the Kingdom: Not Just a Spiritual Idea

THIS ISN'T SYMBOLIC.

This is literal.

The Kingdom will be real, visible, global.

THERE WILL BE:

•A restored priesthood, functioning in purity.

•A rebuilt Jerusalem, not by the hands of political Israel, but by the power of Elohim.

•A Torah-based society, with justice, mercy, and truth.

•A new language, purified from confusion (Zephaniah 3:9).

THIS IS what the disciples meant when they asked Yahusha:

"WILL you at this time restore the kingdom to Israel?" (Acts 1:6)

THEY WEREN'T IGNORANT.

They were hoping for what the prophets promised.

AND NOW, in our generation, that promise is being fulfilled.

VI. The Role of the Remnant Today

WE ARE the forerunners of Zion.

We are not here to assimilate—we are here to announce.

THE DRY BONES are rising (Ezekiel 37).

The fig tree is budding (Matthew 24:32).

The trumpet is sounding.

BUT WE MUST:

•Purify ourselves.

•Unlearn the lies.

•Teach our children who they are.

•Rebuild our communities based on Torah.

WE CANNOT WAIT on the world.

We cannot wait on pastors.

We must become the restored nation within the nations.

VII. This Is the Gospel of the Kingdom

The true Gospel is not just "Jesus died for your sins."

The Gospel of the Kingdom is:
•Yahusha died to restore the covenant with Israel.
•The Kingdom of YAH is coming to reign over all nations.
•The Hebrews are waking up to take their rightful place.
•The Gentiles who humble themselves and receive the Gospel can be grafted in (Romans 11).

THIS IS good news for the whole world—

But it starts with the restoration of Israel.

SUMMARY:

THE RISE of Zion is not a fairy tale. It is the fulfillment of every prophetic word spoken by the Most High. The tribes of Israel are awakening. Judah is leading the charge, but Ephraim and the rest will follow. The covenant is being renewed. The Messiah will soon reign. And the Kingdom will be restored—not by religion, but by power and glory.

THE WILDERNESS PURGE

*E*zekiel prophesied that after YAH gathers Israel from the nations, He will bring them into the wilderness of the people.

"I WILL PLEAD with you there face to face... And I will purge out from among you the rebels, and them that transgress against me."

— Ezekiel 20:35-38

THIS IS THE WILDERNESS PURGE.

JUST AS IN the days of Moses, many who come out of Babylon will not enter the new Jerusalem.

Hidden sins, bitterness, idolatries clung to in secret will be exposed.

THE WILDERNESS WILL REFINE US.

It will strip away everything Babylon gave — pride, greed, lust, division.

Those who endure it, who humble themselves and obey YAH's voice, will cross into the Kingdom.

Those who rebel will perish outside the gates.

The Bride and the Remnant — Who Will Reign with the Messiah?

"Let us be glad and rejoice, and give honour to him: for the marriage of the Lamb is come, and his wife hath made herself ready."

— Revelation 19:7

"And they that are with him are called, and chosen, and faithful."

— Revelation 17:14

I. The Great Misunderstanding: Everyone Is Not the Bride

Modern Christianity preaches a seductive lie:

That everyone who "believes" is part of the Bride of Christ.

But the Scriptures say otherwise.

There is a difference between the crowd and the covenant,

between the churchgoers and the chosen,

between those who shout "Lord, Lord" and those to whom He says:

. . .

"I NEVER KNEW YOU: depart from me, ye that work iniquity."

— Matthew 7:23

JUST AS IN THE WILDERNESS, not all who left Egypt entered the Promised Land.

Just as in Israel, not all who were born Hebrew walked in covenant.

So too today — not all who claim Messiah will reign with Him.

THE BRIDE IS NOT A MEMBERSHIP — it is a position of purity, preparation, and obedience.

II. Who Is the Bride?

"I HAVE ESPOUSED you to one husband, that I may present you as a chaste virgin to Christ."

— 2 Corinthians 11:2

THE BRIDE IS:

•Set apart — not mingled with Babylon's system

•Covenant-keeping — not lawless and worldly

•Loyal to the King — not in spiritual adultery

•Dressed in righteousness — not in religion and rebellion

She is described in Revelation 12 as:

"A woman clothed with the sun... and upon her head a crown of twelve stars."

This is not Rome.
This is not modern Christianity.

This is Zion — the elect of YAH — the remnant of Israel
and those grafted in who walk in the same obedience and reverence.

III. The Remnant: Not Many, But Mighty

"THOUGH ISRAEL BE as the sand of the sea, only a remnant shall be saved."

— Romans 9:27

A REMNANT IS a small portion that remains after judgment, chaos, and cleansing.

IN EVERY GENERATION, YAH preserves a remnant:

•Noah's family in the flood

•Lot and his daughters in Sodom

•Elijah's 7,000 who didn't bow to Baal

•The faithful Hebrews in Babylon (Daniel, Hananiah, Azariah, Mishael)

•The disciples who did not flee after the crucifixion

. . .

THIS REMNANT IS NOT MADE up of perfect people, but of pure-hearted ones.

They repent. They obey. They endure. They overcome.

IN THE LAST DAYS, this remnant will not be the majority.

They will be misunderstood, rejected, slandered, and persecuted.

BUT THEY WILL ALSO BE PROTECTED, EMPOWERED, and crowned.

IV. The Requirements of the Bride

TO BE COUNTED among the Bride, you must:

1.Repent of sin

•Not just confession, but turning away from lawlessness (1 John 3:4)

2.Study and keep Torah

3.Reject Babylon

•Come out of false religion, worldly systems, and spiritual compromise (Revelation 18:4)

4.Keep the commandments and faith in Yahusha

•This is the identifier of the saints (Revelation 14:12)

5.Be ready

•The wise virgins had oil for their lamps; the foolish ones missed the door (Matthew 25:1–13)

YAHUSHA IS NOT MARRYING A HARLOT.

He is not joining Himself to Jezebel, Rome, or compromise.

He is marrying a faithful remnant who knows who He is —

and knows who they are.

V. The Reward: To Reign with the Messiah

"To him that overcometh will I grant to sit with me in my throne…"

— Revelation 3:21

Those who endure to the end and walk in righteousness

will not just be saved — they will rule.

This is not about floating on clouds.

This is about:

•Judging nations with the King (1 Corinthians 6:2)

•Inheriting the land promised to Abraham (Genesis 17:8)

•Governing the earth in righteousness (Isaiah 2:3)

•Healing the nations through the law of YAH (Revelation 22:2)

This is why the enemy fought so hard to keep the true Hebrews enslaved.

Because if Judah doesn't rise, the Kingdom doesn't manifest.

If the Bride doesn't awaken, the wedding cannot begin.

The awakening of the Hebrew remnant is the signal

that Babylon's clock is finished.

VI. Let the Bride Make Herself Ready

"AND TO HER was granted that she should be arrayed in fine linen, clean and white: for the fine linen is the righteousness of saints."
— Revelation 19:8

LET EVERY READER EXAMINE THEMSELVES.

Let every daughter of Zion purify her vessel.

Let every son of Jacob cast off sin.

THE TIME IS SHORT.

THE BRIDE MUST RISE in holiness, truth, and power.

She must reclaim her identity, her purity, her mission.

She must break all covenants with Babylon and return to her Husband.

THE LION of Judah is coming —

not for a church in bed with the world,

but for a woman of fire, fidelity, and faith.

Summary:

The Bride of Messiah is not the Christian church as we know it. It is the purified remnant — the obedient, set-apart, covenant-keeping elect of YAH. This includes the regathered descendants of Israel and grafted-in Gentiles who walk in truth. Not all believers will reign; only the faithful remnant — the Bride — will share in the Messiah's rule. The time to prepare is now. The King is coming.

YAHUSHA'S REIGN FROM ZION

*F*inally, the King returns.

9 AND THE Lord shall be king over all the earth: in that day shall there be one Lord, and his name one.

-Zechariah 14:9 KJV

YAHUSHA WILL RULE FROM JERUSALEM.

Nations will come up year by year to keep the feasts.

The Torah will go forth from Zion, and the word of YAH from Jerusalem.

NO MORE SUPREME Courts redefining marriage.

No more parliaments legalizing abominations.

The law will be the Torah, and Yahusha will judge with righteousness.

. . .

For Hebrews, this is home restored.

For Gentiles who clung to Zion, it is the joy of being grafted into the commonwealth of Israel.

Together, we will rebuild cities long desolate and live under the banner of our eternal King.

The Crown of Thorns and the Throne of David — Yahusha's Role in the Rebirth of a Nation

"The Lord God shall give unto Him the throne of His father David: and He shall reign over the house of Jacob forever; and of His kingdom there shall be no end."

— Luke 1:32–33

"They shall look upon Me whom they have pierced."

— Zechariah 12:10

I. The Suffering Servant Was Always the Reigning King

Let us make no mistake:

The man they mocked, beat, and crucified...

The man the world still depicts as pale and weak...

That man is Yahusha Ha'Mashiach — the Lion of Judah, the Root of David, the soon-coming King.

. . .

He was crowned with thorns by Rome,

but He will return crowned in glory by the Father.

They called Him a heretic.

They nailed Him to a tree.

But He rose with all power in heaven and earth (Matthew 28:18).

His mission was never to start a new religion.

It was to redeem His people, reestablish the Davidic throne, and restore the kingdom of Israel.

II. The Throne of David Is Not Abolished — It Is Reserved

"Of the increase of His government and peace there shall be no end, upon the throne of David…"

— Isaiah 9:7

The Most High promised David that his throne would never be cut off. (2 Samuel 7:12–16)

So where is it?

It's not in the Vatican.

It's not in the Knesset.

It's not among fake monarchies with stolen jewels.

· · ·

IT IS RESERVED IN HEAVEN — and will be revealed in the time appointed.

WHEN YAHUSHA RETURNS, He will:

•Reclaim the throne of His forefather David

•Reign over the twelve tribes of Israel

•Rule all nations with a rod of iron (Psalm 2:9, Revelation 19:15)

HE WAS BORN A HEBREW.

He lived as a Hebrew.

He died as a Hebrew.

And He will return to reign as King of the Hebrews and Ruler of the Earth.

III. Gentile Christianity Rejected His Kingship

THE ROMAN CHURCH accepted the suffering Messiah...

...but rejected the ruling King.

THEY REPLACED ZION WITH ROME.

They replaced Israel with the Vatican.

They said, "The church is the new Israel."

BUT YAHUSHA never made a covenant with Rome.

He made a covenant with Israel and Judah (Jeremiah 31:31).

. . .

THE WESTERN CHURCH:

•Taught a gospel of escape, not kingdom.

•Preached grace, but ignored justice.

•Loved His cross, but hated His crown.

THAT'S WHY REVELATION SAYS:

"HE SHALL RULE them with a rod of iron... and He hath on His vesture and on His thigh a name written, KING OF KINGS AND LORD OF LORDS." (Rev. 19:15–16)

WHEN HE RETURNS, He is not coming as a lamb.

He is coming as a warrior King.

IV. Yahusha's Reign Will Be a Political, Social, and Spiritual Revolution

THE COMING kingdom of YAH will overthrow:

•Corrupt governments

•Greedy corporations

•Hypocritical religions

•Racist systems

•Pagan holidays

•Fake history

•False identities

EVERY KNEE WILL BOW.

Every tongue will confess.

Not to the pope. Not to the president.

But to the Messiah of Zion.

THIS IS NOT ALLEGORY.

This is not metaphor.

This is reality soon to manifest.

V. Yahusha Will Judge the Nations Based on Their Treatment of His People

"INASMUCH as ye have done it unto one of the least of these My brethren, ye have done it unto Me." (Matthew 25:40)

JUDGMENT WILL NOT JUST BE ABOUT personal sins.

It will be about how nations treated the children of Jacob.

•Did they enslave them?

•Did they steal from them?

•Did they mock their true identity?

•Did they oppress them in housing, education, and justice?

"HE THAT TOUCHES you touches the apple of My eye." (Zechariah 2:8)

. . .

THIS IS why Babylon must fall.

It is why America's judgment is unavoidable.

It is why Europe's colonial legacy will burn.

THE MESSIAH IS NOT RETURNING to hand out church pamphlets.

He is returning to bring justice.

VI. The Crown Restored — And the Captives Set Free

"THE SPIRIT of the Lord God is upon Me… to proclaim liberty to the captives, and the opening of the prison to them that are bound." (Isaiah 61:1)

THE REDEMPTION YAHUSHA brings is not just spiritual—it is national.

•The captives in prison? Many are innocent, unjustly targeted Hebrews.

•The brokenhearted? Centuries of trauma passed through generations.

•The bound? A people chained by lies, addiction, poverty, and false doctrine.

HIS ANOINTING BREAKS the yoke (Isaiah 10:27).

HE IS COMING to set His people free, both spiritually and socially.

. . .

WHEN THE LION ROARS, every chain will fall.

VII. His Kingdom Has No End — And We Are Its Firstborn Citizens

WE, the descendants of the scattered twelve tribes, are not just survivors—we are heirs.

"FEAR NOT, little flock; for it is your Father's good pleasure to give you the kingdom." (Luke 12:32)

YAHUSHA DIED FOR US, rose for us, and is returning to rule with us.

THOSE WHO OVERCOME SHALL:

•Sit with Him on His throne (Revelation 3:21)

•Judge the twelve tribes of Israel (Luke 22:30)

•Reign with Him a thousand years (Revelation 20:6)

THIS IS OUR DESTINY.

Not religion.

Not ritual.

Royalty.

Summary:

Yahusha Ha'Mashiach is not just the Savior—He is the rightful King of Israel. His return will not be quiet or symbolic. He is coming to reclaim the throne of David, judge the nations, restore His people, and reign with justice and power. The crown of thorns will be exchanged for a diadem of glory—and His people will rise with Him, never to be brought low again.

The Gospel of the Kingdom — Yahusha, the Lion of Judah

"The Spirit of the Lord is upon me, because he hath anointed me to preach the gospel to the poor... to set at liberty them that are bruised."

— Luke 4:18

"We have found him, of whom Moses in the law, and the prophets, did write, Yahusha of Nazareth, the son of Joseph."

— John 1:45

The Return of the King — Yahusha's Reign from Zion

"And the LORD shall be king over all the earth: in that day shall there be one LORD, and his name one."

— Zechariah 14:9

"The kingdoms of this world are become the kingdoms of our Lord, and of his Christ; and he shall reign for ever and ever."
— Revelation 11:15

I. The Promise Echoed Through the Ages

FROM GENESIS TO REVELATION, the Scriptures tell one overarching story:

A KINGDOM LOST IN EDEN.

A kingdom promised to Abraham.

A kingdom previewed in David.

A kingdom shattered by sin.

A kingdom restored by Yahusha.

THE PROPHETS never preached an abstract heaven — they spoke of a real King ruling on a real throne in a real Jerusalem.

•Isaiah: "Out of Zion shall go forth the law, and the word of YAHUAH from Jerusalem." (Isaiah 2:3)

•Jeremiah: "David shall never want a man to sit upon the throne of the house of Israel." (Jeremiah 33:17)

•Ezekiel: "I will set up one shepherd over them, even my servant David; he shall feed them." (Ezekiel 34:23)

•Zechariah: "YAHUAH my God shall come, and all the saints with thee." (Zechariah 14:5)

. . .

THESE WERE NOT JUST poetic hopes — they were covenant guarantees, sealed in the bloodline of Judah and fulfilled in Yahusha.

II. Yahusha — The Lion of Judah and Son of David

"THE LORD GOD shall give unto him the throne of his father David: and he shall reign over the house of Jacob for ever."

— Luke 1:32–33

YAHUSHA DID NOT COME as a European philosopher or a Greco-Roman mystery deity.

He came as a Hebrew man, born in Bethlehem — the city of David, out of the tribe of Judah.

•His lineage is traced in Matthew 1 and Luke 3, showing legal and blood right to David's throne.

•The wise men did not seek "a savior of souls" — they asked:

"Where is he that is born King of the Jews?" (Matthew 2:2)

AT HIS FIRST COMING, He wore a crown of thorns.

At His return, He will wear many crowns — not only as a savior of souls, but as King of kings, Lord of lords, and rightful heir to the throne of David.

III. The World Will See Him Return in Power

"BEHOLD, he cometh with clouds; and every eye shall see him…"

— Revelation 1:7

. . .

UNLIKE THE QUIET nativity in a stable, Yahusha's return will be:

•Visible: The entire earth will witness the sky split and the King descend.

•Audible: With a trumpet blast, the shout of the archangel, and the voice of YAH (1 Thessalonians 4:16).

•Terrifying to the wicked: Kings, generals, and mighty men will cry for the rocks to hide them (Revelation 6:15–16).

•Glorious to the righteous: The remnant will lift up their heads in joy, knowing redemption has come (Luke 21:28).

HE WILL NOT COME to debate theology — He will come to judge, conquer, and establish His kingdom on earth.

IV. He Will Reign from Jerusalem — Not Rome, Not New York

"AND YAHUAH SHALL BE king over all the earth: in that day there shall be one YAHUAH, and his name one."

— Zechariah 14:9

WHEN YAHUSHA RETURNS:

•The Mount of Olives will split (Zechariah 14:4).

•The nations will gather for judgment (Matthew 25:31–32).

•He will establish His throne in Jerusalem, ruling the entire earth with Torah as the law (Isaiah 2:3).

. . .

THIS IS why the Gentiles have fought so hard to control Jerusalem — because the enemy knows the city is destined to be the seat of the true King.

V. The Twelve Tribes Will Be Regathered and Restored

"AT THAT TIME will I bring you again, even in the time that I gather you... for I will make you a name and a praise among all people of the earth."

— Zephaniah 3:20

NO MORE EXILE.

No more confusion about who Israel is.

No more Gentiles boasting against the natural branches.

•The twelve tribes will be gathered back to the land.

•The land will be divided again by inheritance (Ezekiel 47–48).

•The Hebrews who were despised, lynched, and mocked in Babylon will be crowned as the sons and daughters of Zion.

AND THE NATIONS that humbled themselves will be blessed to serve alongside them — as believers, not oppressors.

VI. The Curse Will Be Broken — Shalom Will Reign

"OF THE INCREASE of his government and peace there shall be no end..."

— Isaiah 9:7

. . .

IN THE DAYS of Yahusha's reign:

•Swords will be beaten into plowshares (Isaiah 2:4).

•Children will play in the streets without fear (Zechariah 8:5).

•The knowledge of YAH will cover the earth as waters cover the sea (Habakkuk 2:14).

•Even the animals will dwell in harmony — wolves with lambs, lions eating straw like oxen (Isaiah 11:6–9).

IT WILL BE the undoing of Eden's curse, the restoration of creation under its rightful King.

VII. Why This Matters for Us Today

THIS IS NOT JUST future prophecy — it is our daily motivation.

•It compels us to endure, knowing our King will avenge us.

•It fuels our holiness, because the Bride must be ready for her Bridegroom.

•It gives us courage to stand against Babylon's threats, because we serve a King whose kingdom cannot be shaken.

THIS IS NOT about going to heaven and playing harps on clouds.

It is about the King returning to earth, to rule from Zion, with us as His royal family.

Summary:

Yahusha, the Lion of Judah and heir to David's throne, is returning not to establish a new religion but to restore the Kingdom of Israel and rule all nations from Jerusalem. The scattered Hebrews will be regathered, the Torah will go forth as global law, and the earth will finally know true shalom under the reign of the righteous King. This is the culmination of every promise ever made to Abraham, Isaac, Jacob, and to us — their descendants.

I. The True Gospel Has Been Hidden, Distorted, and Whitewashed

The "gospel" preached in modern churches is often:

•A gospel of tolerance, not repentance

•A gospel of prosperity, not prophecy

•A gospel of inclusion, not covenant

•A gospel of Rome, not Zion

The Messiah has been remade in the image of Caesar:

A passive pacifist

A whitewashed European deity

A soft-spoken motivational speaker

A tool to justify empires, crusades, and colonization

But the Scriptures declare something entirely different.

. . .

Yahusha HaMashiach — not "Jesus the European" — is:

•The Lion of the Tribe of Judah (Revelation 5:5)

•The Son of the Living Elohim

•The Savior of Israel and the Light to the Nations

•The rightful King of the Earth

•The fulfillment of Torah and the breaker of the curse

He did not come to start a religion.

He came to restore a covenant.

II. Yahusha Was Not a Gentile, Nor a Christian

"For it is evident that our Lord sprang out of Judah..."

— Hebrews 7:14

Yahusha was a Hebrew Israelite — a Black man born into the tribe of Judah, not a European, not a Catholic, and not a Protestant.

His family lineage goes back to:

•David — the warrior king

•Boaz and Ruth

•Perez and Tamar

•Jacob, Isaac, and Abraham

He kept Torah.

He taught the Kingdom.

He celebrated the Feasts.

He condemned religious hypocrisy.

THE ROMAN CHURCH hijacked His identity, renamed Him "Jesus," painted Him white, and stripped Him of His ethnicity thus disconnecting Him from His people.

TO RESTORE the Gospel of the Kingdom, we must restore the identity of the King.

III. What Is the Gospel of the Kingdom?

"And this gospel of the kingdom shall be preached in all the world for a witness unto all nations; and then shall the end come."
— Matthew 24:14

The true gospel is not only about going to heaven when you die. It is the announcement of a coming kingdom on earth. One of righteousness.

It is the good news that:

The power of sin and death is broken
The lost sheep of Israel are being regathered
The curse is lifting off of Jacob
The Messiah reigns as King, not a figurehead
Babylon's system is ending
Zion is rising

THE GOSPEL IS NOT about joining a Sunday church service. Although biblical Fellowship and worship is important.

It's about entering a divine Kingdom through repentance, covenant, and spiritual rebirth.

IV. He Came First as a Lamb — But He Returns as a Lion

"BEHOLD, the Lion of the tribe of Judah, the Root of David, hath prevailed..."
— Revelation 5:5

IN HIS FIRST COMING, Yahusha fulfilled the role of the Passover Lamb:

•Innocent

•Meek

•Sacrificed

•Unjustly condemned

•Rejected by His own

BUT IN HIS RETURN, He comes not to be crucified —

He comes to conquer.

THE LION of Judah returns with:

• Eyes like fire

• A sword in His mouth

• Many crowns on His head

• Judgment and justice

• The cry of vengeance for the blood of the saints

HE IS NOT RETURNING for an unrepentant people.

He is returning for a remnant, purified in fire,

rooted in truth, and dressed in righteousness.

V. Yahusha's Ministry Was to the Lost Sheep of the House of Israel

"I AM NOT SENT but unto the lost sheep of the house of Israel."

— Matthew 15:24

THE CHRISTIAN WORLD teaches that Messiah came for "everyone."

But Yahusha was clear: His mission was first to the Hebrews.

WHY?

BECAUSE THEY WERE:

•The ones given the covenant (Exodus 19:5–6)

•The ones who broke it (Jeremiah 11:10)

•The ones sent into captivity (Deuteronomy 28)

•The ones promised redemption (Isaiah 43:1)

•The ones Yah said He would regather (Ezekiel 36:24)

•The ones who gave birth to the Messiah (Romans 9:4–5)

. . .

GENTILES CAN BE GRAFTED IN — praise Yah!

But they must submit to the King of the Hebrews

and walk in the ways of the covenant people.

THIS IS THE HEBREW GOSPEL — the gospel of the Kingdom.

VI. You Must Choose — Rome's Religion or the King of Zion

THE CHOICE before every soul today is simple but eternal:

DO YOU FOLLOW:

•A whitewashed Messiah who supports Babylon's system?

•Or the true Hebrew King who calls you out of it?

DO YOU TRUST:

•Religion that's been hijacked by colonialism and greed?

•Or the Spirit of Truth calling you back to the ancient paths?

YAHUSHA SAID:

"If you love Me, keep My commandments." (John 14:15)

THE GOSPEL of the Kingdom demands loyalty, not lip service.

Obedience, not just belief.

Faith that produces fruit, not feelings that fade.

. . .

He is not just our Savior — He is our King.

And He is returning.

SUMMARY:

The true gospel is not about religion, race, or Roman politics. It is about the Kingdom of Yah. Yahusha, the Lion of Judah, is the King — a Black Hebrew Israelite born into the tribe of Judah, not a European deity. His gospel is the restoration of Israel, the redemption of the elect, and the coming reign of righteousness on earth. Those who follow Him must reject Babylon's system, keep His commandments, and prepare for the Kingdom.

THE NEW COVENANT FULFILLED

The New Covenant Fulfilled — Torah, Restoration, and Eternal Joy

"Behold, the days come, saith YAHUAH, that I will make a new covenant with the house of Israel, and with the house of Judah…"

— Jeremiah 31:31

"I will put my law in their inward parts, and write it in their hearts; and will be their Elohim, and they shall be my people."

— Jeremiah 31:33

I. Not a New People, But a Renewed Covenant

THE MODERN CHURCH often teaches that the "new covenant" means the Torah is abolished and replaced by grace.

But Scripture says the new covenant is not made with Rome or with the nations — it is made:

•"with the house of Israel and the house of Judah."

•It does not erase the Torah — it writes it on our hearts.

THIS COVENANT IS NOT new in content, but new in location:

•Before: written on tablets of stone, outside of us.

•Now: written in our hearts, by the Ruach, changing us from within.

"I WILL GIVE them one heart, and put a new spirit within them…" (Ezekiel 11:19)

II. Why the New Covenant Was Needed

ISRAEL FAILED under the old covenant not because the Torah was flawed — but because their hearts were hard.

•They chased after Baal, Ashtoreth, Molech.

•They ignored the prophets.

•They trusted in kings and alliances instead of YAH.

So YAH PROMISED a day when He would fix the problem at the root — by giving us new hearts.

"A NEW HEART also will I give you, and a new spirit will I put within you… and I will cause you to walk in my statutes."

— Ezekiel 36:26–27

. . .

THE NEW COVENANT doesn't abolish obedience — it makes it possible.

III. Yahusha — The Mediator of the New Covenant

FROM COVERED by Blood to Cleansed by It

UNDER THE OLD COVENANT, sin was covered — not cleansed.

YAH REQUIRED blood to atone for sin, for as it is written:

"FOR THE LIFE of the flesh is in the blood... it is the blood that maketh an atonement for the soul."
— Leviticus 17:11

AND AGAIN:

"WITHOUT THE SHEDDING of blood there is no remission [of sin]."
— Hebrews 9:22

BUT THE SACRIFICES of bulls and goats were only temporary. They could never change the heart, and they could never permanently remove the guilt of sin.

. . .

THE OLD COVENANT PRIESTHOOD, established under Levi, offered daily sacrifices for the sins of the people (Hebrews 10:11). The blood of animals only covered sin, like a blanket over a stain. But underneath, the sin remained. And the heart of the sinner remain unchanged, not repentant. The conscience remained guilty. The soul remained unchanged.

SIN WAS COVERED — But Not Erased

THE MOST HIGH accepted animal sacrifices as a temporary covering — a foreshadowing of something greater. But even the prophets knew that sacrifices were not the final solution:

"FOR THOU DESIREST NOT SACRIFICE; else would I give it: Thou delightest not in burnt offering. The sacrifices of Elohim are a broken spirit: a broken and a contrite heart."

— Psalm 51:16–17

THE MOST HIGH was never satisfied with outward rituals alone. He desired a heart change — a transformed people.

THE BLOOD OF YAHUSHA — The Perfect Sacrifice

YAHUSHA HAMASHIACH (JESUS the Messiah) did what bulls and goats never could. He entered the Most Holy Place not with the blood of animals, but with His own blood, once and for all:

"BUT CHRIST BEING COME an high priest of good things to come... by

His own blood He entered in once into the holy place, having obtained eternal redemption for us."

— Hebrews 9:11–12

He was the Lamb without blemish, fulfilling what the Passover lamb represented since Egypt:

"Behold the Lamb of God, which taketh away the sin of the world."

— John 1:29

And:

"This is my blood of the new covenant, which is poured out for many for the forgiveness of sins."

— Matthew 26:28

Washed, Not Just Covered

This is the power of the New Covenant:

Sin is no longer hidden — it is washed away.

"And from Jesus Christ... unto Him that loved us, and washed us from our sins in His own blood."

— Revelation 1:5

. . .

"IF WE WALK in the light... the blood of Jesus Christ His Son cleanseth us from all sin."

— 1 John 1:7

THE HEBREW WORD kaphar (כָּפַר) means "to cover," and was used in the Torah to describe atonement through animal blood. But Yahusha didn't just kaphar our sin — He purged it, cleansed it, and gave us a new heart (Ezekiel 36:26).

THE OLD COVENANT WAS GLORIOUS — But It Faded

EVEN THOUGH THE first covenant came with power and fire on Mount Sinai, the New Covenant exceeds it in glory:

"FOR IF THAT which is done away was glorious, much more that which remaineth is glorious."

— 2 Corinthians 3:11

THE BLOOD of animals could not make the people perfect in conscience:

"FOR IT IS NOT possible that the blood of bulls and of goats should take away sins."

— Hebrews 10:4

BUT THE BLOOD of the Messiah does:

. . .

"HOW MUCH MORE SHALL THE blood of Christ... purge your conscience from dead works to serve the living God?"

— Hebrews 9:14

FULFILLED, Not Abolished

YAHUSHA DID NOT COME to destroy the law or the prophets. He came to fulfill them (Matthew 5:17).

The Levitical sacrifices, the Tabernacle, the priesthood, the feasts, and the covenants — all were foreshadows pointing to Him.

A NEW COVENANT Written on the Heart

JEREMIAH PROPHESIED OF THIS MOMENT:

"BEHOLD, the days come, saith YAHUAH, that I will make a new covenant with the house of Israel... I will put my law in their inward parts, and write it in their hearts."

— Jeremiah 31:31–33

THIS NEW COVENANT is not about outward performances — it is about inner transformation.

Not about covering sin — but about killing it, cleansing it, and resurrecting a new creation.

THE BLOOD Still Speaks

. . .

Yahusha's blood is still speaking today — better things than the blood of Abel (Hebrews 12:24).

It speaks forgiveness, redemption, and restoration. It speaks of a second chance and a new birth.

No more sacrifices are needed.

No more altars of stone.

The Lamb has come — and His blood washes us clean.

"He is the mediator of a better covenant, which was established upon better promises."

— Hebrews 8:6

How did Yahusha make this covenant possible?

1.By His Blood:

•His death paid the penalty for our covenant-breaking.

•His blood is the seal of the renewed covenant, just as Moses sprinkled the blood on the people in Exodus 24.

2.By Sending the Ruach (Holy Ghost):

•After ascending, Yahusha sent the Ruach Ha'Qodesh to dwell in us and change our hearts,

making us living temples, empowering us to keep Torah from the inside out.

3.By Taking Up the Throne:

•As King and High Priest, Yahusha intercedes for us, teaches us, and will rule us with perfect justice.

. . .

"FOR THIS IS my blood of the new covenant, which is shed for many for the remission of sins."

— Matthew 26:28

IV. What Restoration Looks Like

IN THE FULLNESS of this new covenant, everything we lost will be restored:

•Relationship:

•No more distance, no more only hearing through prophets.

•Each person will know YAH intimately (Jeremiah 31:34).

•Righteousness:

•Sinful desires replaced by a hunger to obey. Not because we have to, but because we want to.

•Community:

•Israel's tribes reunited.

•No more lines drawn by colonizers.

•A holy nation, living together under the King.

•Land: Back in the promised inheritance.

•Every family with its portion, never to be stolen again.

•Joy:

•The curse reversed.

•Mourning turned to dancing.

•Every tear wiped away by the hand of the King Himself.

. . .

V. Eternal Joy in Zion

"THEREFORE THE REDEEMED of YAHUAH shall return, and come with singing unto Zion; and everlasting joy shall be upon their head."

— Isaiah 51:11

IMAGINE:

•No more rent, mortgages, or debt.

•No more hardships, hospitals, or prisons.

•No more tears of injustice, only tears of worship.

THE FEAST DAYS will no longer be memorials — they will be celebrations with Yahusha Himself.

WE WILL BUILD houses and inhabit them.

We will plant vineyards and drink of the wine thereof.

We will raise children who never taste racism, prison bars, or systemic poverty.

THIS IS the ultimate fruit of the new covenant —

a resurrected people in a restored land under a righteous King forever.

VI. The Role of the Hebrews in the New World

THIS IS why the awakening matters.

Because the covenant is with Israel first, then the nations who join themselves to Israel.

•The Hebrews will teach the nations (Micah 4:2).

•The Hebrews will serve as priests and judges under Yahusha (Isaiah 61:6).

•The nations will come to Zion to learn righteousness — no more colonizers, only seekers.

THIS IS NOT ABOUT racial supremacy — it's about covenant order. This is biblical.

THE WHOLE EARTH will finally see who the Hebrews are, why we suffered, and how YAH has kept His word.

SUMMARY:

THE NEW COVENANT is the fulfillment of every promise made to our fathers. Not by abolishing Torah, but by writing it on our hearts. Not by ignoring Israel, but by restoring her fully. Under this covenant, the scattered Hebrews will be regathered, the land will flourish, the curse will be broken, and joy will fill Zion forever. Yahusha is both the guarantor and the King of this covenant — and we, His people, will live in His presence for all generations.

MANY CHURCHES TEACH that the new covenant abolished the Torah.

But the Bible says:

. . .

"I WILL MAKE a new covenant with the house of Israel and with the house of Judah... I will put my law in their inward parts, and write it in their hearts."

— Jeremiah 31:31-33

THE NEW COVENANT did not erase the law — it internalized it.

Yahusha's sacrifice removed the penalty of sin for those who repent. It did not change the expectation of holiness. In fact Yahusha's sacrifice and his sending of the Ruach Ha'Qodesh made holiness possible.

THIS IS the difference between counterfeit grace that excuses rebellion and true grace that empowers obedience.

Under the new covenant, we keep Torah not to be saved, but because we are saved.

LIFE IN THE AGE TO COME

Zion Restored — Life in the Age to Come

"For YAHUAH shall comfort Zion: He will comfort all her waste places;

and He will make her wilderness like Eden, and her desert like the garden of YAHUAH;

joy and gladness shall be found therein, thanksgiving, and the voice of melody."

— Isaiah 51:3

"They shall not build and another inhabit; they shall not plant and another eat…

My elect shall long enjoy the work of their hands."

— Isaiah 65:22

· · ·

ASAPH MACCABEE

I. From Ruins to Restoration — A Reversal Like Never Before

Look around today — Zion is scattered, bruised, impoverished, often living at the bottom of the nations.

But the prophets foresaw a total reversal.

•The waste places of our cities and souls will be rebuilt.

•The desert places of our scattered families will bloom like Eden.

•The trauma in our DNA will be replaced with songs of deliverance.

The world will finally see the splendor of Zion, not as a people enslaved, but as the crown jewel of YAH's creation.

II. Daily Life Under Yahusha's Rule

Imagine it:

A World at Peace

•Nations no longer wage war.

•No police violence, no gangs, no militaries.

•Children play safely in streets without fear.

Work with Joy, Not Toil

•You plant vineyards and enjoy it's proceeds, without banks or landlords taking it.

•You build homes and live in them, without the threat of eviction or taxes stealing your legacy.

. . .

FAMILIES RESTORED

•No more children growing up fatherless.

•No need for social workers or child protective services.

•Generations sit at tables together, telling the stories of deliverance.

NATURE IN HARMONY

•Lions lie with lambs.

•Bears graze beside cattle.

•Even the serpent no longer strikes.

THIS IS NOT FANTASY — it is promised reality (Isaiah 11, Isaiah 65, Micah 4).

III. A Pure Society — No More Corruption

"VIOLENCE SHALL NO MORE BE HEARD in thy land, wasting nor destruction within thy borders…"
— Isaiah 60:18

UNDER YAHUSHA'S REIGN:

•No prisons filled with our brothers.

•No corrupt judges taking bribes.

•No industries profiting off addiction and poverty.

•No politicians passing laws to oppress.

. . .

TORAH WILL BE THE LAW, perfectly administered by Yahusha and His saints. Justice will be swift, righteous, and compassionate.

IV. Worship in Zion — The Heartbeat of the World

"AND IT SHALL COME to pass, that every one that is left of all the nations... shall go up from year to year to worship the King, YAHUAH of hosts, and to keep the feast of tabernacles."

— Zechariah 14:16

FEAST DAYS Celebrated Worldwide

•Passover will no longer be just a remembrance of Egypt, but a global festival of freedom from all oppressors.

•Tabernacles will be a time when nations stream to Jerusalem to dwell with the King.

•Sabbaths will be honored across the earth.

WORSHIP WITHOUT RESTRAINT

•No time limits. No programs. No denominational walls.

•Instruments will fill the streets.

•Voices from every tongue will sing the songs of Zion.

THIS IS why we are waking up now — to prepare for the wedding supper, for the greatest celebration creation has ever seen.

. . .

V. Health, Wholeness, and Eternal Life

"THE INHABITANT SHALL NOT SAY, I am sick..."

— Isaiah 33:24

•NO HOSPITALS OR FUNERAL HOMES.

•No cancer, diabetes, or mental illness.

•Our bodies will be restored, free from the plagues of Babylon's diet, injections, and curses.

"THERE SHALL BE NO MORE death, neither sorrow, nor crying, neither shall there be any more pain..."

— Revelation 21:4

WE WILL LIVE to see generations without tragedy.

And ultimately, those in Messiah will put on immortality, reigning forever in perfect health.

VI. The Nations Will Know the Name of Zion

"AND THE GENTILES shall come to thy light, and kings to the brightness of thy rising."

— Isaiah 60:3

NO LONGER WILL the world hate us, stereotype us, or exploit us.

They will come to learn from us:

445

•How to walk in righteousness.

•How to keep the feasts.

•How to honor the King.

WE WHO WERE ONCE DESPISED as the "least of the nations" will be seen as the priests and teachers of the world (Isaiah 61:6).

VII. Eternal Joy — The End of All Our Sorrows

"EVERLASTING JOY SHALL BE upon their head... sorrow and sighing shall flee away."

— Isaiah 35:10

NO MORE TEARS for lost sons shot in the street.

No more weeping mothers burying children.

No more anxiety, depression, addiction, or hopelessness.

INSTEAD:

•Laughter echoing through rebuilt streets.

•Songs of deliverance rising at dawn.

•Feasts without fear.

•Love that never ends.

WE WILL SEE Yahusha face to face.

We will dine with Abraham, Isaac, and Jacob.

We will dance in Zion with David.

We will worship as one family, forever free.

Summary:

Zion restored is not an abstract paradise — it is the tangible, promised Kingdom on earth under Yahusha's reign. Every injustice undone, every tear wiped away, every promise kept. We will build, plant, dance, sing, teach, and rule — forever healed, forever holy, forever home. This is the destiny of the Hebrews and all who cling to the covenant.

Imagine a world with no prisons because there are no crimes.

No hospitals because there is no sickness.

No police because there is no injustice.

"The wolf also shall dwell with the lamb… and a little child shall lead them."

— Isaiah 11:6

Hebrews will dwell safely in their land, planting vineyards and drinking its wines.

Gentiles who humbled themselves to cling to YAH's people will rejoice alongside them.

This is not fantasy.

It is the promise of Scripture — a restored earth under Yahusha's reign, where righteousness is the law and joy is the inheritance.

THE RETURN of the Royal Priesthood — Raising a Nation of Kings and Priests

"BUT YE ARE A CHOSEN GENERATION, a royal priesthood, an holy nation, a peculiar people…"

— 1 Peter 2:9

"AND HATH MADE us kings and priests unto God and His Father; to Him be glory and dominion for ever and ever."

— Revelation 1:6

I. FROM SLAVES TO SOVEREIGNS — The Great Reversal

THE WORLD SEES us as felons, failures, and fatherless children.

But the Most High sees us as priests, kings, and firstborn sons.

THEY CALLED US NIGGERS, Negroes, coloreds, and thugs.

But the Father called us: Set-Apart, Chosen, Holy.

THEY HANDED US CHAINS, crack, and condemnation.

But YAH promised us crowns, power, and priesthood.

WE ARE NOT JUST survivors of slavery.

We are the heirs of the Kingdom —

The remnant of a royal bloodline.

The descendants of a divine covenant.

AND THE TIME has come to reclaim our garments and rise as priests once more.

II. The Priesthood Was Never Meant to Be Roman

THE MODERN CHURCH teaches that any believer can be a priest.

But they ignore the biblical origin of the priesthood —

Which began not in Rome,

but in Israel.

•Levi was set apart as the priestly tribe (Exodus 28:1).

•Aaron's sons ministered in the Tabernacle (Leviticus 8).

•Zadok's descendants kept the holiest service (Ezekiel 44:15–16).

•Yahusha, from Judah, is now our eternal High Priest after the order of Melchizedek (Hebrews 7:14–17).

THIS WAS NEVER GIVEN to the Vatican.

Never to Constantine.

Never to the Anglican bishops or the televangelists.

IT WAS A BIRTHRIGHT,

reserved for the children of Israel.

. . .

AND NOW, in the awakening,

the priesthood is being resurrected.

III. Royalty and Righteousness Go Hand in Hand

WE WERE NEVER MEANT to be just kings or just priests — but both.

"HE HATH MADE us kings and priests unto our God." (Revelation 5:10)

A KING without righteousness becomes a tyrant.

A priest without authority becomes ineffective.

BUT WHEN A KING walks in the fear of YAH,

and when a priest knows he is royalty,

he becomes unstoppable.

WE ARE NOT CALLED to beg.

We are not called to assimilate.

We are called to rule and intercede, to govern and sanctify.

THIS IS BIBLICAL TRUTH.

This is prophecy being fulfilled before the world's eyes.

. . .

IV. The Remnant Is Being Sanctified for Service

THIS AWAKENING IS NOT JUST intellectual.

It is spiritual preparation for priestly service.

"PUT ON THY BEAUTIFUL GARMENTS, O Jerusalem, the holy city." (Isaiah 52:1)

•WE MUST CLEANSE ourselves from idols.

•Turn off the Babylonian entertainment.

•Reject the sexual immorality and rebellion.

•Pray with fervor.

•Fast with intention.

•Study with urgency.

•Teach with boldness.

•Intercede for our people and plead before the throne of YAH.

LIKE THE LEVITES BEFORE US, we are being set apart to carry the ark — not of wood, but of truth.

WE WILL NOT BE PERFECT.

But we must be willing.

V. The Role of Hebrew Men and Women in This Restoration

Hebrew men:
You are not just fathers and workers.
You are priests in your home, kings in waiting.
Wash your wife in the Word.
Bless your children.
Speak with authority.
Walk in discipline.
Stop chasing culture — and become culture-shapers.

HEBREW WOMEN:

You are not Babylonian "Jezebels" "only fans girls" or "baddies".

You are daughters of Zion,

mothers of nations,

keepers of the sacred fire.

MODESTY IS NOT OPPRESSION.

Submission is not slavery.

It is a divine order that leads to power and peace.

TOGETHER, man and woman,

we rise to be a holy nation — not fractured, not competing — but unified in purpose.

VI. Priests Must Stand Between Judgment and Mercy

In ancient times, the priest stood between the wrath of YAH and the sin of the people.

Likewise, we are being called to stand in the gap:
•To intercede for the lost.
•To teach the miseducated.
•To reclaim the children from the streets.

•TO PROPHESY AGAINST BABYLON.

•To restore the family.

•To cry aloud and spare not (Isaiah 58:1).

WE ARE NOT CALLED to be passive.

We are not called to retreat.

We are called to war in the Spirit and minister in righteousness.

THE WORLD IS FALLING APART.

The remnant must rise.

VII. We Will Serve in the Kingdom to Come

"AND I SAW THRONES, and they sat upon them, and judgment was given unto them… and they lived and reigned with Christ a thousand years." (Revelation 20:4)

IN THE COMING KINGDOM, the Most High will restore Israel to her rightful place.

. . .

WE WILL:

•Minister in the new Jerusalem.

•Judge the nations with righteousness.

•Be instructors of truth to the Gentiles (Isaiah 2:3).

•Rule under Yahusha Ha'Mashiach.

WE WILL WEAR WHITE LINEN, the righteousness of the saints.

We will offer sacrifices of praise, not blood.

We will teach the Torah and the testimony of Yahusha.

THE WORLD WILL FINALLY SEE who we were all along:

A royal priesthood, born in the fire, raised by the Most High, and redeemed by the blood of the Lamb.

SUMMARY:

THE AWAKENING of the Hebrews is not just an identity revelation—it is a return to the original calling: to be a nation of kings and priests, intercessors and rulers, sons and daughters of the Most High. The royal priesthood is rising again—cleansed, anointed, and ready to serve in the kingdom to come. This is not the end. This is the rebirth of a holy nation.

THE CALL TO PREPARE

The Call to Prepare — Repentance, Righteousness, and the Urgency of Now

"SEEK ye YAHUAH while he may be found, call ye upon him while he is near:

Let the wicked forsake his way, and the unrighteous man his thoughts."

— Isaiah 55:6–7

"NOW IS THE ACCEPTED TIME; behold, now is the day of salvation."

— 2 Corinthians 6:2

I. THIS IS NOT a Story to Admire — It is a Warning to Obey

. . .

ASAPH MACCABEE

WE HAVE TRACED the entire journey of our people:

•From Abraham's promise to Egyptian bondage.

•From Sinai's covenant to Babylon's exile.

•From Roman crucifixions to transatlantic slave ships.

•From plantations to ghettoes.

•From Negro to Nigger to "Black" to African-American, — forgetting we are Hebrews.

WE HAVE UNCOVERED THE TRUTH:

•America is the new Egypt.

•Rome's church is the new Pharisee.

•The global system is the new Babylon.

•Yahusha is still the Lion of Judah the Savior, the Messiah, our Lord and King

•Zion is still our eternal home.

BUT IF WE do nothing with this revelation,

if we only nod our heads and keep living in compromise,

then we will perish with Babylon.

THIS IS a prophetic call to prepare, not just to be informed.

II. Repentance: The True Beginning of Awakening

"If my people, which are called by my name, shall humble themselves, and pray, and seek my face, and turn from their wicked ways…"
— 2 Chronicles 7:14

REPENTANCE IS NOT JUST SAYING sorry.

It is:

•Changing your heart and mind.

•Changing your focus and direction.

•Changing your entire life.

HEBREWS MUST REPENT

•Of embracing Babylon's ways — greed, lust, pride, rebellion.

•Of rejecting Torah.

•Of rejecting Yahusha in favor of tradition, culture, or carnality.

GENTILES MUST REPENT

•Of boasting against the natural branches (Romans 11).

•Of ignoring the truth about who Israel really is.

•Of participating in systems that oppress the people of YAH.

GENTILES, You must repent for greed, pride, lust and complicity. You must repent for the sins of your nation and your personal sins.

· · ·

FOR HEBREW AND GENTILE, repentance is not optional — it is the doorway to salvation and restoration.

III. Righteousness: The Evidence of True Faith

"LITTLE CHILDREN, let no man deceive you: he that doeth righteousness is righteous…"

— 1 John 3:7

IN BABYLON, righteousness is mocked.

But in the Kingdom of YAH, it is the standard.

•Keeping the commandments out of love, not legalism.

•Walking in forgiveness and humility.

•Raising families in truth, rejecting homosexuality, hypersexuality, feminism, gang culture, and all idols.

•Serving one another, building community, preparing for hard times.

FAITH WITHOUT FRUIT IS FAKE.

We must bear the evidence of Yahusha living in us.

IV. Detachment from Babylon: Preparing to Come Out

"REMEMBER LOT'S WIFE."

— Luke 17:32

· · ·

LOT'S WIFE left Sodom with her body, but her heart was still inside the city.

So when the fire fell, she was turned into salt.

MANY HEBREWS TODAY claim they want to see Babylon fall,

but they love her:

•They love her money and luxuries.

•They love her music and entertainment.

•They love her nakedness and sexual license.

•They love her validation on social media.

WE MUST BEGIN DETACHING NOW:

•Practically — buying land, learning skills, growing food, reducing and eventually ending dependence on Babylon's systems.

•Spiritually — cleansing our homes of idols, aligning our calendars to YAH's feast days, living holy.

•Emotionally — longing for Zion, not Hollywood or Wall Street.

V. Urgency: The Time is Short

"FOR WHEN THEY SHALL SAY, Peace and safety; then sudden destruction cometh upon them..."

— 1 Thessalonians 5:3

DO NOT BE LULLED by distractions.

•Babylon will not continue forever.

•America will not remain the global power forever.

•This system is already crumbling — look at the violence, the inflation, the corruption exposed daily.

THE WISE VIRGINS are preparing their lamps.

The foolish are saying, "We still have time."

WE MUST LIVE every day as if the trumpet might sound tonight.

VI. The Hope Beyond the Judgment

THIS IS NOT JUST about surviving judgment — it is about inheriting the Kingdom.

•Seeing Yahusha face to face.

•Being crowned as kings and priests.

•Teaching the nations Torah.

•Rebuilding Zion.

•Watching our children grow up free.

THIS IS the greatest joy ever promised to any people — and it is ours.

VII. Your Decision: Choose Today

"CHOOSE you this day whom ye will serve…"

— Joshua 24:15

. . .

THIS BOOK IS NOT ENTERTAINMENT.

It is a line drawn in the sand.

•Will you cling to Babylon, or come out?

•Will you compromise for comfort, or stand for covenant?

•Will you be part of the remnant Bride, or perish with a falling world?

CHOOSE TODAY.

For tomorrow is not promised — and the King is coming.

Summary:

THIS IS THE FINAL CALL: repent, pursue righteousness, detach from Babylon, and urgently prepare for the coming Kingdom. Hebrews must return to covenant and lead by example. Gentiles must humble themselves and join themselves to Israel. We are at the edge of eternity. The time is now.

THIS IS why we must repent now.

Clean our homes.

Purify our hearts.

Separate from Babylon's systems.

THE TIME of ease is ending.

The wilderness awaits, and only those who walk blameless (not perfect) will pass through it.

Do NOT WAIT for the trumpet blast to start seeking holiness.

By then it may be too late.

"SEEK ye YAHUAH while he may be found, call ye upon him while he is near."

— Isaiah 55:6

CHOOSE THIS DAY

Babylon's foundations are cracking.

Economies will fail.

Wars will escalate.

Pestilence and famine will grip nations.

Artificial intelligence and digital currency will control commerce.

Persecution will rise against those who stand for truth.

Everything that can be shaken will be shaken.

AND EVERY PERSON will have to choose:

•Compromise for comfort — and bow to Babylon's idols.

•Or righteousness at the cost of persecution — and stand with YAH no matter the price.

Joshua's words echo through the ages:

"Choose you this day whom ye will serve... but as for me and my house, we will serve YAHUAH."
— Joshua 24:15

HIS COURAGE WOULD BE ECHOED generations later in the time of the Maccabees.

WHEN ANTIOCHUS EPIPHANES king of the Seleucid Empire desecrated the temple and demanded worship of false gods, many Israelites chose survival over obedience. They abandoned the covenant. They bowed. They ate unclean food. They forsook the laws of YAH.

BUT MATTATHIAS, a priest of the Hasmonean line, stood in the midst of the people and cried out:

"THOUGH ALL THE nations that are under the king's dominion obey him, and fall away every one from the religion of their fathers, and give consent to his commandments:

Yet will I and my sons and my brethren walk in the covenant of our fathers.

God forbid that we should forsake the law and the ordinances.

We will not hearken to the king's words, to go from our religion, either on the right hand, or the left."

— 1 Maccabees 2:19–22

. . .

WITH THAT, Mattathias struck down the apostate who stepped forward to comply with the king's command — and he lit the flame of a holy rebellion. A remnant rose. The temple was reclaimed. The covenant was remembered.

THIS IS the spirit that must return.

HEBREWS MUST CHOOSE:

Not just with their lips, but with their lives.

Not just on Shabbat, but in every decision.

Not just in comfort, but in crisis.

THE DAY IS COMING — and now is — when neutrality will no longer be possible.

You will be forced to stand or to bow.

There will be no middle ground.

"CHOOSE YOU THIS DAY…"

Before the beast system chooses for you.

A FINAL WAKE-UP

*T*his book is not entertainment.

It is a trumpet blast.

It is a blast from the Shofar.

HEBREWS, awaken to who you are, whose you are, and why the world labors so hard to keep you ignorant.

Gentiles, awaken to the deception that blinds you from recognizing and blessing the true people of covenant.

BABYLON WILL BURN.

Zion will rise.

Where you stand in that day will determine everything.

"FOR ZION's sake will I not hold my peace, and for Jerusalem's sake I will not rest."

— Isaiah 62:1

The Testimony of Our Restoration

"THUS SAITH YAHUAH; Behold, I will bring again the captivity of Jacob's tents, and have mercy on his dwelling places;

and the city shall be builded upon her own heap, and the palace shall remain after the manner thereof."

— Jeremiah 30:18

"IN THAT DAY shall YAHUAH defend the inhabitants of Jerusalem...

and it shall come to pass, that at evening time it shall be light."

— Zechariah 12:8, 14:7

I. From Chains to Crowns

WE WHO WERE SOLD on auction blocks...

Who were stripped of names, languages, and dignity...

Who were mocked as "niggers," "slaves," "three-fifths of a man"...

Who filled the cotton fields, the cane plantations, the tobacco rows, the prison yards...

WE ARE the children of Israel.

We are the tribe of Judah scattered to the ends of the earth.

We are the dry bones that stood up and rattled the kingdoms of this world.

. . .

AND NOW — our chains have become crowns.

•Where we were despised, we are honored.

•Where we were crushed, we are restored.

•Where we were last, we are made first.

•Where we wept, we now dance.

•Where we were lynched, we now reign.

II. The World Will Acknowledge Who We Are

"AND THEIR SEED shall be known among the Gentiles, and their offspring among the people:

all that see them shall acknowledge them, that they are the seed which YAHUAH hath blessed."

— Isaiah 61:9

IN THE PLACE where it was said unto them, Ye are not my people, there shall they be called the children of the living God."

— Romans 9:26

THE NATIONS THAT ONCE COLONIZED, enslaved, and ridiculed us will come to Zion and say:

•"Surely our fathers have inherited lies."

•"Truly YAH is in thee; there is none else."

. . .

THEY WILL LAY down their pride, confess the sins of their ancestors, and beg to learn the ways of YAH from us.

NO LONGER WILL we chase validation.

No longer will we imitate Gentile culture to feel worthy.

They will come to us, because YAH has placed His name upon us forever.

III. Our Sons and Daughters Will Be Free

"THEY SHALL NOT LABOUR in vain, nor bring forth for trouble;

for they are the seed of the blessed of YAHUAH, and their offspring with them."

— Isaiah 65:23

NO MORE WILL OUR CHILDREN:

•Be targets for bullets, prisons, or eugenic policies.

•Be brainwashed by Babylon's schools to hate themselves.

•Be lured into hypersexualized, godless identities.

•Be torn from homes by social systems designed to destroy us.

OUR CHILDREN WILL THRIVE in the safety of Zion, taught by YAH Himself.

"ALL THY CHILDREN shall be taught of YAHUAH; and great shall be the peace of thy children."

— Isaiah 54:13

IV. Yahusha Will Be With Us Forever

"Behold, the tabernacle of Elohim is with men, and He will dwell with them…

and Elohim Himself shall be with them, and be their Elohim."

— Revelation 21:3

No more praying to a distant throne.

No more questioning where our God is.

No more needing preachers to mediate.

The Lamb will dwell among us:

• We will see His face.

• We will hear His laughter.

• We will feast at His table.

• We will walk with Him in gardens restored from Eden.

Our King, our Kinsman-Redeemer, our Brother from the tribe of Judah —will wipe away every tear we ever cried.

V. A Song That Will Never End

Then shall be brought to pass the saying:

"Death is swallowed up in victory.
O death, where is thy sting? O grave, where is thy victory?"
— 1 Corinthians 15:54–55

AND WE WILL LIFT up a new song in Zion:

•A song of Moses — for deliverance from Pharaoh's systems.

•A song of David — for triumph over every Goliath.

•A song of the Lamb — for salvation that cannot be stolen.

OUR VOICES WILL ECHO through eternity, saying:

"GREAT AND MARVELOUS are thy works, YAHUAH Elohim Almighty;
just and true are thy ways, thou King of saints."

— Revelation 15:3

VI. To Every Hebrew, To Every Gentile Who Clings to Zion

THIS IS YOUR INHERITANCE.

This is your call.

This is your moment in prophecy.

•Hebrews, return to your King.

•Gentiles, humble yourselves and cling to the covenant.

•All who hear, come out of Babylon and be counted among the righteous.

FOR THE LION of Judah is roaring.

Babylon is burning.

Zion is rising.

AND SOON...

Very soon...

We will be home.

-

From chains to crowns.

From plantations to palaces.

The nations that despised us will marvel at our glory.

The children stolen from our arms will dance in streets paved with righteousness.

YAHUSHA WILL DWELL AMONG US.

He will wipe away every tear.

And we will sing forever as the redeemed of YAH.

THIS IS NOT JUST our hope — it is our destiny.

It is written.

And what YAH has spoken cannot be reversed.

EPILOGUE

-Dedication
-Prayers
-Scripture Highlights for Reflection and Reference
-American Heroes vs the S.O.S.
-The Name of the Most High: From YHWH to "God" and "Lord"
-The Changing of the Name: From Yahusha to Jesus
-Biblical Feasts & Holy Days (Yahuah's Moedim)
-About the Author

Final Benediction

"To Him who is able to keep you from stumbling
and to present you before His glorious presence without fault and
with great joy-
to the only Elohim our Savior be glory,
majesty, power and authority, through Yahusha Hamashiach our
Lord, before all ages, now and forevermore! Amen."
— Jude 1:24–25

DEDICATION

This book is humbly dedicated:

To the Most High YAH, the Elohim of Abraham, Isaac, and Jacob
the Holy One of Israel, our Creator, provider and sustainer, who
keeps covenant to a thousand generations.

To Yahusha Ha'Mashiach, Our Redeemer. The Lion of Judah and the
Lamb slain from the foundation of the world,
whose blood purchased our salvation and whose Kingdom we long to
see established on earth.

To the scattered seed of Jacob — the descendants of the transatlantic
slave trade and beyond —
you who were called "niggers," "negroes," "coloreds," "minorities," and
"the least,"
but are in truth the children of Zion, a royal priesthood, a holy nation.
May you awaken, repent, and return to your covenant,
and stand again in dignity and power under your King.

To every Gentile from every nation who humbles themselves,

clings to the house of Jacob, and seeks righteousness through
Yahusha.
You are no longer strangers or foreigners but fellow citizens of Israel,
grafted into the olive tree, heirs together of the promises.

To our children and children's children —
may you never again doubt who you are, whose you are, or why you
were born.
May you walk in holiness, wisdom, and joy all the days of your lives,
and may you teach your children after you to love YAHUAH with all
their heart, soul, and might.

To my pastor, Bishop Omar Thibeaux, of Philadelphia Christian
Church and The School of the Hebrews —
No man walking this earth has taught me more.
Through your obedience, the Most High used you as a shepherd to
guide me to salvation in Yahusha. And there is no greater act a man
can do for another than to lead his brother into truth and eternal life.
I hold you in the highest respect, honor, and reverence.
May YAHUAH bless you and keep you.
May He cause His face to shine upon you and be gracious to you. May
He lift up His countenance upon you. And bless you with shalom
peace.
May He grant you and your family perpetual shalom, health, wealth,
and prosperity.
May your wellspring of revelation never run dry — may discernment,
knowledge, wisdom, and understanding multiply in your life.
I humbly recognize you as a high priest among the Hebrew nation —
a faithful leader, a prophetic voice, and a vessel chosen for such a time
as this.

Shalom and blessings in Yahusha's name.

"For Zion's sake I will not hold my peace,
and for Jerusalem's sake I will not rest,
until her righteousness go forth as brightness,

and her salvation as a lamp that burneth."
— Isaiah 62:1

To YAHUAH our Elohim, the Holy One of Israel.
To Yahusha our King, the Lion of Judah, who conquers and redeems.
To the scattered seed of Jacob — may you awaken, repent, and be restored.
To every Gentile grafted in by faith — may you cling to Zion and find joy in her salvation.
To our children, may you never again doubt your identity or your inheritance.
To Bishop Omar Thibeaux,
Your are truly a light in the darkness, and your voice has been a trumpet calling Israel to awaken.
May YAHUAH bless you, First Lady Dr. Chantelle Thibeaux, and your family with continued revelation, divine health and protection, generational favor, prosperity, and perfect shalom peace.
You are honored, respected, and eternally appreciated.
In Yahusha's name. Amen. HalleluYah.

PRAYERS

Closing Prayer & Prophetic Blessing

Prayer:
Abba YAH, we exalt You.
Thank You for awakening dry bones and setting captives free.
Seal every word of this book in the hearts of Your people.
Break every chain of deception, addiction, and self-hatred.
Restore marriages, families, and communities.
And prepare us for the reign of our King.

Blessing:

"YAHUAH bless thee, and keep thee:
YAHUAH make His face shine upon thee, and be gracious unto thee:
YAHUAH lift up His countenance upon thee, and give thee peace."
— Numbers 6:24–26

May YAHUAH bless you
May keep you.
May He cause His face to shine upon you

May He be gracious unto you.
May He lift up His countenance upon you and bless you with shalom
peace.
Amen and HalleluYah

May you stand unafraid when nations tremble.
May you inherit Zion's joy forever.

Prayer

Abba YAH,
Elohim of Abraham, Isaac, and Jacob —
the Mighty One of our fathers,
the Keeper of covenant and truth —

We lift up Your great Name in awe and trembling joy.
You have been faithful to awaken us in this generation, to remove the
scales from our eyes, and to call us out of Babylon's lies into the
marvelous light of Your truth.

Thank You for stirring the dry bones.
Thank You for whispering to scattered hearts who had forgotten who
they were.
Thank You for sending Your Son, Yahusha, to redeem us, cleanse us,
and lead us home.

We ask now, O YAH, that every person who reads these pages
would be pierced by Your Spirit, drawn into repentance, clothed in
righteousness, and set ablaze with holy purpose.

Break every chain of confusion, addiction, perversion, fear, and
shame.
Heal the deep wounds of rejection and generational trauma.
Restore the years the locusts have eaten.
Place Your Torah within our hearts, that we may joyfully obey You.

Gather us from every coast and corner.
Let none of our children be lost to the systems of Babylon.
May we stand together in covenant, in love, and in unity under our
King.

Prophetic Blessing Over the Reader

In the name of Yahusha Ha'Mashiach,
I speak this blessing over you:
May the Most High remember you by name in the days of shaking.
May He hide you in the secret place when judgment falls.
May He multiply your provision, heal your body, and bless your
bloodline.

May your sons rise as righteous leaders, strong as oaks of Bashan.
May your daughters be pillars in His palace, adorned with dignity
and joy.
May your home be a sanctuary of shalom, where the Ruach
Ha'Qodesh is welcomed, honored, and obeyed.

May you walk boldly in your true identity as a child of Zion.
May you reject every counterfeit crown and cling to the everlasting
covenant.
May you teach these truths to your children and your children's
children, that the testimony of Israel never be lost again.

And when the trumpet sounds, may you be found watching, ready,
and adorned as part of the Bride —
to dance in the streets of the New Jerusalem, forever free, forever
whole, forever home.

"Now unto Him that is able to do exceeding abundantly above all that
we ask or think,
according to the power that worketh in us,
unto Him be glory in the church by Yahusha Ha'Mashiach throughout
all ages, world without end. Amen."

— Ephesians 3:20–21

SCRIPTURE HIGHLIGHTS FOR REFLECTION AND REFERENCE

Scripture Highlights for Reflection:

- *D*euteronomy 28 – The curses for disobedience and the evidence of who we are.

- Psalm 83 – The conspiracy to erase the identity of Israel.

- Hosea 4:6 – "My people are destroyed for lack of knowledge…"

- 2 Chronicles 7:14 – The blueprint for restoration.

- Ecclesiastes 10:7 – "I have seen servants upon horses, and princes walking as servants upon the earth."

SCRIPTURE REFERENCES

BELOW IS A CAREFULLY curated list of the key Scriptures used (directly or thematically) throughout this book. They provide the spiritual bedrock for every claim, exhortation, and hope declared in these pages.

IDENTITY & Covenant

•Genesis 12:3 — "I will bless those who bless you, and curse those who curse you..."

•Genesis 15:13–14 — Prophecy of 400 years of affliction.

•Deuteronomy 7:6 — "You are a holy people... chosen... above all people on the face of the earth."

•Deuteronomy 28 — Blessings and curses upon Israel.

•Amos 3:2 — "You only have I known... therefore I will punish you."

•Jeremiah 31:31–33 — The new covenant with the house of Israel and Judah.

•Romans 9:4–5 — Adoption, glory, covenants, law, service, promises given to Israel.

CAPTIVITY & Scattering

•Deuteronomy 28:64–68 — Scattering among nations; ships to Egypt again.

•Jeremiah 16:14–15 — No longer speaking of the Exodus from Egypt, but from all lands.

•Ezekiel 36:19 — "I scattered them among the heathen..."

•Luke 21:24 — "Jerusalem shall be trodden down... until the times of the Gentiles be fulfilled."

AWAKENING & Restoration

•Ezekiel 37 — The valley of dry bones coming to life.

•Isaiah 11:11–12 — Gathering the remnant from the four corners of the earth.

•Jeremiah 30:10 — "Fear not… I will save you from afar, and your seed from the land of captivity."

•Zephaniah 3:20 — "I will make you a name and a praise among all the people of the earth."

Repentance & Return

•2 Chronicles 7:14 — "If my people… humble themselves and pray… I will heal their land."

•Hosea 5:15 — "In their affliction they will seek me early."

•Acts 3:19–21 — Repent, be converted, so times of refreshing may come.

Messiah & His Reign

•Isaiah 9:6–7 — "Unto us a child is born… upon the throne of David."

•Luke 1:32–33 — Yahusha to reign over the house of Jacob forever.

•Revelation 5:5 — "The Lion of the tribe of Judah."

•Revelation 19:11–16 — Yahusha returns to judge and make war.

Judgment of Babylon & the Nations

•Isaiah 47 — Judgment on the daughter of Babylon.

•Jeremiah 50–51 — Fall of Babylon and vengeance for Israel.

•Revelation 17–18 — Babylon the Great's sins and destruction.

•Obadiah 1:15 — "As you have done, it shall be done to you…"

. . .

The Second Exodus & Restoration of Zion

•Ezekiel 20:33–38 — The wilderness purge and bringing Israel into the bond of the covenant.

•Micah 4:1–2 — Nations flowing to Zion to learn Torah.

•Zechariah 14:9 — "YAHUAH shall be King over all the earth."

Eternal Joy & Kingdom Life

•Isaiah 65:17–25 — New heavens, new earth, children playing safely.

•Revelation 21–22 — New Jerusalem, no more death or sorrow.

Warnings & Final Urgency

•Matthew 24:4–5, 24 — Many false messiahs; deception so strong it could deceive the elect.

•Revelation 18:4 — "Come out of her, my people…"

AMERICAN HEROES VS THE S.O.S.

American Heroes Who Knew the Truth: Patriots vs. the Synagogue of Satan

Henry Ford and the Hidden Hand

HENRY FORD WAS NOT ONLY an industrial giant — he was one of the most influential voices of early 20th century America. A pioneer of mass production and the modern automobile industry, Ford held the admiration of the common man and the ear of global powerbrokers. But beneath his economic success, Ford harbored growing concerns about a hidden force shaping the world behind closed doors.

IN 1920, through his personal newspaper The Dearborn Independent, Ford began publishing a series of articles that would later be compiled into a book titled The International Jew: The World's Foremost Problem. Drawing from the controversial *Protocols of the Elders of Zion* and his own research, Ford accused an international Jewish elite of manipulating finance, media, and politics for global control. He did not condemn the Jewish people as a whole — he believed most were unaware — but he warned of a powerful cabal embedded within the world's power structures.

THE REACTION WAS swift and brutal. Jewish organizations launched boycotts of Ford products. The media — largely owned by the very interests Ford was critiquing — branded him a bigot. Eventually, under immense pressure and facing lawsuits, Ford issued a public apology, though he never really renounced his convictions.

WHAT IS UNDENIABLE IS THIS: Henry Ford, one of the most revered American entrepreneurs in history, used his immense influence not to stir hatred, but to warn the nation he loved about forces he believed were hijacking its destiny. Today, his writings are nearly impossible to find in mainstream bookstores or libraries. He is remembered for his assembly line — not for his warnings.

AND YET, his voice joins a long line of men — presidents, professors, pastors, and ordinary citizens — who began to see the same patterns. Many were silenced. Others were erased. But their testimonies remain, often whispered, rarely studied.

IN HENRY FORD'S own words:

"THE ONLY STATEMENT I care to make about the Protocols is that they fit in with what is going on."

— The New York Times, 1921

·   ·   ·

HISTORY IS WRITTEN by the victors. But truth is preserved by the courageous.

NIXON AND BILLY GRAHAM: Private Warnings and Prophetic Fears

IN A SERIES of White House recordings from 1972, President Richard Nixon and Rev. Billy Graham — two of the most influential American leaders of the 20th century — had a private conversation that shocked the world when it was later released.

BEHIND CLOSED DOORS, Rev. Graham voiced grave concerns about what he called a "stranglehold" that Jews had on the American media, echoing concerns Nixon himself had long harbored. But their dialogue went deeper. Graham warned the president that if Jewish dominance in media and finance continued unchecked, it could spark a backlash — just as it had in pre-World War II Europe. He feared history might repeat itself in America.

GRAHAM ALSO SPOKE of two types of Jews — a distinction drawn from Revelation 2:9 and 3:9, which speak of those "who say they are Jews and are not, but are the synagogue of Satan." Graham, like many Bible-believers, recognized a difference between the physical descendants of Jacob and those operating under a false banner, using power for corruption, not covenant.

IN THEIR CONVERSATION, Nixon and Graham agreed that while not all Jews were guilty, a small elite — powerful, organized, and unchecked — had gained undue influence in American institutions. They spoke not with hatred, but with deep concern. "A powerful bloc," Nixon called it. "This stranglehold has got to be broken," Graham said. "Or this country's going down the drain."

. . .

WHEN THE TAPES were released decades later, Graham publicly apologized, saying he couldn't recall the words and reaffirming his love for the Jewish people. But the warning had already been spoken — and ignored.

TWO POWERFUL MEN — one political, one spiritual — privately acknowledged what many feared to say aloud: that a pattern of concentrated control and cultural manipulation had taken root, and if America wasn't careful, it would follow the same dark path as Europe before the rise of Hitler.

HISTORY RECORDED THEIR WORDS. But few dared to heed their warning.

Andrew Jackson: The President Who Fought the Bank

Few American presidents were as fiery and unbending as Andrew Jackson — and few were more determined to destroy the growing power of centralized banking in the United States. A war hero and a populist, Jackson viewed the Second Bank of the United States not as a patriotic institution, but as a private cartel — a foreign-owned, elite-controlled monopoly that threatened the freedom of the common man.

HE BELIEVED it was dangerous and unaccountable, wielding more power than the federal government itself. The Bank was heavily influenced by European financiers, many of them Jewish, who used their wealth to manipulate American politics, currency, and credit. Jackson was blunt: "The Bank is trying to kill me — but I will kill it."

. . .

AND HE DID. In 1833, Jackson pulled federal deposits from the central
bank and redistributed them to state banks. The move infuriated the
elites, but it broke the monopoly. When the Bank's charter came up
for renewal, Jackson vetoed it, calling the institution "a hydra of
corruption."

SOON AFTER, in 1835, an assassin named Richard Lawrence
approached Jackson with two pistols and attempted to shoot him at
point-blank range. Miraculously, both guns misfired. Jackson, in his
seventies, reportedly beat the man with his cane until he was
restrained.

SOME HISTORIANS BELIEVE the assassination attempt was not random.
The timing — during Jackson's war with the bankers — and the peculiar failure of both pistols led many to speculate that the attack was
orchestrated by powerful enemies tied to the financial elite he was
dismantling.

JACKSON REMAINS the only U.S. president to completely eliminate the
national debt — a feat not repeated since. His deep distrust of central
banking, foreign control, and elite financial manipulation still echoes
today among those who question the Federal Reserve and the concen-
tration of wealth in private hands.

THOUGH CONTROVERSIAL, Jackson understood something that modern
Americans have forgotten:

"IF THE AMERICAN people only understood the rank injustice of our money and banking system, there would be a revolution before morning."

HE FOUGHT THE BANKS — and survived. But the beast he wounded has grown stronger since.

ABRAHAM LINCOLN: The War Behind the War

WHILE ABRAHAM LINCOLN is most remembered for leading the Union during the Civil War and issuing the Emancipation Proclamation, there is another war he fought—one less taught in classrooms, but just as threatening to the future of the nation.

IN A PRIVATE LETTER, Lincoln is reported to have said:

"I HAVE TWO GREAT ENEMIES, the Southern Army in front of me and the financial institutions in the rear. Of the two, the one in my rear is my greatest foe."

THIS STUNNING STATEMENT reveals that Lincoln understood what many modern Americans do not: that the real power threatening the Republic was not just on the battlefield, but in the banking halls.

DURING THE CIVIL WAR, the U.S. government was desperate for funds, and private European bankers—many of them Jewish banking houses like the Rothschilds—offered loans with crushing interest. Lincoln refused.

. . .

INSTEAD, he bypassed the central banking system altogether and introduced the Greenback — a form of currency backed by the credit of the United States, not by foreign debt. This revolutionary act allowed the government to finance the war without borrowing from the international bankers.

LINCOLN BELIEVED that money creation should belong to the people, not private banks. In 1865, he made this clear:

"THE GOVERNMENT SHOULD CREATE, issue and circulate all the currency and credits needed to satisfy the spending power of the government and the buying power of consumers... The privilege of creating and issuing money is not only the supreme prerogative of government, but it is the government's greatest creative opportunity."

BUT CHALLENGING the bankers came at a price.

ON APRIL 14, 1865, just days after the end of the Civil War, Lincoln was assassinated. Though history attributes the killing to John Wilkes Booth acting alone, some researchers believe that Lincoln's monetary rebellion against international financiers made him a target of far more powerful forces.

AFTER HIS DEATH, the Greenbacks were gradually phased out, and private banking interests—eventually culminating in the creation of the Federal Reserve in 1913—retook control of America's currency.

LINCOLN'S WORDS and actions remain a stark warning:

. . .

THE TRUE ENEMY of freedom may not wear a uniform — he may wear a suit and control a bank.

James A. Garfield: The President Who Knew Too Much

JAMES ABRAM GARFIELD served as the 20th President of the United States, but his time in office lasted only 200 days. What makes his short presidency especially notable is not just how it ended — with an assassin's bullet — but why it may have ended that way.

BEFORE BECOMING PRESIDENT, Garfield was Chairman of the House Appropriations Committee and had deep insights into the nation's financial structure. As a legislator, he had begun investigating the hidden hands behind the economic panics and depressions that plagued America. Garfield understood that the nation's money supply was being manipulated, and he didn't keep his insights private.

JUST WEEKS BEFORE HIS ASSASSINATION, Garfield boldly declared:

"WHOSOEVER CONTROLS the volume of money in any country is absolute master of all industry and commerce, and when you realize that the entire system is very easily controlled, one way or another, by a few powerful men at the top, you will not have to be told how periods of inflation and depression originate."

THIS QUOTE PULLED BACK the veil on the secretive central banking elites—many of them international financiers—who operated behind the scenes, orchestrating economic booms and busts for their own gain. Garfield recognized that these powerful men did not serve the Republic, but sought to control it.

ON JULY 2, 1881, just a few months into his presidency, Garfield was shot by Charles J. Guiteau. He lingered for several weeks before dying on September 19, 1881. Officially, his death was attributed to infection and poor medical treatment. But for many, the timing was too convenient.

HERE WAS A PRESIDENT:

•Investigating the banking system,

•Exposing the power of private financiers,

•Speaking openly about how financial elites control entire economies...

...AND THEN HE WAS GONE.

GARFIELD'S VOICE WAS SILENCED, but his warning still echoes in our time. His assassination — like that of Abraham Lincoln — serves as a grave reminder that opposing the hidden powers behind global finance has always come with a price.

IN THE WORDS of the man himself:

"YOU WILL NOT HAVE to be told how periods of inflation and depression originate."

John F. Kennedy: The President Who Defied the Money Masters

President John F. Kennedy was many things — charismatic, courageous, and deeply aware of the hidden machinery that governed
global power. But one of his boldest, and least discussed, actions was
his quiet war against central banking elites who controlled America's
financial system.

On June 4, 1963, Kennedy signed Executive Order 11110, a directive
that empowered the U.S. Treasury — not the Federal Reserve — to
issue silver-backed currency. This move threatened to strip the
Federal Reserve, a private banking consortium, of its monopoly over
the nation's money supply. By restoring constitutional currency
grounded in real value (silver), Kennedy was undermining the foundation of modern

DEBT-BASED ECONOMICS.

KENNEDY UNDERSTOOD that financial sovereignty was inseparable
from national freedom. He also knew that this system — dominated
by elite, often international financiers, many of them Jewish by
heritage but globalist by agenda — had enslaved the world through
cycles of inflation, debt, and war.

JUST SEVEN DAYS before his assassination, Kennedy gave a chilling
statement:

"THERE'S a plot in this country to enslave every man, woman and
child. Before I leave this high and noble office, I intend to expose this
plot."

— President John F. Kennedy, November 15, 1963

. . .

495

HE NEVER GOT THE CHANCE.

On November 22, 1963, he was shot in Dallas, Texas — broad daylight, motorcade, cameras rolling. The alleged assassin, Lee Harvey Oswald, was quickly silenced. The truth was buried just as swiftly.

KENNEDY'S DEATH marked the last time a sitting U.S. President made a direct move to reclaim control over American currency. Executive Order 11110 was never officially repealed — but it was never used again.

HISTORY REMEMBERS HIS STYLE.

Few remember his fight.

But make no mistake: JFK died at war with the same powers who killed Lincoln, Garfield, and others—the architects of financial enslavement.

<u>Thomas Jefferson – The Philosopher Against Central Banks</u>

Thomas Jefferson, the principal author of the Declaration of Independence and third President of the United States, was a vocal and consistent opponent of central banking and concentrated financial power. His beliefs were not rooted in conspiracy but in a deeply philosophical conviction that liberty could not coexist with financial tyranny.

Jefferson once warned:

"If the American people ever allow private banks to control the issuance of their currency... the banks and corporations that will grow up around them will deprive the people of all property until their children wake up homeless on the continent their fathers conquered."

THIS STATEMENT REFLECTS his understanding that central banks — especially those run by private interests — could quietly and methodically enslave a nation, not by force, but by debt.

JEFFERSON FIERCELY OPPOSED the establishment of a national bank, a project championed by Alexander Hamilton. He believed that financial power should remain decentralized and in the hands of the people, not monopolized by a wealthy elite.

HIS OTHER QUOTE underscores this concern:

"I BELIEVE that banking institutions are more dangerous to our liberties than standing armies."

. . .

ASAPH MACCABEE

JEFFERSON'S INSIGHTS, written over 200 years ago, foreshadow the very warnings echoed by later presidents — that financial systems, if left unchecked, become tools of bondage. Though not assassinated like some of his successors, Jefferson's ideas were increasingly sidelined as the financial elite gained more influence in American affairs. His vision for an agrarian, decentralized republic was eventually overrun by the industrial and banking interests he had long feared.

THOMAS JEFFERSON: Prophet of Financial Tyranny

LONG BEFORE THE Federal Reserve existed, Thomas Jefferson warned America of the danger that private bankers posed to national sovereignty.

HE FAMOUSLY DECLARED:

"I BELIEVE that banking institutions are more dangerous to our liberties than standing armies."

— Thomas Jefferson

JEFFERSON HAD SEEN firsthand how European banks manipulated wars and controlled monarchs through debt. He understood that if America ever surrendered its currency to private interests, the republic would fall not by sword or revolution, but by compounding interest and generational debt.

HE ALSO WARNED:

. . .

"THE ISSUING POWER should be taken from the banks and restored to the people, to whom it properly belongs."

JEFFERSON BELIEVED that a nation's freedom depended on its control of its own money — a truth echoed by later presidents like Lincoln, Garfield, and Kennedy. Today, with a debt-based system that has enslaved generations, his warnings seem less like philosophy and more like prophecy.

LOUIS T. MCFADDEN — The Congressman Who Knew Too Much

LOUIS MCFADDEN, a Republican Congressman from Pennsylvania and former chairman of the House Banking and Currency Committee, spent years exposing the Federal Reserve as a tool of international bankers.

MCFADDEN ACCUSED the Fed of deliberately causing the Great Depression to consolidate power and wealth. In 1932, he boldly declared on the House floor:

"THE FEDERAL RESERVE banks are one of the most corrupt institutions the world has ever seen... They are not government institutions. They are private monopolies which prey upon the people of the United States for the benefit of themselves and their foreign customers."

HE TRIED multiple times to bring articles of impeachment against Federal Reserve officials. He also directly named the Rothschilds and Warburgs as part of the financial conspiracy controlling the United States.

· · ·

McFADDEN DIED under mysterious circumstances in 1936. Official reports said it was from "sudden heart failure" — but rumors persist that he was poisoned. Three prior attempts had been made on his life.

Ezra Pound — The Poet Who Defended Economic Truth

EZRA POUND WAS one of America's most brilliant literary minds — and one of its most controversial. Best known for his poetry and cultural influence, Pound spent the latter part of his life exposing the dangers of usury and the control of money by private banks.

HE FIERCELY CRITICIZED the Federal Reserve and the international banking families behind it. His public radio broadcasts from Italy during World War II included economic commentaries that accused the "synagogue of Satan" of enslaving nations through debt and interest.

FOR THIS, Pound was arrested in 1945 by U.S. forces and labeled a traitor. Instead of a public trial, he was declared mentally unfit and locked in St. Elizabeths Hospital for over a decade — a silencing tactic that removed him from public life without the embarrassment of proving his accusations false.

TO THIS DAY, few intellectuals have paid as high a price for defending economic truth.

Huey P. Long — The Last Populist Who Threatened the Elite

Huey Long, governor of Louisiana and later U.S. Senator, was beloved by the common man and loathed by the elites. His "Share Our Wealth" program proposed heavy taxes on the rich, breaking up corporate monopolies, and returning financial power to the people.

Long didn't just attack domestic oligarchs — he called out the Federal Reserve and international bankers. He proposed replacing their currency control with federal programs funded directly by the Treasury — something similar to Lincoln's greenbacks and Kennedy's silver certificates.

As his national popularity surged and a potential presidential campaign loomed, Long was assassinated in 1935. Officially it was the act of a lone gunman, but the convenient timing and

MURKY CIRCUMSTANCES HAVE LED many to suspect deeper motives.

LONG'S DEATH ended the last major populist movement that directly challenged financial tyranny.

President Andrew Johnson — The Man Who Defied the Bankers and Paid the Price

ANDREW JOHNSON, Lincoln's vice president and successor after the assassination, opposed the reestablishment of centralized banking and the issuance of debt-based currency. He supported greenbacks and wanted economic power to stay with Congress, not a private bank.

WHEN JOHNSON TRIED to remove Edwin Stanton, Secretary of War and ally of the banking elite, Congress struck back. He became the first U.S. president to be impeached — not for criminal activity, but for challenging the growing power of special interests.

THOUGH ACQUITTED by one vote in the Senate, Johnson's presidency was crippled, and Reconstruction fell into the hands of financiers who exploited the South and reshaped America in the image of industrial capital, not freedom.

CHARLES LINDBERGH SR. – The Congressman Who Dared to Expose the Banking Cabal

CHARLES LINDBERGH SR., a U.S. Congressman from Minnesota and father of the famous aviator, was one of the most outspoken political figures in early 20th-century America to challenge the creation and power of the Federal Reserve.

LINDBERGH WAS a principled conservative who believed in the Constitution and the sovereignty of the American people. He became a fierce critic of the Federal Reserve Act of 1913, warning that it would create a private banking monopoly that would rule the U.S. economy from behind the scenes. He declared on the floor of Congress:

"THIS ACT ESTABLISHES the most gigantic trust on earth… When the President signs this act, the invisible government by the money power, proven to exist by the Money Trust investigation, will be legalized."

LINDBERGH ACCUSED ELITE BANKERS — including Paul Warburg (a German-born Jewish banker involved in drafting the Federal Reserve

Act) — of conspiring with Congress to hijack the American financial system under the guise of stabilizing it.

HIS OPPOSITION MADE HIM A TARGET. He was politically isolated, denied renomination, and his writings were suppressed. His 1917 book, "Why Is Your Country at War?", which exposed banking motives behind U.S. involvement in World War I, was banned under the Espionage Act.

LINDBERGH'S BRAVERY in naming names and pointing out the collusion between government and banking power came at great personal and professional cost. But his legacy lives on as one of the first American politicians to call out the central banking cartel before it cemented its grip on U.S. economic life.

CHARLES LINDBERGH SR.: The Congressman Who Exposed the Federal Reserve

OFTEN OVERSHADOWED BY HIS SON, the aviator Charles Lindbergh Jr., Charles Lindbergh Sr. was a brave U.S. Congressman from Minnesota who stood almost alone in opposing the creation of the Federal Reserve in 1913.

HE KNEW what it truly was — a private banking cartel, not a government institution.

He declared from the House floor:

"THIS ACT ESTABLISHES the most gigantic trust on earth... The worst legislative crime of the ages is perpetrated by this banking and currency bill."

— Charles Lindbergh Sr., 1913

LINDBERGH WARNED that the Federal Reserve would cause inflation, depressions, and wars, all under the control of a hidden hand. He authored books exposing this plot, including Banking, Currency and the Money Trust, and was politically punished for his efforts.

HIS ACCURATE PREDICTIONS — including the Great Depression — were ignored.

He paid the price for speaking out.

But his legacy is clear: he was one of the few who saw the monster before it fully rose.

THE NAME OF THE MOST HIGH: FROM YHWH TO "GOD" AND "LORD"

From YHWH to "God" and "Lord"

"I am YHWH, that is My Name; and My glory I will not give to another..."

— Isaiah 42:8

1. YHWH (יהוה) — The Sacred Name

•Original Hebrew Letters: Yod-Heh-Waw-Heh for closer historical accuracy or Yod-He-Vav-He for a closer reflection of modern Hebrew uses. (יהוה)

•Pronunciation: Most likely Yahuah (some say Yahweh, Yehovah, or Yahuwah).

•Meaning: "He who exists," or "I Am that I Am" (Exodus 3:14–15).

•Used in: Ancient Hebrew texts; this is the Tetragrammaton — the true covenant Name of the Almighty.

•Usage in Scripture: Occurs nearly 7,000 times in the Tanakh (Old Testament).

•Why It Was Hidden: By the time of the Babylonian exile, many Hebrews began avoiding saying the Name aloud for fear of misusing it (based on Exodus 20:7). This led to the tradition of saying "Adonai" (Lord) instead.

2. Yah / Yahu — The Shortened Form

•Seen in names like Isaiah (YeshaYah), Jeremiah (YirmeYah), Obadiah (ObadYah).

•Used in halleluYah, which means "Praise Yah."

•This abbreviated form preserves the divine Name in poetic or prophetic use.

3. Adonai — "Lord" (Substitution)

•Hebrew meaning: "Master" or "Lord"

•Replaced YHWH in synagogue readings to avoid pronouncing the sacred Name.

•Later, translators inserted "LORD" (all caps) into English Bibles where YHWH appears.

•Problem: This practice conceals the Most High's actual Name and replaces it with a title.

4. Elohim — "Mighty One(s)" or "Judge(s)"

•Hebrew: אֱלֹהִים (Elohim)

•Used: As a title for the Most High, not His Name.

•Significance: Can mean "mighty one(s)," and occasionally refers to judges, rulers, or even false gods, depending on context (Exodus 22:8–9).

•Not a replacement for His Name, but often used generically and in combination (e.g., YHWH Elohim).

5. God — Pagan Influence & Generic Title

•Origin: Comes from Germanic languages, not Hebrew.

•Rooted in the word gott or gudan, which predates Christianity and was applied to Norse and Germanic deities.

•Not a name, but a title — can apply to any deity, false or true.

•Scripture never called YHWH "God" in the original Hebrew — this came via Greek and Latin translation, then English.

6. Lord — English Substitution

•Derived from: Old English hlafweard, meaning "loaf-keeper" or master.

•Replaced YHWH in nearly all modern Bible translations (e.g., KJV, NIV, ESV), typically written as LORD in all caps.

•This title was also used for pagan deities like Baal (which also means "lord").

•Using "Lord" in place of the sacred Name contributed to the erasure of the personal covenant identity of the Most High.

Why It Matters

•Names carry identity and covenant.

•The Most High said repeatedly: "This is My Name forever" (Exodus 3:15).

•To remove or replace His Name is to remove the relational aspect of faith — He is not just "God," He is Yahuah, the Elohim of Abraham, Isaac, and Jacob.

•Yahusha (Jesus) said: "I have manifested Your Name unto the men You gave Me..." (John 17:6).

THE CHANGING OF THE NAME: FROM YAHUSHA TO JESUS

<u>The Changing of the Name: From Yahusha to Jesus</u>

The true name of the Messiah has traveled a long and winding road—altered by language, culture, and empire. Each transition moved the name further from its original Hebrew root, and in doing so, veiled the powerful meaning it once carried.

1. Yahusha (יְהוֹשֻׁעַ)

Language: Ancient Hebrew

Time: Before 500 B.C.

Used By: The original Hebrew Israelites

Meaning: "YAH is Salvation" or "Yahuah Saves"

The name Yahusha is the original, given name of the Messiah, sharing the same Hebrew root as Joshua (Yehoshua). It combines the shortened name of the Most High (Yahuah or Yah) with the verb "yasha," meaning "to save." This name proclaims the mission of the Messiah: salvation in the name of YAH.

2. Yeshua (יֵשׁוּעַ)

Language: Post-exilic Hebrew / Aramaic

Time: Around 500 B.C. to 100 A.D.

Used By: Jews returning from Babylonian exile; Second Temple-era Israelites

Meaning: "Salvation" (shortened form)

After the Babylonian captivity, Aramaic began to replace ancient Hebrew as the spoken language. Yeshua emerged as a shortened, more Aramaic-friendly form of Yahusha. While easier to pronounce under foreign rule, the name no longer carried the explicit reference to Yahuah (YAH or YAHU). This was the name likely used in everyday speech during this era in Judea.

3. Iēsous (Ἰησοῦς)

Language: Greek

Time: Circa 300 B.C. – 400 A.D.

Used By: Hellenized Jews and early Greek Christians

Reason for Change: The Greek language lacks the letters "Y" (Yod) and "Sh" (Shin), so Yeshua was rendered Iēsous to fit Greek phonetics and grammar.

This form stripped the name of its Hebrew meaning entirely. Greek, the language of empire and philosophy, prioritized form over meaning. Iēsous became widespread as the New Testament was written and circulated in Greek under the Roman Empire.

4. Jesus

Language: Latin > Early English

Time: Circa 1600 A.D. onward

Used By: Roman Catholic Church, then Protestants and modern Christianity

Reason for Change: Latin transformed Iēsous into Iesus. When English began adopting the Latin alphabet, the letter "J" was introduced in the 1500s. The 1611 King James Bible used "Iesus" in early editions, and "Jesus" only became standard in English after the mid-17th century.

By this point, the name had traveled so far from Yahusha that not only its pronunciation but its meaning and sacred connection to the Father's name were completely erased.

When the Messiah was alive — which name did He actually answer to?

When He lived in the flesh among Israel, His people spoke mainly **Aramaic** (a sister language to Hebrew). By that period, the name **"Yeshua" (יֵשׁוּעַ)** was the common, everyday spoken form of His name — much like how "Josh" is a shortened form of "Joshua."

So in everyday life, those around Him probably called Him **"Yeshua,"** because that was the normal speech form of His Hebrew name in the first century.

However, the **original, full, sacred form of His name** — what His name *means* and what the prophets declared — is **Yahusha (יְהוֹשֻׁעַ)**, which literally contains the divine Name "Yahu" and means "Yahuah saves."

So **in meaning and origin**, His name is **Yahusha** — the full, prophetic Hebrew form that declares *"Yahuah is Salvation."*

But when the Messiah walked the earth, His people spoke Aramaic and called Him *Yeshua*, the Aramaic version of the His Hebrew name — the name that carries the Father's Name — is *Yahusha*, meaning

'Yahuah saves.' So Yeshua and Yahusha refer to the same person, but Yahusha expresses the full divine meaning."

Why It Matters

The transition from Yahusha to Jesus was not merely linguistic—it was theological and imperial. The removal of "YAH" from the name conveniently distanced the Messiah from His Hebrew roots. As Rome took over the faith, the name was Romanized, sanitized, and universalized for Gentile consumption.

But Yahusha declared:

"I am come in my Father's name, and ye receive me not..."

— John 5:43

Restoring His true name restores the honor due to the Father. While salvation is not a matter of pronunciation, it is a matter of truth, restoration, and honoring His identity as it was originally revealed.

BIBLICAL FEASTS & HOLY DAYS (YAHUAH'S MOEDIM)

Biblical Feasts & Holy Days (Yahuah's Moedim)

"These are the appointed festivals of Yahuah, holy convocations which you shall proclaim at their appointed times."

— Leviticus 23:4

1. Sabbath (Shabbat)

•Date: Every 7th day (Saturday); for true biblical Sabbath follow the Lunar Sabbath.

•Origin: Creation (Genesis 2:2-3); 4th Commandment (Exodus 20:8-11)

•How to Observe:

•No work, buying, or selling.

•Day of rest, worship, and reflection.

•Gather with family or congregation.

•Optional: Candle lighting and special meals.

•Scripture: Genesis 2:2–3, Exodus 20:8–11, Leviticus 23:3, Isaiah 58:13

2. Passover (Pesach)

•Date: 14th day of the first biblical month (Abib/Nisan) at twilight (usually March–April)

•Origin: Exodus from Egypt; death angel "passed over" Hebrew homes marked with blood.

•How to Observe:

•Remove leaven from homes.

•Eat unleavened bread, lamb (or symbolic), bitter herbs.

•Remember Yahusha as the Passover Lamb.

•Scripture: Exodus 12:1–14, Leviticus 23:5, 1 Corinthians 5:7

3. Feast of Unleavened Bread (Chag HaMatzot)

•Date: 15th–21st of Abib/Nisan (7 days)

•Origin: Commemorates the haste of fleeing Egypt without time for bread to rise.

•How to Observe:

•No leaven (yeast) eaten or in the home for 7 days.

•Holy gatherings on the 1st and 7th days.

•Scripture: Exodus 12:15–20, Leviticus 23:6–8

4. First Fruits (Yom HaBikkurim)

•Date: The day after the Sabbath following Passover (Resurrection Day)

•Origin: Offering of the first ripe barley sheaf to Yahuah.

•Messianic Fulfillment: Yahusha resurrected on First Fruits, as the "firstborn from the dead" (Colossians 1:18).

•How to Observe:

•Acknowledge Yahuah as the source of the harvest.

•Recognize Yahusha's resurrection.

•Scripture: Leviticus 23:9–14, 1 Corinthians 15:20–23

5. Feast of Weeks (Shavuot / Pentecost)

•Date: 50 days after First Fruits (May–June)

•Origin: Commemorates the giving of the Torah at Mt. Sinai.

•Messianic Fulfillment: Holy Spirit poured out (Acts 2).

•How to Observe:

•Study and honor Torah.

•Celebrate the Spirit's guidance and empowerment.

•Gather for teaching and fellowship.

•Scripture: Leviticus 23:15–22, Acts 2

6. Feast of Trumpets (Yom Teruah)

•Date: 1st day of the 7th month (Tishrei) — usually September

•Origin: Day of blowing shofars to awaken repentance.

•Prophetic Significance: Foreshadows the return of Messiah.

•How to Observe:

•Blow trumpets/shofars.

•Reflect, repent, and prepare for judgment.

•Scripture: Leviticus 23:23–25, 1 Thessalonians 4:16

7. Day of Atonement (Yom Kippur)

•Date: 10th of Tishrei (7th month)

•Origin: Annual high holy day of fasting and repentance.

•How to Observe:

•Fast from food and drink.

•Confess sins, seek forgiveness.

•Rest and reflect deeply.

•Scripture: Leviticus 16, Leviticus 23:26–32, Hebrews 9–10

8. Feast of Tabernacles (Sukkot)

•Date: 15th–21st of Tishrei

•Origin: Commemorates Israel living in tents/booths in the wilderness.

•How to Observe:

•Dwell in temporary shelters (sukkahs).

•Rejoice in Yahuah's provision.

•Feast and fellowship for 7 days.

•Scripture: Leviticus 23:33–43, Zechariah 14:16

9. The Eighth Day (Shemini Atzeret)

•Date: 22nd of Tishrei (immediately after Sukkot)

•Significance: A sacred assembly; symbolic of eternity and completeness.

•How to Observe:

•Special assembly.

•Rejoice in the Word and Kingdom to come.

•Scripture: Leviticus 23:36, Nehemiah 8:18

Biblically-Inspired Historical Festivals

These were not part of the original Levitical feasts but were added by the Hebrew people to commemorate historical deliverance and protection. Yahusha also observed these (John 10:22).

10. Purim

•Date: 14th & 15th of Adar (February–March)

•Origin: Celebration of deliverance from Haman's plot (Book of Esther)

•How to Observe:

•Read the Book of Esther.

•Give gifts to the poor.

•Celebrate with feasts and joy.

•Scripture: Esther 9:20–32

11. Hanukkah (Feast of Dedication / Festival of Lights)

•Date: 25th of Kislev for 8 days (December)

•Origin: Rededication of the Temple after victory over Antiochus IV (Maccabees)

•How to Observe:

•Light menorah for 8 nights.

•Remember dedication and faithfulness.

•Celebrate deliverance.

•Scripture: John 10:22, 1 & 2 Maccabees (Apocrypha)

True Sabbath: The Lunar Sabbath

•Structure:

•Begins in the evening the day after the New Moon.

•Then Sabbaths fall on the 8th, 15th, 22nd, and 29th days of the lunar month.

•Why It Matters:

•In the Bible, days of the week were unnamed.

•Feasts and Sabbaths were calculated from the New Moon, not a Gregorian Saturday.

•Example: 1 Samuel 20 shows David recognizing both the New Moon and Sabbath as distinct but interconnected.

May the breath of the Ruach Ha'Qodesh be upon these words

ABOUT THE AUTHOR

Asaph Maccabee is an independent researcher and writer focused on biblical accuracy, history, and identity. Asaph is committed to restoring the true identity of the dispersed Hebrew people. His work examines the intersections of Scripture, culture, and historical memory, with a particular emphasis on reclaiming narratives that have been marginalized, suppressed, or misunderstood. His work focuses on unearthing suppressed history, decoding Scripture through its original cultural lens, and challenging the distortions that have shaped Western religious thought.

Asaph writes for readers seeking clarity in a time of confusion—those hungry for truth, accountability, and spiritual awakening. With a style deeply rooted in Scripture and supported by extensive historical research, he brings together ancient texts, prophetic patterns, and modern realities to reveal the hidden story of a nation once lost and now awakening. Maccabee writes with a commitment to accuracy, clarity, and depth. His goal is to help readers reconnect with forgotten truths and rediscover the biblical foundations of identity, faith, and purpose.

His mission is simple: awaken Israel, warn the nations, and encourage all who seek righteousness to return to the covenant of the Most High. Through his writing, Asaph calls readers back to identity, repentance, and purpose, echoing the mantle of the biblical scribes and watchmen who preserved truth in turbulent times.

Publishing under the imprint Ruach Press, he dedicates his work to dismantling deception, uplifting the oppressed, and proclaiming the restoration promised in Scripture. The Miseducation of the Hebrew and the Gentile is the first volume in a larger movement—supported by the platform TheVoiceOfZion.com—focused on truth, remembrance, and the awakening of Zion.

He is a member of Philadelphia Christian Church pastored by Bishop Omar Thibeaux.

Website:

Thevoiceofzion.com

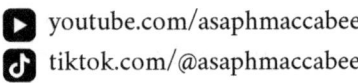

youtube.com/asaphmaccabee

tiktok.com/@asaphmaccabee

www.ingramcontent.com/pod-product-compliance
Lightning Source LLC
Chambersburg PA
CBHW060401130626
46555CB00005B/1963